WRITERS

EXPRESS

A Handbook for
YOUNG WRITERS,
THINKERS, AND LEARNERS

I(T)P®   **International Thomson Publishing**
The ITP logo is a trademark under licence
www.thomson.com

Copyright © 1998 by Great Source Education Group, Inc., a Houghton Mifflin Company.
All rights reserved.

Published in Canada by
I(T)P® **Nelson**
A division of Thomson Canada Limited, 1998
1120 Birchmount Road
Scarborough, Ontario M1K 5G4
www.nelson.com

First published by Great Source Education Group, Inc., a Houghton Mifflin Company.
All rights reserved.

Permission to reprint copyrighted material is gratefully acknowledged. Every effort has been made to trace ownership of all copyrighted material and to secure permission from copyright holders. In the event of any question arising as to the use of any material, we will be pleased to make the necesssary corrections in future printings.

Canadian Cataloguing in Publication Data

Kemper, Dave
  Writers Express: a handbook for young writers, thinkers, and learners

Includes index.

ISBN 0-17-607458-9

1. English language—Rhetoric—Juvenile literature. 2. English language—Juvenile literature. I. Nathan, Ruth. II. Sebranek, Patrick. III. Title.

PEI408.K46 1998   808'.042   C98-930129-X

Printed and bound in Canada
    3 4 5 6 7 8 9 0 / TP / 7 6 5 4 3 2 1 0 9

WRITERS
EXPRESS

A Handbook for
YOUNG WRITERS,
THINKERS, AND LEARNERS

Written and Compiled by
Dave, Kemper, Ruth Nathan, Patrick Sebranek
Illustrated by Chris Krenzke

WRITE SOURCE

GREAT SOURCE EDUCATION GROUP
a Houghton Mifflin Company

Acknowledgments

We're grateful to many people who helped bring *Writers Express* to life. First, we must thank all the students who've contributed their writing and their ideas.

Also, thanks to some of our favourite authors and teachers who helped make *Writers Express* a reality.

Sandy Asher for *Writing Realistic Stories* and *Writing Plays*
Nancy Bond for *Writing Fantasies*
Roy Peter Clark for *Writing Newspaper Stories*
Will Hobbs for *Revising Your Writing*
Toby Fulwiler for *Writing as a Learning Tool*
Stephen Krensky for *Writing Stories from History*
Gloria Nixon-John for *Giving Speeches*
Susan Ohanian for *Writing Tall Tales*
Anne-Marie Oomen for *Writing Poems*
Marie Ponsot for *Sharing Family Stories*
Peter and Connie Roop for *Writing a Classroom Report*
Paula and Keith Stanovich for *Building Vocabulary Skills*
Lorraine Sintetos for *Writing Riddles*
Peter Stillman for *Writing for Fun*
Charles Temple for *Becoming a Better Speller* and *Writing Songs*
Toni Walters for *Using Reading Strategies*
Allan Wolf for *Performing Poems*

Another thank you goes to our team of educators, editors, and designers: Laura Bachman, Laurie Cooper, Marguerite Cotto, Carol Elsholz, Tom Gilding, Julie Janosz, Beverly Jessen, Kathy Juntunen, Lois Krenzke, Heather Monkmeyer, and Sandy Wagner.

Express Yourself!

Writers Express is divided
into four major parts . . .

1   **The Process of Writing** ● Use this section to answer your questions about writing, from selecting a subject to proofreading a final draft.

2   **The Forms of Writing** ● Would you like to start a personal journal, or write a poem, or create a tall tale? Then this section is for you!

3   **The Tools of Learning** ● If your study, reading, or test-taking skills could use a little pumping up, turn to "The Tools of Learning."

4   **The Proofreaders Guide** ● Have a question about punctuation? Spelling? Capitalization? Here's where you can "Check It Out!"

Table of Contents

The Process of Writing

Getting Started

Prewriting and Drafting Guide

Revising and Editing Guide

Building Paragraphs and Essays

Improving Your Writing Skills

The Forms of Writing

The Tools of Learning

Proofreader's Guide: Check It Out

Why Write?

A Note from the Editors

Not too long ago, in a not too faraway place, a bunch of friends got together during summer vacation and started a newspaper. *King's Cove* they called it, after a park in their neighbourhood. Each issue was filled with the local gossip, the latest jokes, lists of stuff for sale, and the names of good books to read. Some writers added stories; others wrote poems. A few wrote basic news reports.

Why did these friends go to all of this trouble and do all of this writing? Why not just hang out and goof around? If you were to ask them, you might be surprised by their answers.

Summer Fun

First, they'd tell you writing a newspaper was fun! Yes, it was a lot of work; but in school they had a classroom newspaper, and it was just plain fun to see their ideas and names in print.

Feeling Good

Second, they would tell you it felt terrific working as a team, helping each other out. And third, they would admit that having the other kids read the newspaper gave them a feeling of pride. They were **being heard** and **feeling useful**.

Why write? This group of young writers, in talking about *King's Cove*, offered some very good answers. They wrote to have fun, to work together, and to be heard. We could not have said it better ourselves.

> **"Writing blows me away! Each time I write, I realize I know more than I thought. Cool ideas pop up out of nowhere."**
>
> — Chris, *King's Cove* writer

The Express Connection

We've created *Writers Express* to help make writing an important part of your life, no matter if you are completing assignments in school or working on writing projects in your own neighbourhood. Many writers, teachers, and students have helped put this handbook together, and it is loaded with all kinds of great writing ideas.

Always have your copy of *Writers Express* right next to you when you write. Then turn to it for help whenever you have any questions about your work.

Once you get to know the handbook better, you will see that it is a writing guide plus much more. It contains information that will help you become a better reader, thinker, speaker, learner, and all-around student. Not bad for one little book!

> **"Why write? Maybe we should ask, Why write and read and think and speak and learn? We hope you find many answers to either question in Writers Express — and we hope that you have a lot of fun along the way."**
>
> — The Editors

The Process of Writing

Getting Started

All About Writing

One Writer's Process

A Basic Writing Guide

Writing with a Computer

Planning Your Portfolio

All About Writing

Wishful Thinking

Let's say that you plot out your next writing assignment on your special computer pad, like this:

Subject:	Class elections
Purpose:	To report on election results
Form:	News story
Audience:	Students at my school

Then you plug your keyboard into the pad, set it on automatic pilot, and eat a piece of pizza or read a good book while your story is being written. This would take all of the work and worry out of writing. By pressing a few buttons, your writing would come out just the way you ordered it, every time.

The Real Story

As you probably know, such a gizmo has not been invented yet. For now, and for years to come, you will have to work very closely with your writing to make sure it is done right. You, and *only you,* are in control of the words and ideas you put on paper. And this is exactly how it should be. Writing is too important to be left in the "hands" of a machine.

Points to Remember

The ideas listed below will help you understand what writing is really all about.

✔ *Writing is a natural thing to do.*

>All of us have the ability to write (even without the help of a special computer pad). This is especially true when you write to learn and to explore your own thoughts and feelings.

✔ *Writing is a lot of different things, and all of them are important.*

>Writing is thinking on paper. Writing is learning new things. Writing is making contact with friends and family members. Writing is dealing with bad days, and much more.

> **"***I have found another side of myself that I've never known before. When I leave this grade, I'm not going to stop writing because I don't want to close up a world that I just unlocked.***"**
>
> — Heidi Bimschleger, student

✔ *Writing is a process.*

>Your favourite writers do a lot of planning, writing, and rewriting to produce the books and stories you like to read. That is why writing is called a process. It's very important for young writers like you to understand and use this process in your own writing. (You will learn more about the writing process on the next pages.)

✔ *Writing is a skill that must be practised.*

>Your handbook says a lot of good things about writing. But there is really only one way to learn how to write, and that is by actually putting pen or pencil to paper, or fingers to the keyboard. That's why it is important to practise all kinds of writing: journal writing, story writing, report writing, and so on. (Even writing notes to friends is good practice.)

The Steps in the Process

When we talk about the writing process, we really mean the steps a writer usually follows whenever he or she writes. We have divided the writing process into the following basic steps:

PREWRITING refers to selecting a subject, collecting details, and any other planning that goes on during a writing project.

WRITING THE FIRST DRAFT refers to the actual writing, when a writer gets all of his or her ideas on paper. (Writers often write more than one draft.)

REVISING refers to the changes a writer makes to improve his or her writing. Ideas may be added, cut, or switched around; sentences may be cut or rewritten.

EDITING & PROOFREADING refers to all of the final changes made in the revised writing. During this step, writing is checked carefully for errors.

PUBLISHING

There is one more important step in he process — publishing. Sharing your story with friends or classmates is one form of publishing; so is sending it to the school or city newspaper. You will naturally work harder at your writing if you know that it is going to be published. (**SEE** pages 54-57 for more information.)

THINK IT OVER

A writer may repeat some of these steps before a piece of writing is finished. For example, after the first draft, a writer may decide to do some more prewriting and planning.

The Writing Process in Action

These two pages provide a basic look at the writing process in action. You will find this information helpful if you have never used the writing process before or if you would like a general guide to follow when you write.

PREWRITING

Prewriting means getting ready to write. Follow these basic steps during prewriting:

- **Select** a subject that really interests you.
- **Collect** details about your subject if you don't know a lot about it.
- **Plan** what you want to say about your subject (the main idea of your writing) and how you want to say it (the form of your writing)

WRITING THE FIRST DRAFT

Once you've collected your thoughts about your subject, write the first draft of your paper.

- **Write** this draft freely, getting *all* of your ideas on paper.
- **Imagine** that you are talking to a group of friends.
- **Let** your prewriting and planning be your guide as you write.

REVISING

When you revise, you try to make improvements in your draft. Follow this basic revising plan:

- **Read** your draft two or three times.

- **Ask** at least one classmate or friend to read and react to your draft.

- **Decide** what changes need to be made.

- **Work** on improving your writing.

EDITING & PROOFREADING

When you edit and proofread, you make sure the revised version of your writing is clear and accurate. Follow this basic editing and proofreading plan:

- **Look** closely at the style of your writing. (Your words and sentences should read smoothly.)

- **Check** your writing for spelling, punctuation, and grammar errors. (Ask for help from a classmate or teacher.)

- **Write or type** a neat final draft of your writing.

- **Proofread** this draft for any additional errors.

One Writer's Process

One Step at a Time

For one of her assignments, Hillary Bachman was asked to write about her favourite teacher. Here's how she used the writing process to complete her assignment.

PREWRITING *Planning Your Way*

Selecting a Subject ● Hillary started by thinking about all of her favourite teachers, past and present. She thought of Mrs. Thompson, Mr. Schwarz, Mrs. Chan, and Mr. Vetter. The one teacher that really stood out was Mr. Vetter, so she decided to write about him.

Collecting Details ● She then freely listed ideas about her subject.

funny, nice, helpful, coach, two boys my age,
helps students, friend, room 203, math,
fun learning, answers questions, laughs,
tells us jokes, we learn, sees when I'm upset,
called Mr. V, . . .

WRITING THE FIRST DRAFT

Mr. Vetter was one of Hillary's current teachers, so she had no trouble writing about him. This is part of her first draft.

<table>
<tr><td>

Hillary starts with words from her collecting list. →

</td><td>

A Great Teacher

Funny, helpful, and friendly. What am I describing? Is it one of your classmates or your best friend? Beleive it or not, Im describing a teacher! His name is Mr. Vetter. We call him Mr. V.

</td></tr>
<tr><td>

She continues by writing freely about her subject. →

</td><td>

One thing that really like about him is the way he makes learning fun.

If math seams boring, he will make it fun by saying something that is so funny so you want to learn. Once I sneezed really loud in the middle of class. Right away, Mr. V. said "googolplex.*" It sounded just the same as gesunthite or bless you.

Mr. V. also . . .

</td></tr>
</table>

*Googolplex refers to a very large number.

REVISING *Improving the Writing*

After reviewing her first draft, Hillary tried to make her writing clearer and more complete. (The comments on the right side of her paper were made by a classmate.)

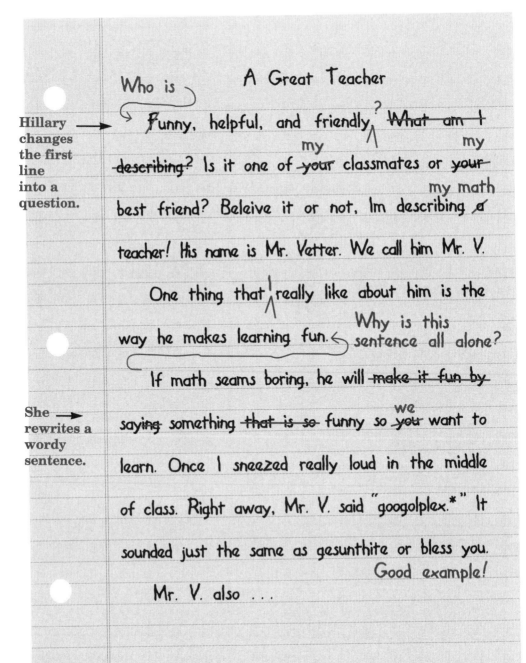

Hillary changes the first line into a question.

A Great Teacher

~~Who is~~ ↱ ~~F~~unny, helpful, and friendly, ~~What am I~~ ?

~~describing?~~ Is it one of ~~your~~ my classmates or ~~your~~ my

best friend? Beleive it or not, Im describing a my math

teacher! His name is Mr. Vetter. We call him Mr. V.

One thing that really like about him is the

way he makes learning fun. ↞ Why is this sentence all alone?

If math seams boring, he will ~~make it fun by~~

She rewrites a wordy sentence.

~~saying~~ something ~~that is so~~ funny so ~~you~~ we want to

learn. Once I sneezed really loud in the middle

of class. Right away, Mr. V. said "googolplex.*" It

sounded just the same as gesunthite or bless you.

Good example!

Mr. V. also . . .

EDITING & PROOFREADING

Hillary then made sure that her writing read smoothly and was free of errors. She paid special attention to spelling and punctuation. (She would check for errors one more time after writing a neat final draft of her paper.)

A Great Teacher

Who is funny, helpful, and friendly? Is it one

Hillary corrects her spelling. → of my classmates or my best friend? Beleive it

or not, I'm describing my math teacher! His

Hillary combines two sentences for smooth reading. → name is Mr. Vetter, *but we* We call him Mr. V.

One thing that I really like about him is the

seems way he makes learning fun. If math seams

boring, he will say something funny so we want to

A comma and capital letter are added to the dialogue. → learn. Once I sneezed really loud in the middle of

class. Right away, Mr. V. said, "googolplex." It

sounded just the same as *gesundheit* gesunthite or bless you.

Mr. V. also . . .

A Basic Writing Guide

Seven Secrets to Success

1 What should I write about?

Repeat this line after me: *I will write about a subject that really interests or excites me*. Say it again. Let this point be your guide each time you start a new writing project.

> 66 Writing has never been my best friend. I always thought it was hard, but now I'm able to pick better topics that I enjoy, and I have grown to love it. 99

— Shaun McDonnell, student

See what I mean? Writing about something that interests you can make all the difference! It's what writing is all about.

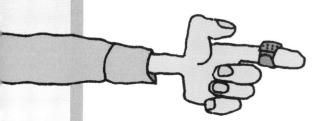

When you can't think of anything to write about, complete one of the selecting activities listed on pages 26-27.

2 Do I have to collect a lot of details before I write?

That depends on the type of writing you are doing. If you're writing about a personal experience (like your first sleep-over), all of the important facts and details may be very clear to you. So you're probably ready to start your first draft right away.

But let's say you decide to write a classroom report about old-time movie monsters. You would have to collect quite a bit of information about this subject before you would be ready to write.

You can start your collecting by talking to someone about your subject or by writing down what you already know about it. Then you can go on from there by reading and trying other collecting activities.

SEE pages 30-31 for basic guidelines and activities to help you collect details for your writing.

3 Should I say everything I know about my subject?

No, your writing would probably go on and on if you say *everything* about it. So you have to think of some way to keep it under control. You can decide what your readers *really* need to know about your subject and write just that information.

In addition, you can think of a focus, or main idea, for your writing. A focus may be a special feeling that you have about a subject, or it may be a certain part of a subject that you really want to talk about. For example, in a story about your best friend, you could focus on one of his or her important personality traits, like kindness or loyalty.

SEE page 32 for more information about planning your writing.

4 How should I write my first draft?

Write your first draft freely and honestly, as if you were telling it to a group of friends. Don't worry about making mistakes or using your best penmanship. In a first draft, you can cross out words, write in the margins, draw arrows, and so on. Remember that first drafts are often called *rough drafts*.

Also, don't worry about saying too much or too little about your subject. A first draft is only your first try at a writing idea; you will make changes later. If you have planning notes or a basic outline, use it as a guide when you write.

SEE page 33 for more on writing first drafts.

5 How do I know what changes to make in my first draft?

You are the best judge of your own writing. If important details seem to be missing, add them. If a certain part doesn't sound right, fix it. But it is also very important to have at least one or two classmates review your work. They may catch some important things that you didn't see.

When you revise, look first at the main points in your writing. Make sure that they are clear and complete. Once all of these ideas are in order, then look at more specific things like word choice and spelling.

SEE pages 37-42 for more information about revising writing.

6 Do I have to find all of the spelling and grammar errors in my writing?

Let's put it this way: No one expects you to be an expert speller or a master of all of the mechanics and grammar rules. But *everyone* expects you to correct as many errors as you can before you publish or share a piece of writing. Writing that contains a lot of errors is hard to read.

Find as many errors as you can on your own. For example, you can make sure that each of your sentences begins with a capital letter and ends with a period. Then ask a classmate or your teacher to check your work. (All professional writers have editors who help them edit and proofread their work.)

SEE page 42 for more information on editing and proofreading.

7 How do I know if my writing is good?

Here is a quick and simple way to evaluate your writing. If you can nod your head after at least three of these questions, you should feel good about your work.

_____ *Did you select a subject that really interests you?*

_____ *Did you think of a special way to write about this subject?*

_____ *Did you make changes in your writing until it said what you wanted it to say?*

_____ *Did you share your work during the writing process?*

SEE page 49 for a basic checklist that will help you evaluate your writing.

Writing with a Computer

Tools of the Trade

People simply can't work or play without the right tools. A family doctor couldn't carry out an examination without a stethoscope or tongue depressor (say ahhh!). A mechanic without socket wrenches and screwdrivers might as well close up shop. A spelunker, someone who explores caves, would be lost without a flashlight and hard hat.

The personal computer will probably be most helpful to you as a revising and editing tool. A spell checker can also be helpful.

All "Keyed Up"

One tool that many writers could not do without is the **personal computer**. Writers will tell you that a computer allows them to say a lot in a short amount of time. They will also tell you that revising and editing first drafts is very easy on the computer.

Coming On-Line

Even if you don't have your own computer, your school is (or soon will be) equipped with them. If you are just learning to use a computer, the following comments about computers and writing will be helpful.

Know Who's in Control ➤ A computer can't think for you (not yet anyway), and it can't write for you. You still have to come up with all of the words and ideas.

Know When to Use Your Computer ➤ Don't put your pencils and paper away once you start using a computer (unless you are a keyboard wizard). You may want to do your planning and first drafts on paper. Then enter or type your work on the computer. At that point, you can make revising and editing changes on the computer screen or on a neat computer printout.

Know What Your Computer Can Do ➤ Word processing programs make a computer the high-tech writing machine it is. All programs allow you to enter your writing on the computer and work with it in many different ways. You can add or cut ideas and move parts around. You can check your work for spelling errors, and so on. (***SEE*** the Bright Idea below.)

Learn the Golden Rule ➤ Expect to lose one of the first few assignments you write on a computer, even if you are very careful. It happens to everyone. Remember the golden rule of the computer age: *Always make a backup copy of your work.*

Learn How to Keyboard ➤ Practise keyboarding as often as you can — before, during, and after school. The faster you get, the more you will like using a computer.

To learn how your word processing program works, enter an old story or paragraph into the computer. Then practise making changes in your writing. (When you get stuck, refer to the program manual or ask a friend or classmate for help.)

Planning Your Portfolio

Organizing Your Own Writing

All writers keep a special collection of their work in a three-ring binder, in file folders, or in some other type of organizer. A collection like this is called a **personal portfolio**. My portfolio is a three-ring binder, but I think of it more as a treasure chest — probably because all of the writing it contains is very special to me.

66Your portfolio represents your work as a writer. The pieces you include in it should say something about your personal talents and your writing process.**99**
— Anne-Marie Oomen

One Writer's Portfolio

I've divided my portfolio into four sections: *new ideas, important drafts, writing just for me,* and *finished writing.* You can learn more about the different sections in my personal portfolio on the next page.

Personal Portfolio Model

Notice that my portfolio is basically organized according to the steps in the writing process.

New Ideas ● In this part of my portfolio, I collect interesting thoughts and descriptions scribbled on notebook paper, dinner napkins, and so on. I go to this section whenever I need ideas for writing.

Important Drafts ● This section includes writing projects that are almost finished. In one case, I may need to talk to someone about the writing. In another case, I may just need to get away from the writing for a while.

Writing Just for Me ● The writing in this section has great personal value to me, but I will never try to publish any of it. Included here are personal letters and special pages from my journal. Sometimes ideas for new writing projects come to mind as I reread this section.

Finished Writing ● I've taken all of these pieces through the entire writing process. They are as good as I can make them. Some of this work has already been published, and some of it I am still trying to get into print.

New Ideas

Important Drafts

Just for Me

Finished Writing

Bright IDEA

You might want to divide your personal portfolio according to the different types of writing you like to do: *poems, stories, plays,* and *letters*. Or you might want to divide it by different audiences: *personal and private, family, friends,* and so on. It's your choice.

Preparing a Classroom Portfolio

If you do a lot of writing in your class, your teacher may ask you to put together a portfolio of your work at the end of the term or grading period. For a basic introduction to the classroom portfolio, read the next two pages.

What is a classroom writing portfolio?

A classroom portfolio is a collection of the best writing you choose to turn in for evaluation. It will also contain basic self-evaluation sheets related to your writing, and maybe a few other things. (Your teacher will provide you with the self-evaluation sheets.)

How is a classroom portfolio different from a basic writing folder?

A writing folder contains all of your in-class writing, from old assignments to the latest story you are working on. A portfolio, on the other hand, contains only your best efforts.

Why would your teacher ask you to put together a portfolio?

Your teacher knows that a classroom portfolio makes the writing process much more real and meaningful for you. You are, after all, going to be judged on the writing *you* decide to include in your portfolio.

❝I used to think of writing as my most dreaded fear. Now it's what I look forward to... When I look over my work, I feel honoured that I wrote it.❞

— Kristen Tomlinson, student

What will you include?

Your teacher will make it very clear what your portfolio should contain. She will tell you how many pieces to include, what types of writing you can choose from, and so on. She will also set a due date when your portfolio must be ready.

What is the most important thing to remember about a writing portfolio?

A writing portfolio is the story of your writing experiences. If you put forth your best efforts, your portfolio will be a success.

Planning Tips

Be Prepared ● It's up to you to understand *all* of the requirements for your portfolio, including what it should contain and what it should look like. (Teachers usually provide special portfolio folders, but you might be able to design your own.)

Stay Organized ● Never, ever lose any of the drafts for writing you are going to include in your portfolio. (We will personally give you six lashes with a wet noodle for each draft you lose.)

Keep on Schedule ● Don't wait to the last minute to complete your writing or other parts of your portfolio. (Remember that it takes time to produce your best efforts.)

Ask for Help ● When you have questions about anything, ask your teacher and classmates for help. (Don't be bashful with something as important as a writing portfolio.)

Do Your Best Work ● All of your work should be neat and in the right place when you turn in your portfolio. (Try to make a good first impression.)

Prewriting and Drafting Guide

Building a File of Writing Ideas

Selecting a Subject

Starting Points for Writing

Collecting Details

Planning and Drafting Tips

Building a Resource of Writing Forms

Prewriting and Drafting Guide

This section contains guidelines, lists, and suggestions for getting ready to write. We hope they help!

BUILDING A FILE OF Writing IDEAS

Most writers are interesting people. They know a lot about all of the different things going on around them. And they try to remember and save as many details from their experiences as they can, knowing that these ideas can be used in their own writing. You can begin to save ideas, just like your favourite authors do, by completing some of the activities listed below. Have fun!

Think and act like a writer! Always keep your eyes and ears open for interesting sights and sounds. On the way to school, you might see two crazy squirrels dashing up and down a tree, as if they were running a shuttle race. In class, you might hear someone whisper, "What's the answer to number five?" Later, at home, you might daydream about being famous someday. Without too much trouble, you could probably think of a story to write, using any one of these ideas.

Helpful Hint   Reserve a section in a notebook or journal where you can list some of these sights and sounds.

Keep track of your experiences! Start a "This Is My Life" list and keep adding to it throughout the school year. Here's what you might include:

- People I'll Never Forget
- Animals I'll Never Forget
- Important Places Near and Far
- Favourite Books and Movies
- Special Skills and Talents
- Unforgettable Moments
- Biggest Blunders
- Important Beliefs
- Prized Possessions
- Wild Ideas

Make new discoveries!   Get involved in many different experiences. Join teams, visit different places, help people out, and have fun with friends. The more you do, the more you know.

Read a lot!   Read books, magazines, newspapers, and whatever else you like. Jot down any names, descriptions, or ideas that jump off the page as you read. These jottings may give you ideas for your own writing.

Write a lot!   Explore your thoughts and feelings in a personal journal or diary, and you will always have a good supply of writing ideas. (SEE pages 106-108 for more information.)

Draw a life map!   Start your life map with your birth and work right up to the present. Choose the experiences you want to picture along the way. This idea comes from two writers names Dan Kirby and Tom Liner. (See the model below.)

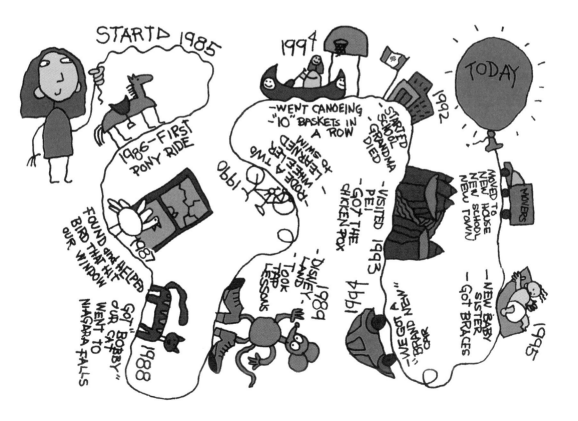

Let's say you've been asked to write about a memorable experience. You say to yourself, "No problem. I'll write about…" But then no ideas come to mind. What should you do? First, see what your handbook has to say about your writing assignment. (Tips for selecting a subject are provided for many forms in "The Forms of Writing" section.) Then check your journal or writer's notebook for ideas. If you still need help, you can talk about the assignment with your classmates, or try one or more of the activities listed here.

Activities for Selecting a Subject

Clustering ■ Begin a cluster by writing an important word related to your assignment. Then list related words and ideas around it. Circle and connect new words as shown in the model.

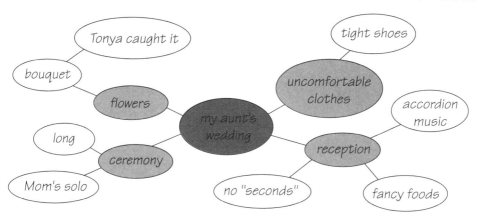

Note: After 2 or 3 minutes of clustering, a writing idea or two may begin to take shape. (Try free writing about one of these ideas.)

Free Writing ■ Write freely for 3 to 5 minutes. *Do not stop and think during this time; just write.* Begin free writing with an idea related to your assignment. As you write, one or two subjects may come to mind. (*SEE* pages 28-29 for ideas for free writing.)

Listing ■ Freely list any ideas that pop into your head when you think of your assignment. You and a classmate can help each other think of possible subjects by listing or brainstorming together.

Sentence Completion ■ Complete a sentence starter in as many ways as you can. Make sure that your sentence starter relates to your assignment. Here are six samples:

I remember when…	I really get mad when…
One place I like…	I just learned…
I wonder how…	School is…

Review the Basics of Life Checklist ■ Many of the things we need to lead a full life fall into the basic categories or groups listed below.

agriculture	faith	love
animals	family	machines
art/music	food	money
books	freedom	plants
clothing	friends	science/technology
community	health	work/play
education	housing	
energy	laws	
environment		
exercise		

MINI LESSON Here's how you can use this checklist to think of possible subjects:

1. Choose one of the categories or groups. (*food*)
2. Decide how this category relates to your assignment. (*memorable experience*)
3. List possible subjects. (*your most memorable meal, a kitchen disaster, and so on*)

When you need a subject or starting point for a writing assignment, look at the prompts and topics on the next two pages for ideas.

Writing Prompts

The following prompts will get you thinking about possible subjects for writing. For example, think of the many ways you could complete this phrase: "The first time I…" You will find this page of prompts especially helpful when you are writing about a personal experience.

Best and Worst
My best day
My worst moment
My biggest accomplishment
My saddest experience

It Could Only Happen to Me!
It sounds unbelievable, but…
I felt so foolish.
I looked everywhere for…

What If… and Why?
What if animals could talk?
What if I had three wishes?
Why is it important to win?
Why do we have to go so fast?

First and Last
The first time I…
My last visit with…
My first goal
The last place I want to go

I Was Just Thinking
I believe in…
I worry about…
Things that make me angry

School Days
I never worked so hard.
I'd like you to meet…
Where did I put my assignment?

Quotations
"Be yourself. Who else is better qualified?"
"Following the crowd can lead nowhere."
"Everyone needs a place to hang out."

"More is not always better."
"We all make mistakes."
"Take life one day at a time."

Writing Topics

As you can see, the following topics are organized according to the four basic reasons for writing. They will be especially helpful when you need ideas for a specific kind of writing (descriptions, explanations, narratives, and persuasive paragraphs).

Describing

People: a relative, a teacher, a classmate, a neighbour, someone who bugs you, someone you spend time with, someone you wish you were like

Places: your room, a garage, a basement, an attic, a rooftop, the alley, the gym, the library, a barn, a lake, a river, a yard, a park, the zoo, a museum

Objects or things: a poster, a stuffed animal, a video game, a book, a drawing, a junk drawer, a photograph, a letter, a pet, a souvenir, a model, a key, a dream

Explaining

How to... make a sandwich, care for a pet, impress a teacher, earn extra money, get in shape, be a friend, stop hiccups, run a race, saddle a horse, teach..., choose..., build..., fix..., grow..., save..., find...

The causes of... rust, acid rain, friendship, hurricanes, happiness

Kinds of... music, commercials, clouds, heroes, cars, pain, groups, restaurants, fun, streets, stores, books

The definition of... love, learning, a good time, friendship, a team, community, a teacher, courage

Persuading

school rules, homework, smoking in public places, shoplifting, bicycle helmets, something that needs improving, something that's unfair, something everyone should see or do, something worth supporting

Narrating (Sharing)

getting caught, getting lost, getting together, making a mistake, being surprised, making the news, learning to _____, being scared, winning

Try writing freely about one of the prompts or topics related to your assignment. As you write, you may discover a number of possible writing ideas.

You really have three basic ways to collect facts and details about a subject. You can...

✔ talk to someone about it,

✔ read and learn about it yourself,

✔ and try one or more of the following collecting activities.

Free Writing ■ Let's say your subject for a writing assignment is the first time you slept over at a friend's house. If you write freely about this time, you will see how many details you really remember about it. *Don't stop and think for this type of writing; just keep the ideas flowing.* (Sometimes your free writing will be so good that you can use it as your first draft.)

To give your free writing a special twist, write to a specific audience: a group of preschoolers, your parents, a student from another country, etc.

Bright
IDEA

5 Ws of Writing ■ Answer the 5 Ws — *Who? What? When? Where?* and *Why?* — to collect basic information about your subject. (Add *How?* to the list for even more details.)

Clustering ■ Use the subject of your writing as the nucleus word for a cluster. Then list, circle, and connect words related to your subject. (*SEE* page 26 for a model.)

Subject Talk ■ Make up a dialogue in which two people (real or imaginary) talk about your subject. Keep the conversation going as long as you can.

Focused Thinking ■ To think carefully about a subject,
write freely about it in two or three of the following ways:

- ☐ *Describe it*. What do you see, hear, feel, smell, taste?

- ☐ *Compare it.* What is it like? What is it different from?

- ☐ *Apply it.* What can you do with it? How can you use it?

- ☐ *Break it down.* What parts does it have? How to
  they work?

- ☐ *Evaluate it.* What are its strengths and weaknesses?

Crazy Questions ■ To help you see your subject in creative
ways, make up some crazy questions about it, and then try to
answer them. Some sample questions follow:

Writing About a Person
What type of clothing is this person like?
Which city or place should this person never visit?

Writing About a Place
What does this place like to do?
What song does it like?

Writing About an Object
What does this object do on weekends?
What does it look like upside down?

Writing to Explain a Process
Where does this process like to shop?
What sport is it like?

Writing About an Experience
(a Narrative)
What movie is this experience like?
What colours does it call to mind?

Collection Sheet ■ Use a collection sheet or gathering
grid to help you keep track of the facts and details you collect.
(**SEE** pages 173 and 226 for examples.)

PLANNING AND Drafting Tips

All successful sports teams start out with a game plan. This plan keeps them organized and focused as the game starts. A game plan (a writing plan) can help you do the same thing when you start a first draft. Here's one way you might draw up your plan.

Developing a Writing Plan

The First Step ➤ Start with these five important points:

Subject: *Who or what are you writing about?*

Purpose: *Why are you writing? (To explain? To describe?)*

Form/Organization: *What form will you use (poem, paragraph, etc.)?*

Audience: *Who are your readers?*

Voice: *How will your writing sound (serious, funny, etc.)?*

A Sample Plan ➤ Let's say I plotted out the following assignment:

Subject: My best friend, Raji

Purpose: To describe why I like him

Form/Organization: Letter

Audience: Classmates and Raji

Voice: Friendly

The Next Step ➤ Next, I would decide on the type of ideas I want to include. I could, for example, write about the funny things Raji does, or the different things we like to do together.

At this point, I would be well prepared to write. I would know whom I was writing about, how I wanted my writing to look, and what I wanted to say. (If something in my plan didn't work out, I could always change part of it.)

Writing a First Draft

Remember that your first draft is your first try at your writing, so it doesn't have to be (and shouldn't be) perfect. Don't stop and think and worry. Just write freely. All you need to do is get your main ideas on paper.

Be Prepared ● It is always easier to write a first draft when you know a lot of facts and details about your subject and you have a basic plan to follow.

Be Willing to Work ● Write your draft while all of your collecting and planning is still fresh in your mind.

Be Open-Minded ● If some new ideas pop into your mind as you write, don't be afraid to include them in your writing.

Be Honest ● Let the real you come through in your writing. This is your paper, so make it sound like you!

You may want to talk about your ideas with a classmate or friend before you actually begin to write. Sharing your thoughts can help you test them out before you write them down. Talking can also help you write more freely and naturally.

Plan the Opening Sentences

Sometimes it helps to plan exactly what you want to say in the opening sentences before you dive into your first draft. Make sure your first lines sound interesting. But also make sure that they state your true feelings about your subject.

You may want to start your writing in one of the following ways:

■ Begin with a surprising fact or quote.

■ Start with a question.

■ Open with some dialogue.

■ Share a brief story about the subject.

■ Introduce some of the main points you plan to cover.

Helpful Hint   **SEE** "Writing a Lead" on page 130 for more ideas and examples.

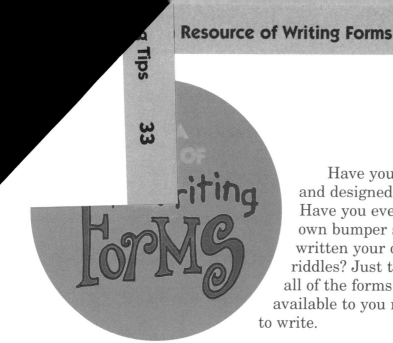

Have you ever written and designed a storybook? Have you ever created your own bumper sticker or written your own book of riddles? Just thinking about all of the forms of writing available to you might help you to write.

Advertisements
Autobiographies
Biographies
Book Reviews
Bumper Stickers
Cartoons, Comic Strips
Descriptions
Dialogues
Dictionaries
Directions (how-to)
Editorials
Family Parables
Instructional Manuals
Interviews
Jokes
Journals, Diaries
Letters

Myths
Narratives
Newspaper Writing
Pamphlets
Photo Captions
Plays
Poems
Proposals
Radio Plays
Recipes
Reports
Requests
Reviews
Riddles
Slogans
Songs
Tall Tales
Time Lines

Other Forms You Might Try

Anecdote ● a little story that describes an interesting incident

Aphorism ● a short, wise saying

Bio-Poem ● a poem about someone's life

Case Study ● a story of one person who represents a larger group

Character Sketch ● a description of a real person

Commentary ● a personal opinion about the state of the world

Dramatic Monologue ● a one-way conversation in which someone tells a lot about him- or herself

E-Mail (electronic mail) ● a message sent between two people using computers

News Release ● an explanation of a coming event using the 5 Ws

Observation Report ● writing that records sights, sounds, and other sensory details

Oral History ● writing down a tape-recorded or filmed conversation about an earlier time period

Parody ● a funny imitation of a serious piece of writing

Pet Peeve ● a personal feeling about something that bugs you

Petition ● a formal request addressed to someone in power

Profile ● a detailed report about a person

Time Capsule ● writing that captures a particular time period

Travelogue ● writing that describes travel pictures (slides, video, film)

THINK IT OVER

You can learn a lot about writing by experimenting with many of these forms. For example, by writing photo captions, you may learn something that will help you write more effective descriptive paragraphs.

Revising and Editing Guide

Revising Your Writing

Editing and Proofreading

Conferencing with Partners

Sharing Family Stories

Publishing Your Writing

Revising Your Writing

Improving Your First Draft

If you say something silly or stupid, there is not much you can do about it. What's said is said. On the other hand, when you write something that sounds kind of dumb, you can always change it. You can, in fact, change it again and again until it says exactly what you want it to say. That's what makes writing so powerful.

Making changes, or *revising*, is the subject of this chapter. You will learn how to turn your first drafts into more complete and creative pieces of writing. Remember that all of your favourite authors spend a lot of time revising their first drafts. It's important that you do the same in your own work.

"Writing a story takes time and energy, but it feels really good when it's done."

— Lauren Brydon, student

What Does It Mean to Revise?

Improve the Ideas ● When you revise a first draft, you make sure that all of the important points about your subject are made. You also make sure that your readers can understand all of your ideas.

Wait with Spelling and Mechanics ● Don't spend a lot of time looking for specific errors in your sentences. First, get all of your main ideas in shape.

How Do You Get Started?

Take a Break ● The first step is easy. Slip your first draft into a folder and forget about it. You need to get away from your writing for a while before you try to change it.

Read and Share ● When you come back to your first draft, read it two or three times. Try reading it out loud. Also have one or two classmates read and react to your draft. Listen carefully to their comments.

What Should You Look For?

Look for the Strong Parts ● Always find one or two things you like in your draft. You may like the dialogue in one part of your writing and a descriptive sentence in another part. Put a star next to these parts. It's good for the spirit.

Look for the Weak Parts ● You must also look for parts that need work. Important details may be missing in one part of your writing, or your sentences may sound confusing in another part. (The checklist on the next page will help you review your work.)

Revising Checklist

Use the following checklist as a guide when you review and revise a first draft.

_____ ***Did I focus on a certain part of my subject, instead of trying to say everything about it?***

_____ ***Do I need to add any information?***
- ✔ Do I need to add a topic sentence, or a sentence that states the main idea of my writing?
- ✔ Do I need to add any important details?
- ✔ Do I need to add a closing or concluding sentence?

_____ ***Do I need to cut any information?***
- ✔ Did I include any details that don't support my main idea?
- ✔ Have I repeated myself in any parts?
- ✔ Have I said too much about a certain idea?

_____ ***Do I need to rewrite any parts?***
- ✔ Are there ideas or sentences that are unclear or confusing?
- ✔ Did I do too much telling and not enough showing? (**SEE** the next page.)
- ✔ Could I improve my explanation in a certain part?

_____ ***Do I need to reorder any parts of my writing?***
- ✔ Do any ideas or details seem to be out of place?
- ✔ Did I place my most important point in the best spot?
- ✔ Did I follow an effective method of organization? (**SEE** page 68.)

Show, Don't Tell

If you do a lot of telling in your first draft, try turning it into writing that shows. If readers can't *see* and *hear* and *touch* and *taste* and *feel* what you've written, it just won't come to life for them. Here's the basic rule:

> ***Use your five senses as you write, and show your readers what you mean.***

One Writer in Action

Here's how author Will Hobbs explains writing that shows.

Let's say I almost drowned last summer, and I'm trying to tell a reader what it was like: "I was drowning. It was really bad. I thought I was going to die. I was really scared..." Now, does the reader feel what it was like? The answer is no. Did I tell, or did I show? I told. I didn't use the five senses.

Don't Use "Telling" Words ■ I try not to use words that tell, like "scared" or "angry." When Cloyd is walking out on a high ledge in my novel *Bearstone*, I didn't want to tell the readers he was scared. I tried to show them instead.

Use "Showing" Words ■ ***"The shape of the rock had forced his body weight out over the thin air, and he was in bad trouble. Stretched tight, the tendons above his heels began to quiver, then to tremble. His strength deserted him in a rush. He paused to rest, but his legs began to shake violently."***

More Revising Tips

Check for Details

"I went to my first basketball game. It was fun."

These two sentences don't say much, do they? We don't know who went to the game, who played, who won, and so on. In other words, a lot of details are missing. Always make sure that you have included enough details in your writing.

Include a Beginning, Middle, and Ending

Your writing should be clear and complete from start to finish. That means it should contain an effective beginning, middle, and ending.

Beginning: Make sure your opening lines grab your readers' attention and tell them something about your subject:

"Listen everybody. Let's keep our buses clean!"

Middle: Stick to the point! All of the ideas in the middle, or body, of your writing should support or explain your subject.

Ending: Add a closing idea to stress the importance of your subject and to keep your reader thinking about it:

"I've seen enough ABC gum, paper wads, and old Kleenex to last me a long time. I hope you have, too."

Add a Title

Once you have all of your main ideas in place, think of a title for your writing. List a number of possible choices, and select the best one. A good title should hook your readers into your writing:

Four Quarters of Fun sounds better than *My First Game*.

Have Garbage Will Travel sounds better than *Bus Litter*.

 You may have to revise your writing two or three times before all of your ideas are clear and complete.

Editing and Proofreading

Polishing Your Writing

This chapter deals with editing and proofreading, the step in the writing process when you get your writing ready to share or publish. Remember that editing and proofreading becomes important *after* you have changed, or revised, any of the main ideas in your first draft.

Make Every Word Count!

The guidelines in this chapter will help you check your writing for style and correctness. All of your sentences and words should read smoothly, and they should be free of careless errors. In other words, this chapter will help you make every word count in your work.

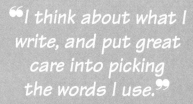

"I think about what I write, and put great care into picking the words I use."

— Catherine Ferrante, student

Checking Your Sentences

Combine Short Sentences ● If you use too many short
sentences one after another, your writing may sound choppy. You
can correct this problem by combining some of your sentences.

Four short sentences:

> *The dog followed Mary.*
>
> *It followed her for half a kilometre.*
>
> *It stayed very close behind her.*
>
> *She forced herself to stay calm.*

■ **Two Longer, Smoother Sentences:**

> *The dog followed Mary for half a kilometre. It stayed very
> close behind her, but she forced herself to stay calm.*

Change Your Sentence Beginnings ● If too many of your
sentences begin in the same way, your writing may sound dull and
lifeless. You can correct this problem by changing the way you
start some of your sentences.

Three sentences beginning with the subject *I*:

> *I slowly ate the cooked carrots. I washed them down with
> milk to cover the taste. I tried to hide some of them when my
> mom wasn't looking.*

How to Change Sentence Beginnings

■ Start with a Modifier:

> *Slowly,* **I ate the cooked carrots.**

■ Start with a Phrase:

> *To cover the taste,* **I washed them down with milk.**

■ Start with a Clause:

> *When my mom wasn't looking,* **I tried to hide some of them.**

Correct Sentence Errors ● There are three basic types
of errors you should look for in your writing: *sentence fragments,
run-on sentences,* and *rambling sentences.* (**SEE** page 87.)

Checking Your Word Choice

Use Powerful Verbs ● As writer Will Hobbs says, "Verbs power sentences, making them fly or jump or sink or swim." They help make your ideas come alive for your readers. Here is a sentence from *Devil on my Back* by Monica Hughes. The powerful verbs (in bold type) give an effective picture of the action.

> He **staggered** over to the door and **grasped** the frame, **stepped** through it into a sunny glade surrounded by wooden houses.

Use Specific Nouns ● Some nouns like *car, fruit, store, flowers,* and *candy* are general and give readers a fuzzy picture. Other nouns like **Honda, kiwi, Zellers, tulips,** and **Snickers** are specific and give readers a much clearer picture. Always try to use specific nouns in your writing.

Choose Colourful Modifiers ● Effective adjectives and adverbs can add colour to your writing.

■ **Using Adjectives:**

> She wandered into the **deep** shade of the **giant** fir trees. (The adjectives make the picture clearer.)

■ **Using Adverbs:**

> Rover ran **wildly** after Rachel. She headed **directly** for the back door. (The adverbs add to the action.)

 Modifiers are very important, but be careful not to *overuse* them. Too many adjectives and adverbs can make your writing sound unnatural.

Select the Right Word ● Make sure that the words you use in your writing are correct. For example, it's easy to confuse words that sound the same — *there, their,* and *they're; know* and *no.* (**SEE** pages 362-369 for a list of words that are often confused.)

Editing and Proofreading Checklist

Use this checklist as a guide when you edit your writing. Also use it when you are ready to proofread your final draft.

Sentence Structure

✔ Did I write clear and complete sentences?

✔ Did I write sentences of different lengths?

✔ Did I begin my sentences in different ways?

Word Choice

✔ Did I use powerful verbs, specific nouns, and colourful modifiers?

✔ Did I use the correct word (*to, too,* or *two; your* or *you're*)? (**SEE** pages 362-369 for help.)

Punctuation

✔ Does each sentence end with an end punctuation mark?

✔ Did I use commas in a series (*Larry, Moe,* and *Curly*)?

✔ Did I place commas before connecting words (*and, but, or*) in compound sentences?

✔ Did I punctuate dialogue correctly? (**SEE** pages 346 and 350 for help.)

Capitalization

✔ Did I start all my sentences with a capital letter?

✔ Did I capitalize nouns that name specific people, places, and things?

Spelling

✔ Did I check for spelling? Did I use the spell checker on my computer? (**SEE** pages 270-273 for help.)

Conferencing with Partners

Sharing and Learning

Writers spend a lot of time thinking and writing by themselves. But sooner or later they need an audience, someone to listen to what they've written. Do you ever nudge your neighbour at school and say, "Hey, Josh, listen to this"? Or at home, do you ever ask your mom or dad to react to something you are writing? If you do, you are acting like a real author.

Getting Started

This chapter is all about working in writing groups and helping one another become better listeners, thinkers, and writers.

Any time writers share ideas about their writing, they are having a conference. You can conference in pairs or in small groups, in school or at home, with classmates or with your teacher, with friends or with family members.

Counting on Your Friends

All good writers (like you!) know they need to find someone who will listen to their writing and help them make it better. We spoke to students at one school, and they gave these reasons why talking with their classmates in writing conferences was helpful:

Conference partners help writers...

- think about all of the ideas in their writing,
- discover new ideas to add to their writing,
- and learn new skills (like writing dialogue).

A good conference partner...

- makes you feel comfortable,
- helps you stay on track (so you don't talk too much about recess),
- shows an interest in your subject,
- listens carefully,
- and gives you straight answers.

"When I conferenced, I became friends with more people. I felt wonderful because I knew some of me was in their writing."
— Damian Broccoli, student

Helping One Another

Conference partners can help you throughout the writing process. Their advice is especially important once you complete a first draft. They can help you identify the parts that work well in your writing, as well as the parts that need work.

They can also help you when you are ready to edit and proofread your work. Good conference partners will catch the spelling or grammar errors that you miss. Finally, they can react to the final draft of your writing. This is the most exciting (and perhaps the scariest) part of the writing process.

Conference Guidelines

During a conference, authors read their drafts to partners who listen and respond. Listed below are tips for conference partners.

Suggestions for Authors:

- Come prepared with a piece of writing you really care about.
- Tell your partner about your interest in this writing.
- Point out any problems you're having.
- Read your work out loud. (Speak clearly and don't rush.)
- Pay attention to what your partner tells you is working or not working in your draft. (His or her questions and suggestions will help you improve your writing.)
- Don't take suggestions personally. Your partner is just trying to help.

Suggestions for Listeners:

- Listen carefully (and take notes) so you can make good observations. (**SEE** "Good Listener Checklist," page 293.)
- Begin your response with positive comments. ("I like the way...")
- Ask questions if you are confused about something or want to know more. ("What do you mean when you say?")
- Make suggestions in a helpful way. (Don't say, "Your writing is boring." Try something like, "Many of your sentences begin in the same way.")
- Always be kind and polite. Writers work hard!

THINK IT OVER

Conference partners should praise a classmate when they like something in his or her writing, but they should really mean it. Writing conferences should not be popularity contests.

Response Sheets

How can you help an author remember all of your comments and suggestions? You can write them down on a response sheet. Your teacher may already have response sheets for you to complete. If not, it is easy enough to make up your own. Here are two ideas.

Memorable

On the top of a half sheet of paper, write the word "Memorable." List the things you really like about a piece of writing under this word.

More

Halfway down this sheet, write the word "More." List one or two suggestions or questions you may have under this word.

Checklist

Organization:
- ✔ Does the writing have a beginning, a middle, and an end?
- ✔ Are all of the ideas arranged in the best order?

Details:
- ✔ Do all of the details support the subject (topic sentence)?
- ✔ Are enough details and examples included?

Style:
- ✔ Is the writing easy to follow?
- ✔ Does the writing contain interesting or descriptive words and ideas?

Mechanics:
- ✔ Is the writing accurate (free of careless spelling and punctuation errors)?
- ✔ Is the writing neatly presented?

Sharing Family Stories

Tell Me Again

Sharing stories can be a very powerful learning tool. Each time you listen to one of your classmate's stories, and tell him or her what interests you about it, you are helping your classmate and yourself grow as writers. Writing and sharing go hand in hand. **We write to share; we share to write better**.

Writing and Learning

As you learn how to write family stories in this chapter, you will also be provided with guidelines for sharing your work. (You will also use some of the conferencing tips included in the last chapter.) The experience you gain here will make it that much easier for you to share your work in the future.

You can also expect to have a lot of fun. Sharing family stories is a very enjoyable thing to do.

> **66Everybody has heard family stories... The fun of hearing about my grandfather's life taught me to listen with pleasure.99**
> — Marie Ponsot

Finding Family Parables

In all my years of school, I've never studied "My Grandpa." But I know him better than the ~~~ table. I've visited him at work. I've watched him ~~ making fine things out of wood. I especially remember the ~~~ boxes and building blocks he used to make. And best of all, I've heard him talk.

What happened around us usually reminded Grandpa of something, and then he'd tell us a story about it. I loved that. Today I call these stories **family parables**.

The Older, the Better

Everybody has heard family parables. Older folks often tell really good ones — the ones that have been told most often, for the longest time. Just think, many grandparents were alive 50 years ago. When they talk about *their* grandparents, they are telling stories that might be 100 years old. But don't forget your parents and aunts and uncles; they, too, have a lot of good family stories to share.

Student Model

Student writer Charles Vodak will never forget the following family story. It has been told to him time and time again. (As you can see, some family stories can be very short.)

My mom always tells me this story when we're at my grandmother's house.

When my mom was a little girl, she had to share a room with my Aunt Ann. My mom's side of the room was clean, but my aunt's side was always a mess. One day my aunt cleaned her closet, and she found some kittens in there. And guess what? They didn't even have a cat!

Iting a Family Story

Lots of family parables are about times of change or about trying something new. Such stories sleep in our memories until a word or an experience calls them to mind. They haunt a happy part of our thoughts. It's a part we can't always get at directly. But stories will come to us, once we search them out.

PREWRITING *Planning Your Writing*

Select a Subject ● Begin your subject search by telling a brief family story to a friend or classmate. Listen to one of hers or his. Tell another. Listen again. As you do, you'll get a feel for one or two stories that you might like to write about.

Helpful Hint If you are working by yourself, complete this sentence starter: "I remember the story of…" Then continue listing ideas until you hit upon a subject.

WRITING THE FIRST DRAFT

Start Writing ● Once you select a favourite family parable, the next step is to write it down from memory. I like to begin my writing with a one-sentence introduction. For instance, I'll write, "This is a story my grandmother told during a thunderstorm." Then I start the actual story in a new paragraph.

Keep It Going ● There are no rules about how long or how short a family parable should be. That will depend on how it was told to you, and how you remember it.

Now, stop reading, choose a favourite story from your list, and begin to write your parable.

REVISING *Improving Your Writing*

Share Your Writing ● Read your first draft aloud to a small group of classmates. Make sure to read loudly enough and slowly enough for everyone to hear your words.

After the reading, members of your group should take turns telling you what they liked about your parable. Listen carefully, so you can do more of these things the next time you write.

Now listen to other members of your group read their stories. Share your ideas about each story. (The more often you respond to someone's writing, the better at writing you will become.)

Review Your First Draft ● After the sharing session is over, review your first draft on your own. Then consider any changes you would like to make in your work.

EDITING & PROOFREADING

Edit Carefully ● Make sure your parable reads smoothly and clearly from start to finish. A family story should be treated with a great deal of respect, so edit it carefully.

Proofread Your Final Draft ● Check for spelling, punctuation, and grammar errors. Then type or write a neat final copy of your work. Check it one last time for any periods or capital letters you may have missed.

MINI LESSON
You should also practise making written observations about shared stories. Follow these steps:

❑ Ask one author to read his or her story aloud.

❑ Write about what you remember. An easy way to practise this kind of writing is to begin with "It interests me that…" and then add whatever you like to complete the sentence. List as many "interests" as you can.

❑ Share your written observations about this story as a group.

❑ Take turns listening, observing, and responding to the stories.

Publishing Your Writing

The Final Step

Publishing is a very important part of the writing process. It makes all of your planning, drafting, and revising worth the effort. And it also gets other people to listen to your ideas.

Publishing can take many forms. Reading a finished story to your classmates is a form of publishing — so is selecting a poem for your classroom portfolio. If your classmates and teacher really like your writing, you might want to explore some of the following ways to publish it.

Mail It!

Greeting cards

Letters to public figures

Requests for information

Thank-you letters to field-trip guides, bus drivers, etc.

Letters that complain about or praise a product or service

Letters to pen pals in other schools, cultures, or countries

Notes to parents about school activities

Perform It!

Plays for school and community audiences
    Puppet shows

Radio shows over the school public address system
    Talking books for the visually impaired

Taped interviews for a class project
    New words for familiar music

Presentations at school board meetings
    Introductions of guests at assemblies

Videotaped documentaries for local TV stations

Print It!

- All-school or classroom collections
- *Stories just for veterinarian clinics, doctors' offices, or other waiting rooms*
- Manuals on how to do certain things
- *School-survival guides for younger students*
- Programs for school productions
- *Newspaper reports of class trips or projects*
- School handbook updates
- *Kid's-eye-view brochures for local travel agencies or chambers of commerce*

Submit It!

There are many magazines published every month that feature student writing. Write to one that you think might publish your work. Ask your teacher for help. Also ask your teacher or librarian for a list of contests you can send your writing to.

Magazines That Publish Student Work

Owl

Topics: Environment/Science/Nature
Forms: Letters, drawings, poetry
Address: *Owl*, Editor
179 John Street, Suite 500
Toronto, ON   M5T 3G5

Kids World Magazine

Topics: General
Forms: Opinions on any subject (in the form of letters to the editor), poetry, very short fiction
Address: 108-93 Lombard Avenue Winnipeg, MB   R3B 3B1

Highlights for Children

Topics: General
Forms: Fiction, poems, true stories, letters to the editor
Address: Children's Mail
810 Church Street
Honesdale, PA 18431
USA

TG Magazine

Topics: General (health, sports, fashion)
Forms: Fiction, essays, poems, letters
Address: TG Magazine Editorial Board
70 University Avenue, Suite 1050
Toronto, ON M5J 2M4

What! A Magazine

Topics: General
Forms: Opinions, poetry, short fiction, journalistic features for teen audiences
Address: 108-93 Lombard Avenue Winnipeg, MB R3B 3B1

❝It feels wonderful to be an author of a real story. I like to publish my writing because it is like making my ideas come alive!❞
— Stephen Greenberg, student

Bind It!

To make or bind your own book for publication, follow these six basic steps. Make sure to add your own personal touches as you put your book together.

1 Stack in order the pages to be bound and add extra pages for titles, etc.

2 Staple or sew the pages together.

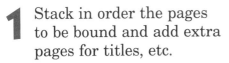

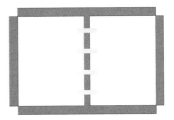

3 Cut two pieces of cardboard one centimetre larger than the page size. Tape them together.

4 Place the cardboard on the cover material (contact paper or glue-on wallpaper). Turn the edges of the cover material over the cardboard.

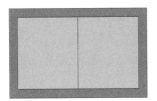

5 Attach construction paper or contact paper to the inside of the book cover.

6 Fasten the bound pages of the book into the cover with tape.

Building Paragraphs and Essays

Writing Paragraphs

Writing Essays

A Writing Sampler

Writing Paragraphs

What Is a Paragraph?

A paragraph is a group of sentences that tells about one subject or idea. Each sentence in a paragraph must give information about the topic. And the sentences must be in the right order, so your readers can understand the information.

A good paragraph presents a complete and interesting picture. The specific subject is stated in one sentence — usually the topic sentence. All of the facts and details in the rest of the sentences add to the readers' understanding of the subject. In other words, all of the parts work together.

In this chapter, paragraphs are explained, the different parts are named, and the basic types are identified. Step-by-step tips for writing good paragraphs are also given.

The Basic Parts of a Paragraph

You can think of a paragraph as a train. The **topic sentence** is the train's engine. It's the main idea that all the other sentences are connected to. The sentences in the **body of the paragraph** are the boxcars. They carry the paragraph's "cargo" — facts, figures, examples. The **closing sentence** is the caboose. It doesn't carry cargo; it just sums up what went before.

The Topic Sentence ● A paragraph begins with a *topic sentence*: a sentence that tells the reader what the paragraph is about. A topic sentence has two main parts — a specific subject and a focus.

The subject: The **subject** of a topic sentence has to be specific or small enough to explain in one paragraph. You couldn't write a paragraph on "the history of baseball." It would be too long! But you could write a paragraph on "yesterday's softball game." That subject is more specific!

The focus: You need more than a subject to write a topic sentence. You also need a **focus**. A focus is usually a feeling or an attitude about the subject. It lets the reader know what you're going to say about the subject.

MINI **LESSON**   Here is a simple **formula** that makes it easy to write good topic sentences. Use it whenever you have to write a paragraph.

> **Subject** (Who? or What?)
> + **Feeling/Focus** (What about it?)
> = **Topic Sentence**

Sample Topic Sentence

In yesterday's softball game (specific subject),
the grade 4 Eagles pounded the grade 5 Hawks (focus).

The Body ● The middle of the paragraph is called the *body.* It includes the sentences between the topic sentence and the closing sentence. These sentences must give the reader all the information needed to understand the topic. Below are sentences that could follow the topic sentence in a paragraph about "yesterday's softball game."

Sample Body

When the Eagles batted, Tim started off with a double. Jamie batted next and hit a home run. The Hawks scored two runs in the third inning to tie the score. After Sarah hit a grand slam for the Eagles in the next inning, the Hawks never scored again.

The Closing Sentence ● A paragraph ends with a *closing sentence.* This sentence may sum up the information in the paragraph, or tell what it means. Below is a sample closing sentence that could be used after the "Sample Body" above.

Sample Closing Sentence

Thanks to Sarah's grand slam, the Eagles won by four runs.

TAKE NOTE If you put the *Sample Topic Sentence, Sample Body,* and *Sample Closing Sentence* together, you'll have a **Sample Paragraph**!

In yesterday's softball game, the Eagles pounded the Hawks. When the Eagles batted, Tim started off with a double. Jamie batted next and hit a home run. The Hawks scored two runs in the third inning to tie the score. After Sarah hit a grand slam for the in the next inning, the Hawks never scored again. Thanks to Sarah's grand slam, the Eagles won by four runs.

Types of Paragraphs

There are four kinds of paragraphs you can write.

- ■ To describe something, write a **descriptive** paragraph.
- ■ To tell a story, write a **narrative** paragraph.
- ■ To express your opinion, write a **persuasive** paragraph.
- ■ To explain something, write an **expository** paragraph.

Descriptive Paragraph

A **descriptive** paragraph describes a person, a place, a thing, or an idea. When you write a descriptive paragraph, you should use words that help your readers see, hear, smell, taste, and feel what you are describing. You should tell your readers what colours things are, how big things are, what things sound like, etc. Your readers should feel as if they are right there with you.

Model Descriptive Paragraph

You can tell a lot about Evan by looking at his face. The first thing you notice are his big brown eyes that always seem so shiny and alert. You wouldn't notice his pug nose except that it seems to be running all of the time. Like many small children, he wipes it with his sleeve rather than a Kleenex. His mouth seems to have two basic positions. He smiles when he's got trouble on his mind, or he clenches his mouth shut when he doesn't want to do something, like eat his lunch. Evan's tongue, which he likes to stick out, is usually orange from his favourite fruit drink. Whenever someone tries to clean his mouth or chin, he squirms and turns away. Evan likes his face just the way it is.

Narrative Paragraph

In a **narrative** paragraph, you tell a story by sharing the details of an experience. A narrative paragraph should pull your readers into the story and keep them wondering what will happen next. It's important to include a lot of colourful details to make the experience come alive.

Model Narrative Paragraph

Evan leaves a trail of trouble even when he isn't trying. The last time I babysat for him, we were painting pictures at the kitchen table. Evan painted a couple of monster faces, and then decided he wanted to do something else. He even offered to help clean up, which surprised me a little. He was carrying the bowl full of dirty water from our paint brushes when disaster struck. He tripped right in front of the sink in the utility room and the dirty water went flying. I did my best to clean up the mess while Evan had a snack. As I worked, I reminded myself never to let Evan help again.

Bright
IDEA

To make sure you have included all the important details in your narrative paragraph, ask the following questions: *Who? What? When? Where? Why? How?*

Persuasive Paragraph

A **persuasive** paragraph gives the writer's opinion on the topic and tries to get the reader to agree with it. When you write a persuasive paragraph, you should give facts and examples to back up your opinion. Otherwise, you won't *persuade,* or convince, your reader that your opinion is the right one.

Model Persuasive Paragraph

Anyone who babysits for Evan should receive an extra bonus. For one thing, you have to put up with Evan's screaming. He likes to sneak up behind you and scream in your ear. He's very good at scaring just about anyone with this move. For another thing, you never get a chance to rest for even a minute. Evan likes to keep things active by teasing the cat, locking himself in his room, overloading the circuits, falling off his bike, and so on. And finally, you have to clean up after him. There is always spilled milk in the kitchen and dumped toys to pick up in every other room. For conditions like these, the regular hourly rate is not enough!

Helpful Hint

Read your paragraph out loud so that you can listen for missing information. Also turn to page 309 in your handbook for more on using facts and opinions in your writing.

Expository Paragraph

The main purpose of an **expository** paragraph is to give information about a topic. It may explain ideas, give directions, or show how to do something. An expository paragraph uses transition words (such as *first, second,* and *most importantly* in the model below). These words help guide the reader through the explanation.

Model Expository Paragraph

Always be prepared when you babysit for Evan. First, make sure to bring a flashlight in case of a blackout. Even likes to overload the circuits. Second, bring a few first-aid supplies like cotton balls and Band-Aids. Evan will get at least two or three scratches or cuts while you are there, and sometimes their first-aid kit is low on materials. You can also use the cotton balls to plug your ears if Evan starts screaming. Most importantly, have a phone number where you can contact Evan's mother. No matter how prepared you are, you can't babysit for Evan all by yourself. You will need to call his mother at least once for help or advice.

TAKE NOTE

Sometimes it's helpful to list the facts or examples you are going to include in your paragraph. That way, you can put your supporting ideas into the best possible order before you begin.

Sample Listing

Topic Sentence: ***Always be prepared when you babysit for Evan.***

- ✔ ***Bring a flashlight***
- ✔ ***Bring first-aid supplies***
- ✔ ***Have a phone number to contact his mother***

Writing the Paragraph

1 **Plan your paragraph.** To begin planning your paragraph, you can ask yourself the following questions:

Subject: *Who or what will I write about?*

Purpose: *What feeling about my subject will I focus on?*

Audience: *Who will be reading my paragraph?*

Form: *What kind of paragraph will work best?*

2 **Gather information.** Once you've answered these questions, you are ready to begin gathering details for your paragraph. This chart will help you decide what information you need to collect.

For a...	you'll need...
descriptive paragraph	lots of details about how things look, sound, smell, taste, and feel
narrative paragraph	details about an experience you want to share: how it began, what problems occurred, how it ended
persuasive paragraph	facts, figures, and examples to back up your opinion
expository paragraph	facts to explain the thing or process you're writing about

3 **Put the information in order.** The topic sentence is first. Next comes the body — the sentences that tell about the topic sentence. At the end is the closing sentence that sums up the paragraph, or tells what it means. (**SEE** pages 60-61.)

4 **Check your work.** Read your paragraph. Imagine that you are reading it for the first time. Does it tell everything you need to know to understand the topic sentence? Is it interesting and clear?

Details in a Paragraph

Details are an important part of any paragraph. They are the facts and examples that bring the paragraph to life.

Personal Details

Most of the details you use in your paragraphs will be personal details — things you know from your own experience. Here are the different kinds of personal details you can use:

Details from Your Senses ● These details come from the world around you and are picked up by your five senses. They are things that you see, hear, smell, taste, and touch. You will need a lot of these when writing a descriptive paragraph.

Details from Your Memory ● These details come from memories of things you've done and experienced. In an expository paragraph, such details will help you to explain how to do something. In descriptive and narrative writing, they will help you to bring the past to life.

Details from Your Imagination ● These details come from inside your mind and deal with your hopes, wishes, and wonders. *What if Evan were a teacher?* Thoughts like this one can make narrative paragraphs interesting and fun.

Details from Other Sources

When you write a paragraph, first think about what you already know about the subject. Then add details from other sources:

■ Ask people who may have the answers you need — teachers, parents, neighbours, friends.

■ Ask an expert on the subject. For example, if you are writing a paragraph about the flu that's going around, talk to a doctor or a nurse.

■ Check newspapers, magazines, and books. Check the ones you have at home and the ones in your library.

Putting Things in Order

The sentences in the body of a paragraph must be organized so that the reader can follow the information from one sentence to the next.

Time order. It is easy to understand things that are explained in the order in which they happened. You may use words like **first, second, next,** and **finally.**

> **When** the fourth grade batted, Tim started off with a double. Jamie batted **next** and hit a home run. The fifth grade scored two runs in the third inning to tie the score. **After** Sarah hit a grand slam for the fourth grade in the next inning, the fifth grade never scored again.

Place order. When things are described in the order in which they are located, the description usually goes from left to right or from top to bottom. Place order can work well when you are writing a descriptive or an expository paragraph. Use words and phrases like **above, below, to the left of,** and **in front of** to guide your reader.

> **Looking at** the infield from home plate, the batter sees the third baseman on her far left. **To the right** of the third baseman is the shortstop. **To the right** of him is the second baseman, and **to the right** of her is the first baseman.

Order of importance. News stories are often organized this way. They tell the most important news first. Persuasive or expository paragraphs are also organized in this way, with the most important detail coming first *or* last.

> Very early this morning, an adult male ostrich escaped from the zoo. He was found about a kilometre north of the zoo running along Adams Boulevard. Zoo officials say the ostrich was safely back in captivity within 15 minutes of his escape.

Transition or Linking Words

Words that can be used to **show location**:

above	around	between	inside	outside
across	behind	by	into	over
against	below	down	near	throughout
along	beneath	in back of	off	to the right
among	beside	in front of	on top of	under

Words that can be used to **show time**:

about	during	until	yesterday	finally
after	first	meanwhile	next	then
at	second	today	soon	as soon as
before	third	tomorrow	later	when

Words that can be used to **compare two things**:

in the same way	likewise	as
similarly	like	also

Words that can be used to **contrast things** (show differences):

but	otherwise	on the other hand	although
yet	however	still	even though

Words that can be used to **emphasize a point**:

again	for this reason	in fact

Words that can be used to **add information**:

again	and	for instance	as well
also	besides	next	along with
another	for example	finally	

Words that can be used to **conclude or summarize**:

as a result	finally	in conclusion
therefore	last	in summary

Finding Paragraphs

You know how easy it is to go on and on when you have something important to say to one of your friends. "Guess what I did…" Well, the same thing can happen when you are writing about something that means a lot to you. You may start out writing a simple paragraph and end up filling a whole page or two with great ideas.

Keeping Your Ideas Together

When your writing does go on and on, make sure it is organized into paragraphs before you share it. Otherwise, your readers may have trouble following your ideas. The guidelines that follow will help you find the paragraphs in your writing so that it is ready to be enjoyed.

"When I thought about my message, it became important for my readers to understand it."

— Erik Olsen, student

How You Do It

To find the paragraphs in longer pieces of writing, repeat these three steps — *Label, Name, Find* — until you come to the end of your work.

1. Label: Put a paragraph sign (¶) before the first word in your paper.

2. Name: Identify the first main idea in your writing.

3. Find: Locate the first sentence that is **not** about this idea.

* * * * * *

1. Label: Put a paragraph (¶) sign before the sentence you have found (#3 above).

2. Name: Identify the main idea of this paragraph.

2. Find: Locate the first sentence that is **not** about this idea.

* * * * * *

1. Label: *Repeat the process until you are done.*

Sample Writing

Here is part of an autobiography by student writer Elizabeth Hartfield. As you can see, it is not divided into paragraphs. (We took them out so you can see how the three-step process works.)

My name is Elizabeth Frances Hartfield. I'm going to tell you about my life starting with the day something exciting and sad happened. What happened was that I moved from my home in Winnipeg to a house in Toronto. I was nervous and scared. I didn't think that I would make a lot of friends but I did. Since I moved to Toronto, I have gone to three different schools. The first one I went to was Saints Simon and Jude. I went there for grades one and two. I went to Sacred Heart Academy in Mississauga for grade three, and now I go to Villa Maria Academy. I am now in grade six. I like to draw a lot. On April 25, 1997, I won an award for a piece of artwork that I did. My favourite activities besides art are reading and dancing...

Following the Steps

Finding the paragraphs in this autobiography is easy if you follow the three-step process.

1. Label: Put a paragraph sign (ꝗ) next to the first word
ꝗ *My name is...*

2. Name: Identify the main idea of the first paragraph.
Moving to Toronto

3. Find: Locate the first sentence that is **not** about this idea.
Since I moved to...

* * * * * *

1. Label: Put a paragraph sign before this sentence.
ꝗ *Since I moved to...*

2. Name: Identify the main idea of this paragraph.
Different schools I've attended

3. Find: Locate the first sentence that is **not** about this idea.
(See if you can find the last paragraph!)

Writing Essays

Think Before You Write!

Even if you've never written an essay before, you've probably thought out many of them. For example, if you've just read something interesting — maybe about saving trees — and decide to tell someone about it, you are "thinking" an essay. Or, if you're trying to figure out why you are such good friends with someone, you are also thinking an essay.

Facts and Feelings

An essay is a form of factual writing that is more than one paragraph in length. Some essays are informational and sound like basic classroom reports. Other essays are freely written and include a lot of personal feelings. Most essays fall somewhere in between. They present a lot of good information about a specific subject, plus some of the writer's personal feelings.

The guidelines and model in this chapter will help you write a very basic informational essay — maybe your first essay ever! Good luck, and remember to think before you write.

What an Essay Can Do

There are three basic reasons to write essays: *to present information, to share a strong opinion,* and *to make everyone think.*

➤ Present Information

If you want to present important facts and details about a subject, you can write an *informational essay.* In this type of writing, your goal is to inform your readers about something new or important. (An informational essay is like a classroom report, only shorter and not as detailed.)

Subject Ideas: **Reasons for Recycling Newspapers**
Introducing a New Computer Game

➤ Share a Strong Opinion

If you want to share an opinion about something going on in your school or community, you can write a *persuasive essay.* In this type of essay, your goal is to convince your readers to agree with your way of thinking. It's important that your opinion is supported by believable facts and details.

Subject Ideas: **Keeping the Buses Cleaner**
Why a Computer Club Is Needed

The most common type of persuasive essay is the letter to the editor. (***SEE*** page 131 for an example. Also, see pages 308-311 for other helpful information.)

➤ Make Everyone Think

If you want to share your thoughts about a fun or serious subject related to your personal life, you can write a *personal essay.* Your goal is to entertain your readers, or to express your feelings about your subject.

Subject Ideas: **Fashion Trends with My Friends**
Living with Allergies

Writing an Informational Essay

Writing an essay is no trouble at all if you know the **ins and outs** of the process.

PREWRITING *Getting Started*

To begin planning, answer three basic questions:

Subject ● Who or what am I writing about? (Make sure that your subject really interests you and that you already know something about it.)

Audience ● Who will be reading my essay? (Are you writing for your classmates, for another group of students, or for someone else?)

Voice ● How do I want my writing to sound? (Do you want to sound serious, funny, or somewhere in between?)

PREWRITING *Collecting and Organizing*

Next, decide on the type of information you plan to include:

Explore ● Write down all that you know about your subject.

Focus ● Review your writing, and decide what part of your subject you would like to cover. (For example, if your subject is recycling newspapers, you might focus on the ways it helps the environment.)

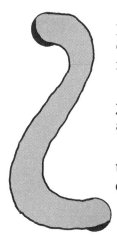

Collect ● Gather more information about your subject if you feel that you need to know more about it.

Organize ● Decide what details you are going to include in your essay and how they will be organized. (***SEE*** page 77 for help.)

WRITING THE FIRST DRAFT

When you are writing an essay, remember that each part — the beginning, the middle, and the ending — plays a special role:

Beginning ● Your first paragraph should say something interesting or surprising about your subject to get your readers' attention. It should also name the specific part of the subject that your essay will cover.

Middle ● The middle should include all of the ideas (facts, figures, examples) that explain the subject. This information must be clearly organized. (This part may be more than one paragraph.)

Ending ● The final paragraph summarizes the main points covered in the essay. It should also remind readers why the subject is important, or help them remember it better.

REVISING & EDITING

The following checklist will help you improve your:

✔ Have I written a title that helps identify my subject?

✔ Have I introduced my subject in an effective way?

✔ Have I included enough facts and details to support my subject? Are they clearly stated?

✔ Will readers understand why my subject is important or interesting?

✔ Do I like the sound of my words and sentences? Have I checked for errors?

Model Essay

The following informational essay deals with a very important subject, recycling. As you will see, all of the ideas are clearly stated and organized.

Why My Family Recycles Newspapers

Beginning
A personal story introduces the subject.

In my family, we recycle our newspapers. My sister talked my parents into it after she studied recycling in school. I learned from her that old newspapers can be made into usable paper again. I also learned how recycling newspapers helps the environment.

Middle
Basic facts explain the subject.

There are three basic benefits when old paper is recycled. First, recycling saves trees. As more and more paper is recycled, fewer trees have to be used to make paper. Second, recycling saves energy. It takes less energy to recycle paper than to start the papermaking process by cutting down trees. Third, recycling old paper is cleaner than making paper in the old way. This means recycling causes less pollution.

Ending
The main points are summarized.

It's easy to recycle old newspapers. We just put them in paper bags and drop them off at the recycling centre every Saturday. It's worth the little time it takes because we are saving trees and energy and helping keep our air cleaner. Have you started recycling yet?

THINK
About It

The question at the end of this essay will help readers remember the subject by encouraging them to start recycling, too.

Organizing Your Essay

To help you organize the supporting facts and details in your essay, try *listing, clustering,* or *outlining.*

Listing ● For some essays, you can simply list the supporting details in the order you want to write about them.

- Recycling saves trees.
- Recycling saves energy.
- Recycling causes less pollution.

Clustering/Webbing ● When you have a lot of information, you may want to try a cluster or web. (**SEE** pages 26 and 222-223.)

Outlining ● Or, you may want to organize your ideas in an outline. An outline helps you arrange information from general to specific. A *topic outline* contains only words and phrases. (See the sample below.) You can also write a *sentence outline* if you want to add more detail.

Sample Topic Outline

Aids for the Visually Impaired

I. Aids for reading and learning  Main Idea
    A. Braille ← Examples
        1. Each letter enlarged and encoded as "bumps" by special machine
        2. Readers feel large raised letters  Supporting Details
    B. Talking books
    C. Enlarged-print books
II. Aids for moving about
    A. Special walking cane
    B. Trained dog
    C. Sonar device

YOU DON'T SSSS SAY

In an outline, everything comes in sets of two or more. If you have a *I*, you must have a *II*. If you have an *A,* you must have a *B,* and so on.

A Writing Sampler

Making Contact

All of the different *people, places, events,* and *objects* in your life have something special to offer you and your readers — if you take the time to write about them. You will see what I mean when you read the personal narratives and essays on the next five pages. They do more than just retell what happened to the writers. They show that the writers have carefully thought about their experiences and formed new ideas about them.

Learning About Yourself

Writing about your personal experiences will help you practise storytelling. Part of becoming a good writer is being able to tell a good story. It will also help you understand that writing is much more than putting a few words on paper. You will learn that writing can be a very meaningful way to share, and even celebrate, parts of your life.

> **❝Writing from experiences is easy because I know all the details. Once I start, I can't stop.❞**
>
> — Mike Franzago, student

Writing About a Special Person

Writing about another person is a very important form of writing. It is sometimes called biographical writing. A *biography* is the story of another person's life.

Selecting a Subject ● Write about someone you know well, or someone you would like to know well.

Collecting Details ● *List* details that describe your subject. *Remember* important things he or she has done. *Compare* your subject to other people. Who is he or she most like? *Ask* others abut your subject, and *explain* why your subject is important.

Student Model

Adam Garelick had a lot to say about his father in this story. His writing includes a lot of examples and real feelings.

Beginning
The writer
introduces
the subject.

Someone Who Cares

My dad is very special because he does so many things with me. He helps me with my homework, and if I ask him to take me somewhere, he'll do it. He even gives me confidence when I am having trouble with baseball.

Middle
One main
activity is
described.

My dad and I do so much together. Last summer, we took a trip across the country. We got to talk to each other a great deal. My dad told me about the time he was in the middle of nowhere and ran out of gas. After that story, I watched the gas gauge every other minute! He said he had made the same trip when he was 23 years old with his best friend. Now, it was just the two of us.

Ending
Real
feelings are
expressed.

I wish everyone could have a companion like my dad. We all need an ally, or friend, in our lives; because if we have problems or need to express our feelings, we need a responsible person to turn to. I have my dad.

Writing About a Special Place

Writing about a place is part descriptive writing and part narrative writing. You need to include details that describe your subject, but you also need to tell a good story about it.

Selecting a Subject ● Write about a place that has played an important role in your life. It can be a big place like a house you used to live in, or a small place like a certain tree in a yard.

Collecting Details ● If possible, *visit* this place, and *jot down* what you see, hear, smell, and feel. *Remember* personal experiences related to it. *Compare* your subject to other places. And *explain* what you like or dislike about it.

Student Model

In this sample, Terra Wilcoxson remembers a special tree. She uses a lot of descriptive words and similes in her writing.

It Was Tall and Mighty

Beginning
The writer remembers the tree.

Even though it lay on its side, it somehow seemed tall and mighty, like a friendly bear protecting me. When I climbed across it, nothing existed beyond the short range of the tree. My pudgy little hands could grasp branches that stuck out like spikes. I'd lift myself up and scamper across the trunk, afraid of plunging into the ditch of leaves below. When I finally reached the end, a sense of accomplishment and pride came over me.

Middle
The writer's feelings change.

Day after day passed, and I slowly drifted away, until my tree seemed to move into another dimension, isolated. Now it no longer stands tall or mighty. It just hangs there, like an old toy, forgotten.

Ending
Sadness is expressed.

Sometimes, I glance out the window at the weeping tree. It reminds me of all the hours I've spent climbing the bear it used to be.

Writing About an Event

When writing about an event, make the action come alive for your readers, but don't try to say everything about your subject. It's better to focus on one exciting part of it. (**SEE** pages 110-115 for a related form of writing.)

Selecting a Subject ● Write about any recent event, or an event you plan to attend. For example, you may have attended a sporting event or a concert, watched a parade, and so on.

Collecting Details ● *Write down* all of the details related to your subject. Include sights, sounds, and smells. Also try to answer the 5 Ws (*who? what? when? where?* and *why?*) related to it. Then *decide* why this event is worth sharing.

Student Model

In this personal story, Manon Leblanc recalls the time she met her skating idol. She makes this event sound very exciting.

The Unforgettable Autograph

Beginning
The writer wonders about meeting her idol.

I couldn't imagine really getting her autograph. What would it be like? I felt faint. She is my idol because she skates so well. She has been Canadian National champion three times.

Middle
The main activity is described.

While I was walking toward the practice rink, in my head I was hoping I would at least see her warm up. I was sure my sister was thinking the same thing. Then, suddenly, there she was, Josée Chouinard, wearing a jacket over her costume and listening to headphones. My sister and I ran over to her as fast as horses to a finish line. I stared at her with butterflies in my stomach. She actually signed my paper, and I felt like nothing else mattered.

Ending
The writer feels closer to her subject.

Later, while I was watching her skate, it might have been my imagination, but I thought she winked at me!

Writing About a Special Object

When you write about an object, think of an interesting story to tell about it, a story that will help your readers know why this object is special to you. This is more important than describing the object in great detail.

Selecting a Subject ● Write about an object that you know well. You may have a special stuffed animal, a favourite baseball glove, a lucky charm, or a useful gadget of some type.

Collecting Details ● *List* details that describe the size, shape, and smell of your subject. *Remember* interesting stories related to the object. *Ask* yourself if your feelings about your subject have remained the same or have changed over time.

Student Model

Michele Dreiding shares her feelings about an object that once played an important role in her life.

I'm Growing Up

Beginning
The writer gives background information.

When I was little, I was scared of the dark. I thought monsters or ghosts would come out and yell "Boo!"

Finally, I got a flashlight, and that worked like a charm. It lit up my room a little so I could sleep better. Through the years, I enjoyed having my flashlight right next to my bed.

Middle
The story about the flashlight is told.

Now I am older, and I don't need it anymore. I no longer have a fear of the dark. Every time I take my flashlight out of the socket, my mom puts it back in again. I want to say, "Stop, Mom! I am growing up. I am not a baby anymore. You have to understand that I like the dark."

Ending
The ending ties into the title: "I'm Growing Up."

I know she is only trying to help, but...

Writing About the Condition of Things

Some personal essays or stories are about the way things are, or about the *condition of things*. An essay about having allergies or about being too tall would fall into this category. In this type of writing, you share your feelings about a certain part of your life.

Selecting a Subject ● Write about some part of your life that makes you angry, happy, sad, or proud. You might write about wearing glasses, sharing a bedroom, or watching TV.

Collecting Details ● *Write down* all of your thoughts about your subject. If possible, *list* details that help answer *who? what? when? where?* and *why?* about the condition. Then *think* of the different ways this condition has affected your life.

Student Model

In this essay, Christopher FitzSimons asks himself why he has to have allergies. A lot of honest feelings are expressed.

Why?

Beginning
The writer asks questions about his condition.

Rachel has one problem — me. Wait. It's not me. It's my allergies! So why do I feel so guilty? Why do I think I'm shattering someone's dreams when my allergies are out of control? How come I feel like I've stabbed my sister in the heart when I can't stop my eyes from watering, tingling, itching?

Middle
The questions continue.

Most of all, why do my allergies start right when everything is going so well, like when my family is about to buy a pet, or when we're playing with a kitten, or even when I'm watching my favourite TV show and I'm snuggled up in a warm, furry blanket.

Ending
The final lines are filled with emotion.

I feel empty, like there's nothing inside of me, no love or compassion. I want to be in control, but I can't do anything about it.

Rachel can't get a cat because of me . . . me . . . ME!

Improving Your Writing Skills

Writing Basic Sentences

Combining Sentences

Writing with Style

Modelling the Masters

Writing Terms

Writing Basic Sentences

Keeping Your Ideas Under Control

Let's say the tracking on Joe's VCR goes bonkers right in the middle of a good video. He tries everything, but the picture keeps jumping up and down like it has a bad case of hiccups. Finally, he gives up and turns off the machine.

Your readers may end up doing the same thing if your sentences seem out of control. If they can't follow your ideas, they will simply give up on your writing. That is why it is so important to use complete sentences. The guidelines in this chapter will help you write clear, correct sentences so that all of your ideas will be easy to follow.

Always check your writing for sentence errors. This may be your most important job when you edit and proofread your work.

SENTENCE REVIEW

Sentences are not hard to figure out. They are groups of words that express complete thoughts. You already know a sentence when you hear one because your mind is tuned in to complete thoughts. ***Your job as a writer is to listen carefully and write complete sentences.***

The Basic Parts of a Sentence

All sentences have two basic parts — the subject and the verb.

Subject ● The subject usually tells us who or what is doing something.

> *JOE watched his favourite video.*

Verb ● A verb expresses action or links the subject to another part of the sentence. (The verb is sometimes called the **predicate**.)

> *Joe WATCHED his favourite video.* (action)

> *He IS nuts about adventure movies.* (linking)

Additional Words ● Most sentences also contain additional words that describe or complete the thought.

> *Joe watched HIS FAVOURITE VIDEO.*

Compound Subjects and Verbs ● A sentence may include more than one subject or more than one verb.

> *His MOM and BROTHER were in the kitchen.* (two subjects)

> *Then the tracking WENT bonkers and RUINED Joe's fun.* (two verbs)

Compound Sentence ● Two sentences may be connected with and, but, or or.

> *Later, Joe's mom fixed the tracking, AND he watched the video.*

TAKE NOTE You can find more about sentences in the "Check It Out" section. (**SEE** pages 370-373.)

SENTENCE ERRORS

Sentence Fragments ● A **sentence fragment** is a group of words that does not express a complete thought. It is missing important information.

> **Sentence Fragment:** *Thinks she is so cool.* (The subject is missing.)
>
> **Corrected Sentence:** *Martha thinks she is so cool.*
>
> **Sentence Fragment:** *Not cool to me.* (The subject and verb are both missing.)
>
> **Corrected Sentence:** *She is not cool to me.*

Run-On Sentences ● A **run-on sentence** occurs when two sentences are joined without punctuation or a connecting word.

> **Run-On Sentence:** *I thought the lopsided game would never end the score just kept getting worse and worse.* (Punctuation is needed.)
>
> **Corrected Sentences:** *I thought the lopsided game would never end. The score just kept getting worse and worse.* (Punctuation has been added.)
>
> **Corrected Sentence:** *I thought the lopsided game would never end, and the score just kept getting worse and worse.* (Punctuation and the connecting word *and* have been added.)

Rambling Sentences ● A **rambling sentence** happens when you put too many little sentences together with the word *and*.

> **Rambling Sentence:** *I went skating down at the pond and three kids from my school were there and we fell on our fannies again and again and we laughed so much our stomachs hurt!* (Too many *and*'s are used.)
>
> **Corrected Sentences:** *I went skating down at the pond, and three kids from my school were there. We fell on our fannies again and again. We laughed so much our stomachs hurt!*

SENTENCE AGREEMENT

Make sure the parts of your sentence "agree" with one another. If you use a singular subject, use a singular verb; if you use a plural subject, use a plural verb. (Your subject and verb will then be in *agreement*.) The examples below will show you how this works.

One Subject ● In most basic sentences, you have one subject at the beginning of a sentence followed by the verb. Since they are often right next to each other, it is easy to check for subject/verb agreement.

> *Amy wants* **to go bowling.** (*Amy* and *wants* agree because they are both singular.)

> *Her parents want* **to go bowling, too.** (*Parents* and *want* agree because they are both plural.)

Compound Subjects Connected by AND ● If a sentence contains a compound subject connected by *and*, it needs a plural verb.

> *Harry and Earl spend* **most of their time teasing girls.**

> *Suyin and Jesse sing* **like squawking chickens.**

Compound Subjects Connected by OR ● If a sentence contains a compound subject connected by *or*, the verb must agree with the subject nearer to it.

> *Either the cat or the dog wakes* **me up each morning.**
> (A singular verb is needed because *dog* is singular.)

> *Anna or her brothers feed* **the pets each evening.**
> (A plural verb is needed because *brothers* is plural.)

THINK IT OVER

Sometimes the subject will not come at the beginning of the sentence. This will happen in questions and sentences beginning with the word *there*. Check these types of sentences very carefully for subject/verb agreement.

SENTENCE PROBLEMS

Check your sentences for these problems:

Double Subjects ● Avoid sentences in which a pronoun is used immediately after the subject. The result is usually a double subject.

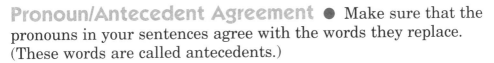

> **Double Subject:** *Some cats they eat all the time.* (The pronoun *they* should be omitted.)

> ***Corrected Sentence: Some cats eat all the time.***

Pronoun/Antecedent Agreement ● Make sure that the pronouns in your sentences agree with the words they replace. (These words are called antecedents.)

> **Agreement Problem:** *If my brother and his friend each eat three Big Macs, she will really be stuffed.* (The pronoun he is singular. The words it replaces — *my brother and his friend* — are plural.)

> ***Corrected Sentence: If my brother and his friend each eat three Big Macs, they will really be stuffed.*** (Now the pronoun and the words it replaces agree; they are both plural.)

Double Negatives ● Do not use two negative words, like *never* and *no* or *not* and *no,* in the same sentence.

> **Double Negative:** *Never give no one a note in class.*

> ***Corrected Sentence: Never give anyone a note in class.***

> **Double Negative:** *I didn't have no mistakes in my paragraph.*

> ***Corrected Sentence: I didn't have any mistakes in my paragraph.***

Confusing OF for HAVE ● Do you use *of* in a sentence when you really mean *have*? (When *have* is said quickly, it sometimes sound like *of.*)

> **Incorrect Usage:** *We should of won the game.*

> ***Corrected Sentence: We should have won the game.***

Combining Sentences

One Plus One Equals One

Sentence combining is making one smoother, more detailed sentence out of two or more shorter sentences. For instance, take a look at the following sentences:

My dog loves to run fast.
He loves to jump fences.
He loves to chase rabbits.

These three sentences are fine, but see what happens when they are combined. All of the ideas flow more smoothly.

My dog loves to run fast, jump fences, and chase rabbits.

The guidelines in this chapter will help you learn how to combine sentences. Learning this skill will help you write with more style.

Sentence combining will come in handy when you are checking your writing for sentences that don't read smoothly.

Combining with a Key Word or Series

Use a Key Word ● Ideas from short sentences can be combined by moving a key word from one sentence to the other. This key word may be an adjective or an adverb.

Short sentences: *Kelly's necklace broke. It was beaded.*

■ *Combined sentence with an* **ADJECTIVE***:*
   Kelly's **beaded** *necklace broke.*

Short sentences: *I am going to start my book report. I'll start it tomorrow.*

■ *Combine sentence with an* **ADVERB***:*
   Tomorrow *I am going to start my book report.*

Use a Series of Words ● Ideas from short sentences can be combined into one sentence using a series of words or phrases.

Short sentences: *The gym teacher is strict. The gym teacher is organized. The gym teacher is fair.*

■ *Combined sentence with a* **SERIES OF WORDS***:*
   The gym teacher is **strict***,* **organized***, and* **fair***.*

All of the words or phrases you use in a series should be *parallel* — stated in the same way. Otherwise, your sentences will sound like they are out of balance. (Look at the example below.)

Awkward series: *The dog was friendly, playful, and he was pretty smart, too.*

■ *Corrected sentence:*
   The dog was friendly, playful, and smart.

Note: This sentence is now correct because all the words in the series — friendly, playful, smart — are single-word adjectives. They are parallel.

Combining with Phrases

Use Phrases ● Ideas
from short sentences
can be combined into
one sentence using
prepositional or
appositive phrases.
(***SEE*** pages 346 and 386.)

Short sentences: *Our cat curls up.*
He curls up on top
of my homework.

■ ***Combined sentence with a* PREPOSITIONAL PHRASE:**
Our cat curls up on top of my homework.

Short sentences: *Mrs. Keller makes the best cookies on the block.*
Mrs. Keller is our next-door neighbour.

■ ***Combined sentence with an* APPOSITIVE PHRASE:**
*Mrs. Keller, **our next-door neighbour,** makes the best cookies*
on the block.

Use Compound Subjects and Compound Verbs ●
A compound subject includes two or more subjects in one sentence.
A compound verb includes two or more verbs in one sentence.

Two short sentences: *Tom danced around the room.*
Mary danced around the room, too.

■ ***Combined sentence with a* COMPOUND SUBJECT:**
***Tom** and **Mary** danced around the room.*

Two short sentences: *John slipped on the ice.*
He fell on his rear end.

■ ***Combined sentence with a* COMPOUND VERB:**
*John **slipped** on the ice and **fell** on his rear end.*

Combining with Longer Sentences

Use Compound Sentences ● A compound sentence is made up of two or more simple sentences joined together. The conjunctions *and, but, or, nor, for, so*, and *yet* are used to connect the simple sentences. (Place a comma before the conjunction.)

Two simple sentences: *My puppy has hair hanging over her eyes.*
She looks just like a dust mop.

■ *Combined sentence with* **AND:**
My puppy has hair hanging over her eyes, **and** *she looks just like a dust mop.*

Two simple sentences: *Our dog likes to eat shoes.*
He won't touch my brother's smelly slippers.

■ *Combined sentence with* **BUT:**
Our dog likes to eat shoes, **but** *he won't touch my brother's smelly slippers.*

Use Complex Sentences ● A complex sentence is made up of two ideas connected by words called subordinate conjunctions (*after, when, since, because, before*, etc.) or relative pronouns (*who, whose, which,* and *that*).

Two short sentences: *My best friend shares his lunch with me.*
He doesn't like what his dad packs.

■ *Combined sentence with* **BECAUSE:**
My best friend shares his lunch with me **because** *he doesn't like what his dad packs.*

Two short sentences: *Very cold weather closed school for a day.*
The cold weather came down from the North.

■ *Combined sentence with* **WHICH:**
Very cold weather, **which** *came down from the North, closed school for a day.*

Writing with Style

Learning by Doing

Style comes in many shapes and sizes. You may like to perform a certain stunt that gets you and your skateboard high off the ground. That's part of your own special style. You may like pepperoni on your pizza. That's also part of your style. You may like to wear your hair cut short or long or half-and-half. That's your style, too. What's *in style* for you depends on your own interests and tastes.

> **"Writing isn't just words on paper anymore. It's me."**
>
> — Meredith Dempsey, student

The Way You Write

As a young writer, you have your own special way of expressing your thoughts and feelings on paper. This is your writing style, and it will develop naturally as you write more and more. However, you can help your writing style along if you follow our suggestions in this chapter.

Developing a Sense of Style

Your writing style will grow strong and healthy if you follow the advice listed below.

➤ **Practise often.** Keep a daily journal. This is the best way to develop your writing style.

➤ **Try different forms.** Write poems and riddles; write news stories and personal stories. Each form of writing has something different to offer you.

➤ **Write about ideas that are important to you.** If you write about subjects that really interest you, your writing style will have a better chance of developing.

➤ **Please yourself.** If you don't feel good about your writing, try again. Make it sound like the real you.

➤ **See how other writers do it.** When you read, look for sentences that read smoothly or contain eye-catching words. Write some of these sentences down. Then see if you can write your own sentences in the same way.

➤ **Write with details.** Writing without details is like baking cookies without flour. One of the most important ingredients is missing. Use details that help readers see, hear, smell, taste, and feel your subject. Also use similes (like the sentence about cookies) and metaphors.

➤ **Know when your writing doesn't work.** Watch for sentences that all sound the same as well as sentences that sound boring or lifeless. Then try to fix these!

MINI LESSON   This activity will help you write sentences with style. List five or six sentences from your writing (your best or your worst). Then try to change each sentence so it sounds better. You might change the order of the words in one sentence and use a different descriptive word in another one.

Modelling the Masters

Follow the Leaders

Beginning artists learn a lot about art by studying the work of famous painters. In the same way, you can learn a lot about writing by studying the work of your favourite authors. When you come across sentences or short passages that you especially like, practise building sentences of your own that follow an author's pattern of writing. This process is sometimes called "modelling." Here are some guidelines you can use for doing your own modelling.

Guidelines for Modelling

- **Find** a sentence (or short passage) that you especially like.
- **Select** a subject for your copy change.
- **Follow** the pattern of your model sentences as you write about your subject.
- **Build** your sentence one small section at a time.
- **Review** your work, and change any parts that seem confusing or unclear.

One Writer's Experience

Kate has enjoyed Roald Dahl's stories for a long time, so every once in a while she tries to write like him. Here is one sentence from Dahl's book *Danny the Champion of the World:*

> **Grown-ups are complicated creatures, full of quirks and secrets.**

Here's Kate's sentence, modelling Roald Dahl's sentence:

Cats are complex beasts, going from lazy to crazy in no time.

Kate might have written, "Some cats can be really nutty. They can go from being couch potatoes to crazy blurs of fur in no time." While this is fine, her modelling has taught her that she can create powerful ideas with fewer words. She has discovered a new pattern of writing.

Later, Kate tried modelling a longer passage from L.M. Montgomery's short story, "The Magical Bond of the Sea." (This paragraph describes the heroine, Nora Shelley.)

> **He had never seen her look so beautiful. The shawl had slipped down to her shoulders and her head rose out of it like some magnificent flower out of a crimson calyx. The masses of her black hair lifted from her face in the rush of the wind and swayed back again like rich shadows.**

Kate especially liked the sound of this passage. She also liked the descriptive language it contained (*like some magnificent flower out of a crimson calyx* and *the sea's sharp caresses*). Here's what Kate wrote: (Notice that she is still thinking about her cat!)

I had never seen her look so intent. She was crouched low on her haunches, and her tail moved slowly back and forth, like some exotic seaweed in a troubled sea. Her long white hair rippled along her back in the gentle breeze and left peaks of white, like angry waves.

...ng **Terms**

...ist contains words used to describe different parts of the ...ng process. It also includes certain writing devices, or special ways of stating an idea.

Anecdote ● A brief story that describes an interesting or amusing incident. Anecdotes are often used to make a point or to illustrate a character trait.

Arrangement ● The way details are organized in writing. (**SEE** page 68 for more information.)

Audience ● Those people who read or hear what you have written.

Body ● The main part of the writing that comes between the opening and closing ideas. The body of a piece of writing contains the specific details that support or develop the main idea.

Brainstorming ● Collecting ideas in groups by freely sharing all of the different possibilities.

Cliché ● A familiar word or phrase that has been used so much that it is no longer a good way of saying something, such as *good as gold* or *bright as the sun.*

Closing/Concluding sentence ● The sentence that sums up the main point being made in a paragraph.

Composition ● Writing in which all the ideas work together to form a finished product.

Conferencing ● Working and sharing in writing groups.

Description ● Writing that paints a picture of a person, a place, a thing, or an idea using specific details.

Details ● The specific facts, examples, and words used in a piece of writing to support or explain the main idea.

Diction ● A writer's choice of words. In a story about everyday life, a writer may use very informal, everyday language. For a business letter, a writer will use more formal or proper language.

Editing ● Checking your writing to make sure the ideas are clear and that the words and sentences are strong and read smoothly.

Exaggeration ● Words that stretch the truth. Exaggeration is used in tall tales: *The mosquito is so big it needs a runway to land.*

Exposition ● Writing that explains, such as a report or research paper. (Also called expository writing.)

Figure of speech ● A special way of writing to create an effective word picture. A figure of speech usually involves making a comparison of some type. (**SEE** *simile, metaphor,* and *personification.*)

First draft ● The first complete writing about a subject.

Focus/Main idea ● Concentrating on a specific part of a subject. When writing about a favourite person, for example, you could focus on his or her sense of humour.

Form ● The shape of writing — a poem, an essay, a novel, a play, and so on. (**SEE** pages 34-35 for a complete list.)

Free writing ● Writing freely and rapidly to discover new ideas.

Generalization ● A statement that gives the general meaning rather than the specific details of a subject. "Writing helps you learn" is a generalization. (**SEE** *topic sentence.*)

Grammar ● The rules and guidelines of a language, which are used when you want to be correct in your writing and speaking.

Irony ● Using a word or phrase to mean the exact opposite of its normal meaning: Having the flu is *so much fun,* don't you think?

Journal ● A daily record of thoughts, feelings, and ideas.

Limiting the subject ● Narrowing a general writing subject to a more specific writing idea: *Pets — dogs — Labradors — older Labs — caring for older Labs.*

Metaphor ● A figure of speech that compares two different things without using a word of comparison such as *like* or *as*: *The streetlight was my security guard.*

Modifier ● A word, or group of words, that describes another word or idea. (**SEE** "Adjectives" and "Adverbs" on pages 384-385.)

Narration ● Writing that tells a story or recalls an experience.

Objective ● Writing that includes facts, with no opinions or personal feelings.

Parallelism ● The repeating of phrases or sentences that are written in the same way: Josie *scratched her head, bit her nails,* and *shrugged her shoulders.*

Personal narrative ● Writing that tells a story from the writer's life.

Personification ● A figure of speech in which an idea, object, or animal is given qualities of a person: *The rock refused to move.*

Persuasion ● Writing that is meant to change the way a reader thinks or acts.

Prewriting ● Planning a writing project. *Selecting a subject* and *collecting details* are prewriting activities.

Process ● A way of doing something that involves several steps; the writing process includes prewriting, writing the first draft, revising, editing and proofreading, and publishing.

Proofreading ● Checking a final draft for spelling, grammar, and mechanics errors.

Prose ● Regular writing in sentences and paragraphs.

Pun ● A word or phrase used in a way that gives it a funny twist: That story about rabbits is a real *hare raiser.*

Purpose ● The main reason a person has for writing.

Revising ● Changing a first draft to improve it.

Sarcasm ● Praise that actually means the opposite, and is meant to put someone down: That's *just great!*

Sensory details ● Details that help us to see, feel, smell, taste, and hear a subject.

Simile ● A figure of speech that makes a comparison using either *like* or *as*: *A summer wind feels like a soft cotton sheet.*

Slang ● Special words and phrases used by friends when they are talking to each other. "Chill out" is a slang term.

Style ● A writer's choice of words, phrases, and sentences.

Subjective ● Writing that includes personal feelings.

Supporting details ● The details used to develop a subject or bring a story to life.

Theme ● The central idea or message in a piece of writing.

Topic ● The specific subject of a piece of writing.

Topic sentence ● The sentence that contains the main idea of a paragraph. (*SEE* pages 60-61.)

Transitions ● Words that help tie ideas together. (*SEE* page 69.)

Voice ● The way a writer expresses ideas. Writing that sounds believable is often written in an honest, natural voice.

The Forms of Writing

Personal Writing

Writing in Journals

Writing Personal Narratives

Writing Friendly Letters

Writing in Journals

Your Very Bad Day

Your old friend Bobbi Jones told everyone that your socks didn't match. Your mother packed you a cheese sandwich and two carrot sticks for the third day in a row. You never got a chance to bat during gym class. And on the way home from school, you left your favourite folder on the bus. Repeat after me: "It was a terrible, horrible, no-good, very bad day!"

How should you deal with a day like this? You could head straight for the Oreo cookies in the kitchen, "chill out" in front of the TV, or give your pillow a couple of body slams. But what happens when you can't look at another Oreo or watch another rerun? Your "very bad day" will still be there.

Here's what I would do: After a couple of cookies, I would get out my personal journal and write about all of the things that happened. Writing helps me sort out my thoughts. It helps keep me in control. It helps make bad days not seem so bad. And I almost always feel better when I'm done.

Why Should You Write in a Personal Journal?

There are many reasons to write in a journal. You can...

✔ **make notes of interesting things you see and hear,**

✔ **collect ideas for stories, poems, and reports,**

✔ **practise writing on your own,**

✔ **deal with your bad days,**

✔ **and relive all of your good times.**

Here's how to get started...

1 Gather the right tools. All you need is a notebook and some pens or pencils (or a computer).

2 Find a special time and place to write. Get up early in the morning and write while it is quiet in your house. Write at a regular time during school. Or plop down on your bed right after dinner and see how that works.

3 Write every day. Write freely, exploring your thoughts and feelings as they come to mind. Don't worry about what you say or how you say it. Just keep writing for as long as you can (at least 5-10 minutes at a time).

4 Write about those things that are important to you. Write about something that is bothering you or something you want to remember. Write about what you did last weekend or something silly you saw. Write about one thing and then later go on to something else.

5 Keep track of your writing. Put the date on the top of the page each time you write. Read through your journal writings from time to time. Underline ideas you find interesting or surprising and ideas that you would like to write more about in the future.

A Closer Look at Journal Writing

Journal writing works best when you can *reflect* or really think about your experiences and learn from them. When you can do this, your writing becomes more exciting — and full of surprises.

➤ *Reflect*

Thinking and writing in the following ways will help you explore and reflect upon your experiences.

Ask questions: As you write, ask yourself some questions: *"What was fun or interesting about this experience?" "How do I feel about it now?"* Or simply ask yourself *why?* at different points in your writing, and try to discover some answers.

Wonder: Also think about what you have learned from an experience. *Compare* it to others you've had. *Wonder* what you could have done differently, or *predict* what the experience will mean to you in the future.

Read the model journal entry on page 108, and you will see that this student was writing and thinking (reflecting) about his father.

➤ *Push Yourself*

If you push yourself in your writing, you are sure to make some interesting discoveries.

Keep it going: When you start a new journal entry, pick up right where you left off in your last entry. When you find an idea that surprises you, try to say more about it. When you think that you have said all that you can about a certain subject, keep going for at least a few more lines.

Make connections: And if you want a challenge, try to make connections between ideas that seem really different. You can also make connections to events in the news, movies, songs, and so on.

Kinds of Journals

If you enjoy exploring your thoughts in a personal journal, you might also enjoy writing in one of the special journals listed below.

Dialogue Journal ● In a dialogue journal, you and a friend, parent, or teacher write to each other about experiences you've had, books you've read, or ideas you wonder about. (**SEE** the sample on the next page.)

Diary ● A diary is a personal record of daily events as they happened. (You keep track of personal things in a diary.)

Learning Log ● In a learning log or class journal, you write about subjects like math and science to help you understand them better. (**SEE** pages 338-339 for more information.)

Response Journal ● Do you ever have strong feelings about the stories and books you read? You can write about these feelings in a response journal. (**SEE** page 137 for a list of writing ideas.)

A Special-Event Journal ● You may want to write about your experiences while participating in a sport, while preparing for a new member of the family, or while doing a special project.

Sample Journal Writing

In the first sample, a student thinks and writes about his father, a peace keeper.

Oct. 26

I never imagined growing up without a father. He could have died in Bosnia. I never thought of it that way. I'm sure my mother did. The subject never comes up at home. But I think about my dad's military service a lot.

I wonder what I would do if I was in the army. Lt. Craven, it has a nice ring to it. Jogging 30 kilometres, 50 push-ups, and cheap food.

Just watching the news I know what my father went through. I'm glad he's home, and everyone's happy...

Dialogue Journal

In this second sample, a student and teacher carry on a conversation about a book.

Feb. 3

Dear Susan,

That part in <u>Mrs. Frankweiler</u> where the kids are hiding in the bathroom made me think of the time I hid from my mom in K-Mart. I didn't want to go home, so I hid behind the shower curtains. She was so mad! I thought of this because my heart was beating really fast whenever Mom got close to me, like the kids' hearts in the book. (Hey, when does your heart beat fast?)

Sincerely,
Mrs. N

Dear Mrs. N.

Thanks for your letter. You hid from your mother? That's funny. My heart beats fast (1) when we have spelling bees, (2) when I'm reading my book to the class, and (3) when you call on me to answer a math problem and I'm not sure where we are! (I have to number my problems!)

Your friend,
Susan

Writing Personal Narratives

The Stories of Your Life

Have you ever wished you could be the main character in a story? Well, guess what? You already are. You're the main character in the story of your life. A true story about yourself is sometimes called a **personal narrative**.

A personal narrative is a story about a personal memory. But it's not about any old memory. It's about a time so important you don't ever want to forget it.

First Thoughts

Think about the different chapters (or experiences) in the story of your life. Some of them might make you laugh; some might make you shudder. Then again, maybe some of them make you feel angry or happy or sad or excited. Any experience that has caused you to feel a strong emotion is a good subject for a personal narrative.

> **❝It's not easy to travel back into your memory and gather details. But it's worth it. They help your reader understand what happened. And they help you remember the very important chapters in the story of your life.❞**
> — Sandy Asher

Model Personal Narrative

Here's a true story about me and my family. When it happened, I felt scared, sad, and then happy. (I'm sure you have plenty of your own exciting stories to share.)

THE GREAT GERBIL ESCAPE

When my daughter Emily was nine years old, she had a pair of gerbils named Farrah and Festus. One day, Festus escaped from our bathtub!

It sounds silly to have gerbils in your tub, but it's not. The sides are too high to jump over and too slick to climb. We plugged the drain. We put in toys and sunflower seeds. The gerbils could exercise and play safely.

But one day, I accidentally left a fuzzy blue bath mat over the edge of the tub. When Emily and I came back, Festus was gone. He'd grabbed the mat and climbed out!

The only place he could have gone was down the heat vent in the wall. We knelt beside the vent. We could hear him! "Scritch-scratch. Scritch-scratch." We lowered a rope into the vent, but he didn't climb out. We stuffed in a towel, but he didn't climb that either.

And when we pulled the towel out, there was no more "Scritch-scratch." Oh, no! I thought. We've pushed him down the vent into the furnace. We've baked our gerbil!

Emily was heartbroken. I felt terrible. We put Farrah back in the cage and went downstairs. Then I noticed another heat vent in the hall, right below the one upstairs in the bathroom. And sure enough, we could hear Festus again: "Scritch-scratch. Scritch-scratch!"

Finally, Emily remembered that gerbils love to explore boxes. We took all the tissues out of a small tissue box. Emily lowered the box into the vent as far as her arm could reach. Then Festus climbed aboard and rode to safety in his own private elevator. And that's how the Great Gerbil Escape became the Great Gerbil Rescue!

The story is organized according to time (describing what happens first, second, third, and so on).

Each new action adds suspense and interest to the story.

Gathering Story Ideas

You can start gathering ideas for personal narratives by writing in a daily diary or journal, or by making lists of personal experiences. A good way to find ideas is to ask yourself the following types of questions:

■ **Who are the important people in your life?**

> Family members? Friends? Classmates? Neighbours? Think about the times you've shared with each one. What do you remember best? What would you just as soon forget?

■ **Where have you been?**

> Every place you visit is an adventure, whether it's the doctor's office, the principal's office, or Disneyland. Think of the biggest place you've been, and the smallest. Think of comfortable places, and places that cause you to squirm. Think of special meeting places from your past.

■ **What do you like to do?**

> Do you enjoy drawing or cooking or caring for animals? Do you like to play ball or just hang out? Do you like to talk on the phone or read at night when you're supposed to be asleep?

■ **What do you *not* like to do?**

> Study? Clean your room? Babysit? Get up early? There are a lot of ways to answer this questions, aren't there? And a lot of strong feelings involved, too. Isn't it nice to know that even the *worst* times you can remember are at least good for story ideas?

If you **don't know where you're going,** you'll **probably end up somewhere** else.

Writing a Personal Narrative

PREWRITING *Planning Your Way*

Select a Subject ● Choosing a subject for a personal narrative should be easy. You're looking for a memorable experience that happened over a short period of time. (**SEE** "Gathering Story Ideas" on the previous page for help.)

Collect Your Thoughts ● If the experience you select seems really clear in your mind, go right to your first draft. Write it all out as best you can. If you're a little fuzzy about all of the details, try doing a cluster or making a list.

As soon as you can answer the 5 Ws — *Who? What? When? Where?* and *Why?* — about the experience, you're probably ready to write.

WRITING THE FIRST DRAFT

Start at the Beginning ● Put your self at the beginning of the experience ("There I stood" or "As I entered the room") and continue to add details as they come to mind. Don't worry about saying everything. You can fill in any gaps later when you revise.

REVISING *Improving Your Writing*

Review Your Work ● Look over your first draft. Have you left out any important details, or put things in the wrong order? Ask a classmate to review your writing as well. Then make the necessary changes in your story. (**SEE** "Striking It Rich in Your Story" on page 114 for helpful writing reminders.)

EDITING & PROOFREADING

Check for Errors ● Finally, make sure that your writing makes sense and reads smoothly. Then write a neat, error-free final draft and proofread it.

Striking It Rich in Your Story

Here are some special reminders to help you develop your personal narrative:

Add Physical Details ● Take another look at my gerbil story. Can you see what I saw? There are two gerbils in the tub, with its high, slick sides. There's the fuzzy blue bath mat and the heat vent in the wall. It's important that you help your readers see the details that matter. You do this by adding important facts and by leaving out facts that are less important to your story.

Add Sounds, Tastes, Smells, and Textures ● Sounds make readers feel as if they were there, living the adventure with you. I emphasize one important sound in my story: "Scritch-scratch!" What about taste, smell, and touch? Did I include all of those in my gerbil tale? Only touch. I mentioned that the tub was slick and the bath mat was fuzzy. Taste and smell weren't important in my story, but they might be in yours.

Add Dialogue ● Dialogue always makes a story seem real. Here's how I might have started my story with dialogue:

> *"Mom, look!" Emily shouted.*
> *"Festus is gone!"*
> *"Gone?" I asked, rushing into*
> *the bathroom after her. "What do you mean?"*

Add Thoughts and Feelings ● What helped you understand my thoughts and feelings in "The Great Gerbil Escape"? Comments like "Oh, no!" and "I felt terrible" surely helped. A narrative without the writer's thoughts and feelings would not have that special personal touch that can make this type of writing so much fun to read.

TAKE NOTE Write the way you feel. If your subject makes you laugh, try to make your readers laugh. Or, if your subject makes you feel sad or excited, try to make your readers feel the same way.

Student Model

In this model narrative, Jessica Gilbert recalls a motorcycle ride that taught her an important lesson.

When I Got Burned on My Dad's Motorcycle

As I was going outside, I was happy because I was going to ride on my dad's motorcycle. It was always fun.

"Come on. Get up," said my dad cheerfully.

"Okay," I answered. But just as I was getting onto the seat, I burnt myself on one of the accelerator pipes!

"Ow!" I yelled as I started to cry.

"Are you all right?" asked my mom.

"No," I answered.

"Come here," said my mom. "Let's take a look at that burn. It's really bad. I don't think she should go for a ride on the motorcycle."

I felt really glad that my mom had said that.

"Aw, come on. It won't hurt her anymore than she's already hurtin'," said my dad. I started to get really angry. I mean, I was only five years old. I hurt! Why should I have to ride the motorcycle?

Then he picked me up and set me on the seat of the motorcycle.

"Dad, I don't wanna go!" I said, still crying.

"Nonsense. Now stop crying," said my dad. And we took off.

I have to admit that during the ride, I started to laugh. My burn hardly hurt anymore. I was still sniffling a little when we got back, but it had been a fun ride.

I'm really glad my dad made me get on the motorcycle. If he hadn't, I probably never would have gotten on it again. From that day on, I knew I would never give up after I got hurt. I would just get back up and try it again.

Dialogue makes the story seem real.

The writer shares her thoughts and feelings with the reader.

Writing Friendly Letters

Keeping in Touch

Do you ever run to the mailbox to see if anything is addressed to you? Everyone enjoys receiving mail, especially letters. Letters from friends make friendships stronger. Letters from relatives make you feel closer. The best way to make sure you receive a letter is to send one.

Parts of a Friendly Letter

Friendly letters have five parts: the *heading,* the *salutation*, the *body*, the *closing*, and the *signature*.

➤ The **heading** includes your address and the date. Write it in the upper right-hand corner.

➤ The **salutation** or greeting usually begins with the word *Dear* and is followed by the name of the person who will receive the letter. Place a comma after the name. Write a salutation at the left-hand margin, two lines below the heading.

➤ The **body** of the letter contains your thoughts and ideas. Begin writing on the second line after the salutation. Keep the paragraphs short for easy reading.

➤ Write the **closing** two lines below the body of your letter. Capitalize only the first word and follow it with a comma. Put your **signature** under the closing.

Model Friendly Letter

Tracy introduced herself in this letter to her new pen pal, Grace.

Heading

165 Ranch Glen Drive NW
Calgary, AB T3G 1S2
February 8, 1997

Salutation

Dear Grace,

My name is Tracy, and I am your new pen pal. I go to Riverview School in Calgary, Alberta.

I'll start by telling you about some of my hobbies. I am taking keyboard lessons because I got a keyboard for my birthday, and I think it will be fun. I'm not very good, yet, but I can play two songs. Have you ever played a keyboard?

Another hobby of mine is horseback riding. Have you ever been horseback riding? When my dad was 15, besides school, he worked at a horse ranch. I think that is neat.

I really like to draw, paint, and read stories. I also love to read mystery books and fiction books. My favourite mystery series is Nancy Drew. Do you like to read?

Body

I have three people in my family: my mom, my dad, and me. My mom is in advertising, and my dad is a car mechanic. I also have ten pets: seven fish, two parakeets, and a dog. My dog's name is Hershey. My family and I named her that because she's all brown, like a Hershey's chocolate bar. My two birds, Sammy and Tweedy, are green, blue, yellow, and black. Tweedy bites, and because of that, it's really hard to train her. Sammy is trained and can ride on my shoulder in the house.

As you probably have noticed, I love animals. I want to work with animals when I grow up, especially with whales. What do you want to be when you grow up? Please write and let me know all about yourself.

Closing

Sincerely,

Signature

Tracy Randlett

P.S. Write back soon!

Writing a Friendly Letter

PREWRITING *Planning Your Letter*

Choose a Friend ● This part is easy! Write to someone who wrote to you, someone you haven't seen in a long time, or a special person you want to talk to in a letter. Maybe you'd like to have a pen pal as Tracy did.

Gather Ideas ● List all of the ideas you want to include in your letter. Gather all the details you will need to make each idea clear. Here are some ideas to get you started:

- Share a good story.

- Tell what's been on your mind.

- Describe something you like to do.

- Tell about the latest book you've read.

- Share a favourite poem, or write one of your own.

- Provide a few questions for your friend to answer.

WRITING

Get Started ● Begin by telling all about one of the ideas on your list. Any one will do! Tracy started by telling all about her hobbies and the things she likes to do. Then she told about her family and pets.

Write Back ● If you are writing back to a friend, you can • start by answering the questions he or she may have asked. Then add the new information about yourself.

THINK IT OVER

Writing a friendly letter gives you a chance to think about your own life. In this way, you benefit from writing a letter as much as the person who receives it.

REVISING   *Improving Your Letter*

Try to make your letter easy to read and entertaining. Read the sentences over to be sure they make sense. Remember to start a new paragraph each time you switch to a new story or idea.

EDITING & PROOFREADING

Check your letter for spelling, punctuation, and capitalization. Also check the form of your letter, especially if you are writing to someone who is not a close friend or relative. Then neatly write or type a final copy if you need to. A correctly written letter will make a good first impression.

P.S.   If you have already finished your letter and then remember something you forgot to say, add a P.S. (postscript) at the bottom under your signature.

Address the Envelope

Address the envelope clearly and correctly so it is sure to reach its destination. Also make sure to fold your letter so that it fits neatly into the envelope. (**SEE** page 146.)

Ms. Tracy Randlett
165 Ranch Glen Drive
Calgary, AB   T3G 1S2

Ms. Grace Jackson
25 Deer Valley Crescent
London, ON   N6J 4K5

Writing Social Notes

Sometimes you will need to write a special kind of friendly letter — a thank-you note or an invitation. These are often called social notes.

Parts of Social Notes

A social note begins with a **salutation** *(Dear ___ ,)*. The middle of your note, the **body,** is usually one or two paragraphs. The paragraphs are short and to the point. "Your friend" or "Love" are common **closings.** Don't forget to sign your note with your **signature.**

Invitations ➤ When you are inviting someone to come to a party or special event, you'll need to write an **invitation**. Be sure to include these items:

- *What:* a party, a celebration
- *When:* the date and time
- *Where:* the place and address
- *Who:* who the party is for
- *Why:* birthday, bar mitzvah, going away

Ask for an answer in your letter if you want to know whether or not the person will be coming to your event. You can also add R.S.V.P. and your telephone number in the lower left-hand corner.

Thank-You Notes ➤ When writing a *thank-you note,* be specific. If you are thanking someone for something special he or she did, explain why it was important to you. If you are thanking someone for a gift, tell why you like it and how you are using it.

Bright IDEA

You can make your own customized notes and invitations with rubber stamps, watercolours, coloured markers, stickers, or special lettering. Be creative!

Sample Invitation

Dear Josh,

My twelfth birthday is coming up, and my dad said I could have a party. He's going to take us to the zoo, and the director said we could go on a scavenger hunt.

The party will be on my birthday, April 29th. You can be dropped off at 12:30 and picked up at 4:00 p.m.

My address is 3200 Main Street North. Bring a raincoat if it looks like rain. Please call me to let me know if you can come.

Mei
R.S.V.P. 639-2231

Sample Thank-You Note

THANK YOU
THANK YOU
THANK YOU
THANK YOU
THANK YOU
THANK YOU
THANK YOU
THANK YOU
THANK YOU
THANK YOU
THANK YOU
THANK YOU
THANK YOU

Dear Josh,

Thanks for coming to my party. The book and paper-making kit you gave me are great. I started reading <u>50 Simple Things Kids Can Do to Save the Earth</u>, and I'm already working on some of the ideas.

I started collecting junk mail to use for the paper-making kit. I'll show you how my first paper turns out. Thank you very much for the presents. I really like them.

Your friend,
Mei

Subject Writing

Writing Newspaper Stories

Writing Book Reviews

Writing Explanations

Writing Business Letters

Writing Observation Reports

Writing Newspaper Stories

Look!
Up in the Sky!
It's a Reporter!

How would you like to be Superman for a day? Would you like to zoom through the sky? Leap over tall buildings? Discover secrets with your X-ray vision?

You may remember that Superman, when he wasn't flying around in his long underwear, had a real job. As Clark Kent, he worked as a newspaper reporter.

> **Starting today, you can be a reporter in your own classroom, school, and community. All you need is a little curiosity, an interest in people, and, of course, a reporter's notebook! With a little energy and creativity, you can even produce your own newspaper.**
> — Roy Peter Clark

Real-Life Reporters

Some reporters think that writing stories about important events and memorable people is more interesting than being a comic-book hero. As you read this chapter, maybe you'll see why.

The Parts of a Reporter

A curious mind to think of story ideas

Eyes to see interesting details

Ears to listen for good quotes

A nose for news

A mouth to ask the right questions

Heart to understand people

Feet for following up on good stories

Hands for writing down good notes

Interviewing

Many wonderful stories result from interviews. During an interview, the reporter asks people questions about their experiences. The result can be a dramatic and funny adventure, like this one:

JAWS!

By Karin Fraser

One day last summer during school vacation, a boy named Billy Shannon was at a beach. He was swimming in the Gulf of Mexico. He was swimming near the deep water markers, and he felt something rubbery slide against his leg and saw a fin.

He called "Help!" about four or five times. A few people went out of the water. The movie <u>Jaws</u> flashed through his mind. The lifeguard went to him in a jet-ski. He pointed out that they were dolphins.

Billy swam back to the shore. He went to the pool where his parents were. He was quite embarrassed. He told them the story, and they thought it was funny. His brother made fun of him, and Billy punched him in the jaw.

Tips for Interviewing

✔ Prepare a list of questions beforehand.

✔ Start with a question from your list, but then try to make the interview seem like a *real* conversation.

✔ Listen carefully, write quickly.

✔ When you take notes, politely say, "I want to write that down." The person will stop so you can write.

✔ Ask the person to spell any names you're unsure of.

✔ Remember that **the meaning is more important than the exact words.**

Finding News Stories

A news story tells readers about an important or unusual event. The more important the event, the more interesting the news. An old joke says that when a dog bites a man, it is not news. But when a man bites a dog, that's news!

The headlines below show the difference between news that is news, and news that is not news.

News:

Daily Chronicle

Class Makes Flying Saucer

Not News:

Daily Chronicle

Saucer Breaks in Cafeteria

News:

Daily Chronicle

Flu Hits Laurier School

Not News:

Daily Chronicle

Student Gets Headache

News:

Daily Chronicle

Artists Receive Awards

Not News:

Daily Chronicle

Art Teacher Draws in Class

MINI LESSON   Newspaper stories are about real events, not make-believe ones. Make a list of interesting things that have recently happened at your school. Put stars next to the ones that you think would make good news stories.

Three Types of Stories

Here is a list of stories written by one group of students for their school newspaper. They decided to name their newspaper the *Cougar Chronicle,* after the school mascot. The newspaper's motto is "If a student needs to know it, we print it." You will notice that these stories are listed under three general story types: news stories, human interest stories, and opinion letters to the editor.

News Stories

- A power outage kills fish in the school aquarium.
- Mr. Krauss, the school custodian, cannot catch the raccoon that lives in the school attic.

Human Interest Stories

- What is it like to see a baby being born?
- Who is the fastest reader in the school?
- Our math teacher plays in a rock band.
- Your friend mistakes a dolphin for a shark. (**SEE** "Jaws!" on page 125.)

Opinion Letters to the Editor

- There should be a greater variety of nutritious foods in the school cafeteria.
- We should have more time for reading and more books available in our classroom.
- People should not give pets as gifts because the pets are often abandoned.

About It

A good reporter sees the world as a storehouse of story ideas. Look around, be curious, read, and ask questions. You'll discover stories everywhere — in your classroom, school, and community — enough to fill up the pages of any classroom newspaper.

Daily Chronicle

① Lakewood Girls Win Soccer Championship!

② by Anna Flanagan

③ The girls of Lakewood made history yesterday. They became the first team from Burnaby to win a provincial soccer championship. They beat Rockledge by a score of 1-0.

④ "The girls played well," said Coach Bill Carter. "I'll always remember this team. In my eyes they were all stars."

⑤ Ever since Susan James broke the team record by scoring five goals against Central, no one could stop Lakewood. Susan and her teammates, Darcy Smith and Olivia Hum, played such good defence that only one goal was scored against them in their last three games.

They have set a new record for their school, ending the season with a record of 7 wins and 0 losses.

⑥ Coach Carter smiled as he said, "Eight members of our soccer team will return next year. I am ready for the season to start right now."

Parts of a Newspaper Story

① The **Headline** is a title that tells the story in bold type:
Lakewood Girls Win Soccer Championship!

② The **Byline** gives the writer credit for the story.

③ The **Lead** tells the reader the most important news:
"The girls of Lakewood School made history yesterday. They became the first team from Burnaby to win a provincial soccer championship. They beat Rockledge by a score of 1-0."

④ A good **Quote** gives life to a story:
"The girls played well," said Coach Bill Carter. "I'll always remember this team."

⑤ The **Body** of the story answer questions for the reader:
- Who played well?
- How many games has the team won this season?

⑥ The **Ending** gives the reader something to remember:
"Eight members of our soccer team will return next year. I am ready for the season to start right now."

Writing a News Story

PREWRITING   *Planning Your Writing*

Select a Subject ● Write about a *newsworthy* subject — something important, interesting, or unusual that your readers will want to read about.

Collect Details ● You can do this by interviewing people, making eyewitness observations, and so on. A good starting point is to ask the 5 Ws and H — *Who? What? Where? When? Why?* and *How?* (Try to include enough information to answer any questions your readers may have.)

WRITING THE FIRST DRAFT

Write the Lead or First Paragraph ● Begin with the most important or interesting detail. If at all possible, put a person in the lead paragraph — for example, a baker spinning a pizza crust, or a lifeguard hearing a shout for help. (**SEE** page 130.)

Write the Main Part of Your Story ● Remember that the most important is usually stated early in basic news stories. Try to leave your readers with something to think about in the ending.

REVISING   *Improving Your Writing*

Review Your Work ● Make sure you have included all of the important facts an details in your story. Also make sure your information is correct and in the best possible order.

EDITING & PROOFREADING

Check for Careless Errors ● Pay careful attention to the spelling of names! Have your teacher or a classmate review your work as well. Write the final copy of your story.

Writing a Lead

The beginning of a newspaper story is called a **lead** because it leads the reader into the rest of the story. The lead can be a short sentence or a paragraph. When it is well written, the lead pulls the reader into the story, and prepares the reader for what comes next.

Remember Karin Fraser's lead for the story "Jaws!"? She begins the story with a bit of danger, so the reader will want to find out if Billy Shannon is going to be the victim of a shark attack.

Student Models

Here are some leads written by student reporters. Read them and then imagine what the rest of the story will be about:

I rode six hours in a little yellow Datsun, but it was worth it. I finally got to see the greatest concert in years.

Picture in your mind the most beautiful sunset you've ever seen, the one sunset that you'll remember forever.

Everybody was in uniform, out on the field, and ready for the final game of the season.

Tommy Walton is "The World's Greatest Singing Hot-Dog Salesman," a 58-year-old man with the heart and soul of a teenager.

Lead Sampler

The samples listed here will help you write leads for human interest stories.

■ **Question Lead:** *Have you ever watched a true hot-dog lover in action?*

■ **Suspense Lead:** *Should she hold the pickle relish or mustard? Tanya Robinson couldn't decide.*

■ **Surprise Lead:** *A dog with the works is worth the indigestion.*

Writing A Letter to the Editor

One way to exercise your right to free expression is to write a letter to the editor of a newspaper. Good newspapers will publish letters written by young people. They know that young writers have strongly felt beliefs and that their opinions are important. Here is one student's letter:

BUDDY SNIDER
351 HERRING COVE ROAD
HALIFAX, NC B3R 1V9

CANADA

LETTERS TO THE EDITOR
THE CHEBUCTO CHRONICLE
1734 CONNAUGHT AVENUE,
HALIFAX, NS B3H 4C8

351 Herring Cove Rd.
Halifax, NS B3R 1V9
October 15, 1997

Editor
The Chebucto Chronicle
1734 Connaught Ave.
Halifax, NS B3H 4C8

Dear Editor:

During the last six years that I have been going to Bay Point Elementary School, the lunches have been getting smaller, and the prices have been getting bigger! I have noticed that the little mustard and ketchup containers have taken one whole space on the tray that used to be filled with a vegetable or something else.

We are also getting smaller main courses. When I get home from school, I eat a lot; sometimes my mom has to tell me to stop.

Maybe it is because I'm getting older and I eat more, but I think that the school lunches are getting smaller.

Your truly,

Buddy Snider

Buddy Snider

Writing Book Reviews

Sharing Your Views

The students in one school in New Brunswick really enjoy sharing their thoughts and feelings in book reviews. Their school library is loaded with books to choose from. And after reading each other's reviews, the students always know which books they want to read next.

In a book review you share your *understanding of* and *opinion about* a book you have read.

Becoming an Expert

The students also enjoy this form of writing because it gives them a chance to write about subjects that really interest them. For example, two students named Devon and Amina are both crazy about sports. When they read good sports stories, they *want* to write about them. And when other students want to read sports stories, they turn to Devon and Amina (and their reviews) for suggestions.

Model Book Review

The following model is a review of *Lost in the Barrens*, by Farley Mowat. Each paragraph in this model answers one of three basic questions: *What is the book about? What is the book's theme or message? What do I like about this book?*

Lost in the Barrens

What is the book about?

<u>Lost in the Barrens</u> by Farley Mowat is an adventure story set in the area around Keewatin, in Northern Ontario. Jamie Macnair, a sixteen-year-old who lives with his uncle, a trapper, makes friends with a Cree boy called Awasin. Together, the boys decide to join a Chipewyan hunting party headed for the isolated Barrenlands in search of food. Unfortunately, disaster strikes and the two friends are separated from the others. Stranded in the hostile wilderness, with winter coming on, the boys hole up in a cabin. In the adventures that follow, the boys must draw on all the survival skills they know, as well as learning new ones.

What is the book's theme or message?

I think the author, Farley Mowat, wanted to tell his readers that we need to respect nature and be self-reliant. Jamie is not sure they will be able to survive. Both boys learn to rely on themselves and each other. I think the book is also about not judging people based on what other people tell you. All through the book, Jamie and Awasin are terrified that they will run into the fierce Eskimo tribe. When they finally do meet them, things are far different from what they expected.

What do I like about this book?

<u>Lost in the Barrens</u> is exciting! I couldn't put it down. I especially liked the detailed descriptions of how the boys survived in the cabin. These details made the whole story very believable. Farley Mowat clearly loves the North, and he made me want to go there, too.

Readers don't have to know everything that happens in your book, or all of your reasons for liking it. Try to say enough so they can decide if they want to read it themselves.

Writing a Book Review

PREWRITING *Planning Your Review*

Select a Subject ● The type of book you review is really up to you. It could be a mystery, or an adventure story, or maybe a new book about your favourite sports figure. Just make sure that you enjoyed the book, or that you have strong feelings about it.

Collect Your Thoughts ● Your book review should answer three basic questions: *What is the book about? What do I like about the book? What is the book's theme or message?* (The "Collection Sheet" on the next page will help you gather information.)

WRITING THE FIRST DRAFT

Include the Right Stuff ● The first paragraph in your review should give the name and author of your book, and also answer the "What is the book about?" question. The other two questions should be answered in separate paragraphs.

REVISING *Improving Your Writing*

Make It Clear ● Carefully review your first draft, checking for ideas that seem unclear or out of order. Also make sure that no paragraph says too much or too little. Saying too much can sometimes be a problem, especially in the first paragraph.

EDITING & PROOFREADING

Check It Out ● Make sure your review reads clearly from start to finish. Also check for spelling and punctuation errors. (Remember that titles should be underlined.) Then write a neat final draft and proofread it.

Collection Sheet

The ideas listed below will help you form answers for the three basic review questions. (Notice that there are separate ideas for fiction and nonfiction books.)

1. **What is the book about?**

   Fiction: *What events happen in the story? (A book review should highlight a few events rather than give the whole story away.)*

   Nonfiction: *What is the basic subject of this book? Is there one part of the book that seems really important?*

2. **What do I like about the book?**

   Fiction: *Does the book start in an exciting or interesting way? Does the book contain a lot of action or suspense? Does the main character show courage or strength? Does the book end in a surprising way?*

   Nonfiction: *Does the book contain interesting information? Is the information easy to follow? Does the book contain colourful illustrations?*

3. **What is the book's theme?**

   Fiction: *What message about life is the author trying to make?* (Here is a sample message: It's not easy to stand up for your rights.) *How do you know that this is the message?*

   Nonfiction: *Why do you think the author wrote this book? What basic information or message does the author want to share?*

YOU DON'T SSSSSSAY

As you collect your ideas, you can write possible answers to each question on separate index cards.

A Review with a Special Focus

Another way to write a book review is to give it a special focus. Writer Heather Monkmeyer feels that *The True Confessions of Charlotte Doyle* is a very suspenseful book. As you will see, this feeling of suspense ties all of her ideas together. It is the focus of her review.

The True Confessions of Charlotte Doyle

The first paragraph tells what the "focus" of the review is.

"Not every thirteen-year-old girl is accused of murder, brought to trial, and found guilty. But I was such a girl..." That is the opening line of <u>The True Confessions of Charlotte Doyle</u> by Avi. From the first line to the final paragraph, Avi creates suspense by telling just enough to make readers ask questions that need good answers.

In the first chapters, Avi creates suspense by setting up strange circumstances. As Charlotte boards the ship that will take her to America, she learns that she is the only passenger. That really made me begin to wonder.

Three suspenseful events are highlighted.

Sometimes Avi creates suspense by the things Charlotte does. She tries to stop the captain from killing an innocent man and slashes the captain's face in the process. What will the captain do to her?

Avi packs in a double helping of suspense when the cruel captain sentences Charlotte to be hanged for a murder she did not commit, while at the same time, the crew turns against her.

In the closing, the writer invites others to read this book.

If you like tales of danger, mystery, and suspense wrapped into a story about courage, <u>The True Confessions of Charlotte Doyle</u> will keep you reading far into the night.

Writing in a Reader Response Journal

A **reader response journal** is a notebook or journal in which you write freely about the books you read. In one writing, you may write about why you think the main character acts in a certain way. In a second writing, you may try to guess what will happen next in the story. In still another writing, you may relate some part of the story to your own life. The choice is yours.

How to Respond

A response journal is very much like any other type of personal journal. You turn to it whenever you feel like writing about something you have read. The point is to make discoveries for yourself, so write as openly and honestly as you can. *Some of the ideas in your journal will help you write book reviews.*

Ideas for Responding

For novels and other longer books, try to write in your journal at least four or five times. The following ideas will help you write responses at different points in your reading.

First Feelings ● What did you like about the opening chapter or two? How do you feel about the characters?

On Your Way ● Are the events in the reading clear to you? How do you feel about the characters and story now? What do you think will happen next?

The Second Half ● What seems important now? What questions or concerns do you have? Does the book keep your interest? Why or why not?

Summing Up ● How do you feel about the ending? How has the main character changed? How have you changed? What do you like most or least about this book and why?

Bright
IDEA

Here are some more ideas to try: Carry on a conversation with a character, express your feelings in a poem, draw a picture, or try adding to or changing the story.

Writing Explanations

Recipe for a Baseball Card Collection

By James Lambert

First, place the autographed rookie card in a plastic wallet. Then, neatly arrange your complete set of Upper Deck cards with the Juan Gonzalez card on top. Next, make sure that the Cal Ripken card is separated from the other cards (otherwise, you'll never find it). Finally, place all of these hot cards on a shelf to cool, and check them from time to time.

How to Do Something

While this set of directions is obviously not real, there are times when you really do have to explain things. For example, you might be asked to explain how to do something, how something works, or how to get from one place to the other. On the next three pages, you will find helpful guidelines and models for this form of writing.

Writing an Explanation

PREWRITING *Planning Your Writing*

Select a Subject ● Think of something you know how to do or make, or some skill you are interested in learning about. You may be skilled at shooting free throws, making pancakes, or *eating* pancakes. Or you may be interested in exploring caves, buying a guitar, or starting a fan club.

List the Steps ● List the steps involved in completing your skill. Or learn as much as you can about a new skill through reading, observing, interviewing, and participating.

WRITING THE FIRST DRAFT

Explain It Clearly ● Explain how to carry out your skill from start to finish. Start your explanation with a topic sentence that identifies the subject.

Helpful Hint   Use linking words like *first, second, next,* and *then* to help readers move from one step to the next.

REVISING *Improving Your Writing*

Test It Out ● Carefully reread your first draft, making sure the directions are clear and complete. If possible, have someone else try to do what you've explained by following your directions. This will help you see if you have missed any important points.

EDITING & PROOFREADING

Check It Out ● Make sure that the revised draft of your writing reads smoothly and is free of careless errors. Proofread the final copy before sharing it.

Student Models

How to Make Something ● Here are the steps to a real recipe, stated very carefully and clearly.

My Favourite Food

by Kimberly Tso

This is how my grandma makes fried bread. First she puts some flour in a bowl. She puts baking soda and salt with the flour. She gets some warm water. She puts in a little bit of water at a time while mixing the flour to make a dough. She kneads the dough to make it soft. Then she covers it with a cloth. She lets it set for 5 minutes. She puts a pan on the stove with grease in it. She waits until the grease gets hot. By that time the dough is ready. Then she starts making fried bread. She fries pieces of bread until they are golden brown, and they taste really good.

How Something Works ● The following model explains how the digestive system works.

Digestion

by Lauren A. Kitchell

The digestive system is really a cycle. It starts as soon as you put food in your mouth. The food gets chewed up by the teeth. Then the salivary glands make a digestive juice called saliva. The saliva covers the chewed-up food, and the food goes down the esophagus or throat to the stomach. In the stomach the food gets churned up and covered with some more digestive juices. After the stomach does its job, the liver and pancreas add digestive juices for use in the small intestine. From the small intestine the digested food passes into the bloodstream. The wastes of the digested food go into the large intestine. In the large intestine the waste is stored and then finally goes out of the body.

How to Get Someplace ● In the following model, Hillary Bachman provides directions for the driver of a stretch limo that took Hillary and her friends on a special birthday ride.

Birthday Ride

For my birthday ride, I want to go from my house to Chi-Chi's restaurant in La Crosse following this route. First, drive north four blocks until you reach Montgomery Street. Then take a left. Continue past the senior high and take the second left after you pass the school. This road will take you in a big loop back to where you first turned. After you pass the senior high again, turn right and drive past Lawrence Lawson Public School. Then take the second left. Drive until you reach Water Street and take a right. This will take you through downtown and past Tim's house (please honk) right after you pass the Morrow Home. Turn right when you come to Roadside Diner. This highway (16) will take us directly to Chi-Chi's. Thank you!

How to Create a Feeling ● You can also use your imagination with explanations that create a feeling or a mood.

Recipe for a Cosy Winter Day

1 snow-filled evergreen forest
1 small one-room log cabin
4 good friends who know lots of songs
1 blazing fireplace
4 mugs of hot chocolate
1 plate of chocolate chip cookies
4 marshmallows

Directions: Take small one-room log cabin. Place it in the middle of a snow-filled evergreen forest. Fill the cabin with four good friends in front of a blazing fireplace. Serve each friend a mug of hot chocolate. Put one marshmallow into each mug. Pass around one plate pile high with chocolate chip cookies. Mix in singing voices, and your cosy winter day will be complete.

Writing Business Letters

When You Mean Business

A **business letter** is different from a letter you write to an aunt in another city or to a pen pal in another country. It looks and sounds more business-like and focuses on only one subject.

You may write a business letter for different reasons:

- **when you need information** (*a letter of request*),

- **when you have a problem with something you ordered** (*a letter of complaint*),

- **or when you have a problem with a situation in your city or school** (*a letter to an editor or official*).

But no matter what type of business letter you write, you should follow the guidelines given in this chapter. Your letters will bring better results if you do them right. Pay special attention to the sample letter on page 145.

Types of Business Letters

There are three types of business letters described below: **a letter of request, a letter of complaint,** and **a letter to an editor or official.**

Letter of Request ● You want to go to Banff National Park on your vacation next summer, but you need to convince the rest of the family. You decide to write a letter of request asking for information. Here are some guidelines you could use. (**SEE** the model on page 145.)

✔ Explain why you are writing.

✔ Ask any questions you have.

✔ Describe what you would like to receive (and when).

✔ Thank them for their help.

Letter of Complaint ● You ordered a pair of high-tops and received two left shoes. How will you get the shoes exchanged or ask for your money back? You could write a letter of complaint.

✔ Describe the product.

✔ Describe the problem and possible causes.

✔ Explain how you have tried to solve the problem

✔ End with what you would like the reader (or company) to do.

Letter to an Editor or Official ● The traffic on your street makes it dangerous for children. How will you get the city to do something about the situation? You could write a letter to your local newspaper, or to a public official. (**SEE** page 131 for a model.)

✔ Describe the situation.

✔ Tell what you think about the situation.

✔ If you have ideas for improvement or change, explain them.

✔ Support your ideas with facts and examples.

✔ End by asking that the situation be changed.

Parts of a Business Letter

Heading ● The **heading** includes the sender's address and date. Write the heading about 3 centimetres from the top of the page at the left-hand margin.

Inside Address ● The **inside address** includes the name and address of the person or company you are writing to. Place it at the left-hand margin, four to seven spaces below the heading. If the person has a special title such as park superintendent, add it after his or her name. (Use a comma first.)

Ms. Hedy Shore, Park Superintendent

Salutation ● The salutation is a greeting, a way of saying hello. Write it on the second line below the inside address. Always use a colon at the end of the salutation.

➤ If you know the person's name, write:
   Dear Ms. Shore:

➤ If you don't know the person's name, write:
   Dear Park Superintendent:
   Dear Sir or Madam:
   Greetings:

Body ● The **body** is the main part of the letter. Begin this part two lines below the salutation. Double-space between each paragraph. Do not indent. Keep the information brief and simple so the reader clearly understands what you are asking for or explaining.

Closing ● Place the **closing** at the left-hand margin, two spaces below the body. Use **Very truly, Yours truly, Yours sincerely**, or **Sincerely** for a business letter closing. Capitalize the first word but not the others. Always place a comma after the closing.

Signature ● End your letter by signing your name beneath the closing. If you are typing your letter, skip four lines and type your full name. Then write your **signature** between the closing and your typed name.

Sample Business Letter

79 Cricklewood Crescent
Thunder Bay, ON L3T 4T8
January 1, 1998

Ms. Hedy Shore, Park Superintendent
Banff National Park
Box 400
Banff, AB T0L 0C0

Dear Ms. Shore:

We are having a contest in my family to see who can plan the best summer vacation. I want to convince everyone that a trip to Banff National Park would be better than going to the Yukon or even to Disneyland for a week. This is not going to be easy!

I would appreciate any help you could give me. I am most interested in some up-to-date brochures of the park with photos and maps. I will also need information on where we can stay and what we can do there.

Thank you for your help. Maybe I'll see you next summer.

Sincerely,

Luke Iliescu

Luke Iliescu

Folding Your Letter

When you finish your letter, fold it in three parts.

Like this:
- Fold bottom one-third up.
- Next, fold top one-third down.
- Crease the folds firmly.
- Insert into envelope.

Or like this:
- Fold letter in half.
- Next, fold into thirds.
- Crease folds firmly.
- Insert into envelope.

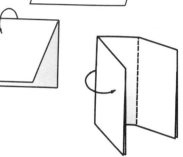

Sending Your Letter

Address the Envelope

- Place the full name and complete address of the person to whom the letter is being sent slightly to the left of the middle of the envelope.
- Place your return address in the upper left-hand corner of the envelope and the stamp in the upper right-hand corner.

MR LUKE ILIESCU
79 CRICKLEWOOD CRESCENT
THUNDER BAY, ON L3T 4T8

MS HEDY SHORE
PARK SUPERINTENDENT
BANFF NATIONAL PARK
BOX 900
BANFF, AB T0L 0C0

When addressing your envelope, the post office prefers that you use all capital letters, no punctuation, and the two-letter abbreviations for provinces. (**SEE** page 357 for a list of abbreviations.)

Writing a Business Letter

PREWRITING *Planning Your Letter*

- ✔ Check your handbook for the requirements for the different types of business letters: **Letter of Request, Letter to an Editor or Official, Letter of Complaint.**
- ✔ Gather all of the details and facts you need.
- ✔ Organize your ideas for your writing.

WRITING THE FIRST DRAFT

- ✔ Write naturally, but keep the style somewhat formal.
- ✔ Explain your main points clearly.
- ✔ Write short paragraphs.

REVISING *Improving Your Writing*

- ✔ Make sure you have included the necessary facts and details.
- ✔ Make sure you have written honestly and sincerely.
- ✔ Make sure your letter is easy to read.

EDITING & PROOFREADING

- ✔ Make sure you proofread for punctuation, capitalization, and grammar errors. (Pay special attention to the heading, inside address, and salutation.)
- ✔ Make sure you've included all the necessary "parts" of a business letter. (*SEE* page 144.)
- ✔ Make sure your letter is neatly written or typed.
- ✔ Centre the letter and keep the margins even.
- ✔ Use only one side of the paper.

Writing Observation Reports

I hear kids shouting. There is a strange scent in the air. There is a faint breeze. It is 9:35 Saturday morning, and the playground is filling up with kids. Cars keep whizzing past. Suddenly an in-line skater zooms by...

Using Your Senses

You have just read part of an observation report. The subject is a playground where the writer observes different *sights, sounds, smells,* and *physical feelings.* In other words, all of the writer's senses are focused on his subject. In an observation report, there is no need to get involved in any action. You simply select a location and look, listen, and learn.

Writing an Observation Report

PREWRITING *Planning Your Writing*

Select a Location ● Observe a room in your school, a street corner, a bus or subway car, a small store, an entrance to a mall, a kitchen. The choice is yours.

Observe and Write ● In a notebook, write down what you see, hear, smell, and feel at this location. If there is a lot of activity, take quick notes so you don't miss anything. (Spend at least 15 minutes at this location.)

You may find a camcorder helpful for collecting, but check with your teacher before you do any recording.

WRITING THE FIRST DRAFT

Prepare Your Report ● You can write your observation report in two different ways.

1. You can share all of the details in the order that you listed them. In this way, your report will flow from one sight or sound to another. This is how the model at the beginning of the chapter is written.

2. You can organize your observations around a main idea just as you would in a descriptive paragraph. (See the model on the next page.)

REVISING *Improving Your Writing*

Decide What Changes Need to Be Made ● Review your first draft once to make sure that it contains all of the important observations (sights and sounds). Review it a second time to check for sentence, spelling, and punctuation errors. Make all of the needed changes; then proofread the final draft of your report.

Model Observation Report

The main idea in this model paragraph is stated in the first sentence. All of the observations that follow relate to this idea.

The Big Chill
by Todd Michael

As we wait for the Grey Cup parade, everyone looks cold. My little brother sits on my mom's lap, trying to hide from the wind. The little boy and girl sitting next to my mom have snowsuits on, plus they have a green blanket wrapped around them. Two or three different times they say, "Mom, can we pleeease have some hot chocolate?" The man standing behind us says, "I'm from Victoria, and I'm not used to the cold." I hear another voice say, "Just wait until it starts to snow." Five boys next to me are playing tackle tag to keep warm. They all wear colourful ski jackets and ear warmers. The road in front of us looks drab and grey under the streetlight. One family on the other curb is wrapped inside a big blue quilt. Just then a siren sounds. The parade is finally about to begin.

THINK IT OVER

Always try to show rather than tell in your writing. A *showing* sentence like "My little brother sits on my mom's lap, trying to hide from the wind" says much more than a *telling* sentence like "It was windy." (**SEE** "Show, Don't Tell" on page 40 for more examples.)

Science Observation Report

In your science class, you may be asked to write an observation report on an experiment or project. For one of his science projects, Emery Sanford observed how mould grows on different kinds of bread. Part of his final report follows.

Observing Mould on Bread

PROCEDURE: On October 27, I brought my bread to school. I had four different kinds of bread: Clausen's white bread, Roman Meal bread, French bread, and pita bread. I put each piece of bread in a sandwich bag and waited a few days for the mould to grow.

OBSERVATIONS: The Clausen's bread started growing mould first. The mould was green and white. Before this, I had never seen anything other than green mould on bread. This was the first thing I learned about mould...

The Roman Meal started by getting little white speckles on it. In four days there was mould on the bread. It got green, white, and yellow mould at first. Now I had found yellow mould. I had seen two new colours that I had never seen before...

The French bread got stale very quickly. It got very hard and then it started getting mouldy. The mould grew on the inside of the bread, not on the outside like the others.

The pita didn't grow mould at all, probably because it is made from whole wheat and oat bran. It did get hard. That's something I didn't know, that pita bread can get stale, but not mouldy.

CONCLUSIONS: I learned a lot of things during this observation. I learned that there are different coloured moulds, why the bread shrinks (which took some thinking), how mould grows, what mould looks like under a microscope, and how it forms. And most important, I learned what kind of bread to buy if you want it to last: either pita or Roman Meal.

Writing Tales and Stories

Writing Fantasies

Writing Tall Tales

Writing Realistic Stories

Writing Stories from History

Writing Fantasies

Inventing Impossible Things

Do you ever daydream? Have you ever had an imaginary friend? Have you ever made believe you could fly, or wished you were an explorer? Have you ever invented your own private world, or pretended to be one of the characters in your favourite book? If so, you've been using your imagination, and when you do that, *anything* can happen — even impossible things.

Animals That Talk?

Any time you write stories, you use your imagination. In one special kind of story, you get to make up all the rules yourself. It's called *fantasy,* the type of story where even a spider can save a pig. So let's begin by reading a fantasy story by a student writer.

> **When you write a story, you can imagine it any way you want, just as long as your readers believe you.**
> — Nancy Bond

Student Model

In this story, a girl named Penny and her barnyard friends try to figure out why Montgomery the cat is acting so strangely.

MONTGOMERY MEWS MYSTERIOUSLY
by Katie Ambrogi

The setting is described in the opening paragraph.

There was a dusty barn made of old grey wood. The nails marked their age with signs of permanent rust. An old silo stood next to the barn. It looked odd and was every bit as old as the barn.

Just then, Penny appeared in front of the barn. The animals looked up at her in surprise. Penny never came into the barnyard at this time of day!

"I insist on a barnyard meeting, now!" declared Penny.

Sandy the pig stopped rolling in the mud. Mr. Winkle, otherwise known as Perry the rooster, stopped stalking the barnyard. Freedom the dog stopped lapping up week-old water. Oxford, the biggest ox you've ever seen, let out a great big bellow from the barn.

Then the characters and their problem are identified.

Baanie the sheep said to Penny, "What's the matter?"

"Yeah, what's wrong?" chorused all the animals.

"Have any of you seen Montgomery?" Penny inquired.

"No," chorused the animals.

"Well, neither have I, and I'm beginning to worry. She's hardly ever around," said Penny.

"Well," began Oxford, who was always a close observer, "Montgomery looked different today in a way I can't put my finger on, but she was very nice to Sandy. That's a sure sign that something is wrong."

"Mr. Winkle, do you think we should pry into the cat's business?" Freedom asked.

Sandy, who was listening to the conversation, stepped in and said, "No... but there could be something wrong with Montgomery. Not that I really care."

"Okay," began Oxford, "here's the deal. Winkle, you are the chief administrator of the spy office. We will run around, watch Montgomery closely, and report our messages to the office."

"What about me?" asked Penny.

"Penny, you record everything the spies report," Mr. Winkle said.

Just then, Montgomery slid into the barn. "Why is everyone staring at me like that? I'm fine." Montgomery quickly turned around and made her way out of the barn.

Hours later, they still had no clue to what was wrong with Montgomery. Sandy sat at her desk and tapped her fingers. Mr. Winkle fluffed up his feathers and started to twiddle his thumbs. Penny jotted down reports, but nothing was good enough to lead them to an answer.

Then the barnyard door swung open a crack. Montgomery slid through it. Six pairs of eyes travelled to the door. "You know," Montgomery began, "I guess I should have told you." The animals listened in suspense.

"You know how cats love privacy," Montgomery started again. Just then, two kittens timidly stepped in. "They were born three weeks ago," Montgomery said, her voice full of pride. She introduced the kittens. "The little one I call Mouse..."

So, somewhere in a barn in Saskatchewan, there are six happy barnyard adults, two happy kittens, and one happy girl.

The characters decide how they will deal with their problem.

After hours of suspense, the problem is solved.

One Writer's Process

When I write a fantasy, I want to make my readers *believe* my story. I want them to think it could happen, just the way I've imagined it. I want them willing to pretend with me. Here's how I usually get started on my stories.

➤ Keep a Writer's Notebook

Ideas can come from anywhere at any time. I find it helps to write them down before I forget them. I can't use everything I put in my notebook, but sometimes just writing down a word or two can start a story growing in my imagination. I write down anything that interest me: funny names, unusual objects, silly thoughts. Then when I need an idea, I can look back and see what I've got.

➤ Ask Questions

When I write a story, I ask myself lot of questions about what's going on. I'll show you what I mean. Almost everyone's imagined what it would be like to fly like a bird. Suppose we want to write a story about a girl who can really do it. To me, the most interesting thing is not so much that she can fly. I want to know how she does it and what it feels like.

➤ Make Choices

The first thing we have to do is get the girl into the air. But how? Have you ever seen a Canada goose take off from a pond or a riverbank? Maybe *that's* how she does it, by running faster and faster and flapping her arms.

Maybe she flies by concentrating on feeling light. Or perhaps she has to think of nothing at all. Remember Peter Pan? He told Wendy, John, and Michael to "think lovely thoughts, and up you go!" That's another way. Have you got other ideas?

➤ Ask More Questions

Let's go a little further. Now our girl is in the air, however we decided to get her there. Let's ask some more questions. How does it feel? Does she ride the wind like a kite? Or does she have to keep flapping her arms like a bird? When she's up in the sky, what do the clouds feel like? Are they wet and cold, or soft and warm like down comforters? Maybe they're sticky, like cotton candy.

➤ Start the Story

To describe this girl in action and build some excitement into my story, I might write something like this:

> Cynthia had no warning. One minute there she was, floating on soft pillows of warm air. Her wings were stretched wide while she admired her neighbourhood. Here and there among the trees a swimming pool glinted at her, a miniature car winked in the sun, and tiny people followed sidewalks, never thinking to look up to see Cynthia Bean gliding over their heads.
>
> Suddenly she blinked. It was all gone: the sun, the warmth, the houses on her block. Grey blankness filled her eyes. In a blind panic, she curled into a ball, hugging her wings tight around her, and dropped like a stone out through the bottom of the cloud...

Why was Cynthia falling? What will happen to her? How could this action lead to other exciting events? I would try to answer these questions as I wrote the rest of my fantasy.

THINK IT OVER

Can you think of someone else who might fly into a story? How about a young boy who finds himself floating in air on his way home from school? Why is he floating? What will he do about it?

Writing a Fantasy

PREWRITING *Planning Your Story*

Invent Characters ● Fantasy characters can be real people, talking animals, dragons, unicorns, or creatures you invent yourself. (Think of a main character and maybe one or two others.)

What are your characters' names? What do they look like? What do they like to do? Write about them and find out.

Choose a Problem to Solve ● In a fantasy, the main character's problem may be finding out why a cat is acting strangely, searching for a treasure, finding the way back home, or whatever you imagine. (The way your main character solves his or her problem is the plot, the main part of your story.)

Find a Setting ● Fantasy can take place anywhere or anytime — in your neighbourhood or a magical place. (Describe the setting so that your readers can see it in their minds.)

WRITING THE FIRST DRAFT

Get Started ● Begin your story by introducing the main character or setting. Or begin with something happening, like two characters arguing, a narrow escape, or an explosion. This action should lead to the main problem in the story.

Keep It Going ● As you continue, try to make the main character's life more and more difficult because of the problem. Include lots of dialogue. This will keep your readers interested.

Stop When You Get to the End ● The end of the story comes when the problem is solved. That sounds obvious, but sometimes writers go on to explain what their stories are about and end up writing too much.

REVISING　*Improving Your Writing*

Let It Sit ● After you've written your story, let it sit for a while. Then, when you read it again, try pretending someone else wrote it, and see what you think. You'll never be able to fool yourself totally, but you'll be able to see it a little more clearly.

Make It Believable ● Remember that your story should be imaginary *and* believable. Ask, "Do my characters act in a way that fits the story? Do the actions make sense in my setting?"

Share Your First Draft ● Listen carefully to the questions your friends ask after reading or listening to your story. This can be hard to do, but when you write a story for other people, you want them to understand it. One of your friends may be confused by something you have said in the introduction. Another friend may think that a part of your story isn't believable.

If you're not sure about your story's ending, try removing the last sentence or paragraph. See if the story seems complete without it.

EDITING & PROOFREADING

Edit ● Take a close look at the specific words and sentences in your story once you have made all of the major changes. Have you picked the best words to describe the setting, character, and action? Are your sentences interesting and clear? Have you used enough dialogue and punctuated it correctly?

Proofread ● Also make sure to proofread the final draft of your story before you share it.

Writing fantasies can be fun, but reading them can be even more enjoyable. Have you read these popular fantasies?
- *Sandwriter* by Monica Hughes
- *The Secret World of Og* by Pierre Berton
- *A Wrinkle in Time* by Madeleine L'Engle

Writing Tall Tales

Monster Mosquitoes!

Throughout history, **tall tales** have been told by people struggling to survive. These tales contain extraordinary heroes and heroines who can defeat anything and anybody. And they are filled with humour and exaggeration:

> *The mosquitoes up here are so big and so fierce that as you walk through the woods you may find a pile of bones. That's where a mosquito chews up a whole village, pauses to digest his meal, and spits out the bones.*

People still enjoy inventing tall tales. When you use language like "she was so mean" or "he was so strong," you are well on your way to inventing a tall tale.

> **66** **For tall tales, ordinary, run-of-the-mill, polite little lies won't do, no sirree. Tall tales need lies so big and exaggerated that they make you laugh out loud and beg for more.** **99**
> — Susan Ohanian

Model Tall Tale

In the following tall tale, Paul Bunyan's father is faced with a big problem: he has to look after his unusual son!

THE ORIGIN OF THE BAY OF FUNDY TIDES

Paul Bunyan is described using exaggeration.

Many stories are told about Paul Bunyan, the giant logger. When he was a baby, Paul was so big that his parents had to keep 14 cows to supply milk for his porridge. Every morning they discovered that he had grown 60 centimetres taller.

The writer describes a problem, then a solution.

When Paul was only a few weeks old, his parents had to fix him a bed outdoors as he could no longer get through the cabin door. Paul's father decided to build him an enormous cradle and anchor it near the entrance to the Bay of Fundy. Then he hired a crew of men who kept busy every day rowing back and forth from the shore to the cradle carrying boat loads of food for the fast-growing child.

More exaggeration provides a fun ending to the story!

One night, Paul had a stomach ache. He tossed and rolled around so much that he sent a 20-metre tidal wave racing up the Bay of Fundy. In fact, the waves were so high that they almost made an island out of Nova Scotia. Even today the waters have not calmed down, and powerful tides still sweep up the Bay of Fundy twice a day.

Writing a Tall Tale

PREWRITING   *Planning Your Story*

You can build your own tall tales by following these guidelines:

Choose a Hero or Heroine ● Remember that these heroes are always strong, brave, and smart. Use exaggeration when you describe this person. Your hero or heroine may be

> ... so strong that he could pull crooked paths straight.
> ... as smart as a city full of brain surgeons.

Create a Problem the Hero Must Solve ● Think of a difficult problem that your hero must solve. This problem may be

> ... a thick cloud of polluted air that has settled over your city. In twelve hours there will be no air left to breathe.
> ... a blizzard that buried your community in 16 metres of snow overnight. The forecast is for more snow.
> ... a large meteorite that is speeding toward earth.

Show the Cleverness of Your Hero ● To defeat a foe or solve the problem, your hero or heroine may be able to

> ... battle a mosquito so big it needs a runway to land.
> ... lasso and tame a powerful cyclone.
> ... dig the St. Lawrence River to make the boundary between Canada and the United States.

A Tall Cast of Characters

Knowing something about three famous tall-tale heroes may help you plan your own story:

● *Big Joe Mufferaw, a lumberjack in Ontario, carries his logs down the river on his shoulders because he does not have any horses.*

● *Pecos Bill ties rattlesnakes together and invents the clothesline.*

● *Old Sally Cato crawls into the belly of the giant Billy Bally Bully and shakes out clouds of dust to make the giant wheeze and sneeze.*

WRITING YOUR STORY

Tall tales are meant to be fun and entertaining. So remember to include a lot of exaggeration and humour in your writing. If you use dialogue, have the main character say things that are funny or clever, and have other characters say things that sound a little silly or simple. (More writing tips are provide below.)

Think of yourself as an old-time storyteller with a group of eager listeners around you. Your job is to tell them a good story. A good story has a beginning, a middle, and an end.

Start by Catching the Reader's Attention   A good story catches your attention right at the beginning and makes you want to keep reading. In the story about Paul Bunyan, the writer begins with some examples that show that Paul was a most unusual baby. Right away, the reader knows that looking after this child will not be easy. Most writers find the opening of the story is the most difficult part to write. One of the best ways to learn how to write attention-grabbing beginnings is to look carefully at the openings of some stories that you really enjoy.

Keep It Going   In most stories, the main character must try to solve some kind of problem. (What problem does Paul's father have to deal with? How does he finally solve this problem?) Before you start to write your story, decide what your main character wants. Try not to make things too easy for your hero. He or she may have to do some searching, fighting, building, waiting, and so on. When you write a tall tale, put your imagination to work. Remember to exaggerate!

End Your Story   In a tall tale, the main character almost always wins in the end. Will your hero win because of her or his strength, craftiness, or a combination of the two? Will there be any surprises at the end of your story?

Writing Realistic Stories

Amanda Comes to Life

Amanda Lowe is 11 years old. Her long red hair curls wildly, like fire flaming out of control. She is the shortest student in her class.

Amanda hates being short. And she wishes she could be brave enough to tell everyone to stop treating her like somebody's kid sister. But what would happen if she did? Amanda isn't sure she wants to find out.

What are realistic stories?

Ideas for realistic stories often come from a writer's own experiences or interests. But the finished products are more fiction (made-up) than fact.

What I have just described is an idea for a **realistic story**. The main character in a realistic story may remind you of someone you know. For instance, you may know someone like Amanda. Her problem (being too short) may sound very believable. But a realistic story has not actually happened. It only *seems* real.

Student Model

In Lorraine Kenny's story, Keith and Matt have a real problem — just like Amanda — which they solve in a clever, humorous way.

THE VACATION

The main characters are introduced in the opening paragraph.

Keith and Matt lived with their Uncle Mark since the accident, which for both boys was as far back as they could remember. Mark was very good to his nephews. The boys' model train set was spread out all over the living room floor during vacation, and they were pestering Mark to buy them some bridges for the tracks. At last Mark could stand no more.

"Listen!" Mark said. "I've bought a lot of new parts for that train set already. And I am tired of tripping over those tracks every time I want to cross the room! Clean this place up!"

"Spoilsport!" murmured Keith, as he began to pick up the tracks.

The dialogue makes the story seem more real.

"You guys need a quiet hobby. How about painting or reading?" said Mark. Fifteen minutes later he was surprised when the boys asked to go out.

"I don't know if I want to do this!" moaned Keith as he and Matt walked down the street, toward the library.

Mark was astonished to see them come back with a pile of very big books! But he was also happy. "Maybe things will finally be quiet around here."

The trip to the library builds suspense into the story.

Matt and Keith hurried to their room, and all was silent for a very long time. "I've got to see what those two are up to!" Mark thought, "It's just not like them to suddenly want to read a book. Not without a battle at least." Mark walked quietly up the stairs and gently pushed open the boys' bedroom door. Keith and Matt were sitting on the floor with the books, but they weren't reading. They had used them to build bridges for their trains!

"Switch on!" yelled Keith, and Matt pressed the button. The trains screeched around the tracks and over and under the book bridges.

"Oh no!" groaned Mark, shutting the door quickly. "You can't win with these two guys!" With that thought in mind, Mark went to look for his old railroad engineer hat and gloves.

Writing a Realistic Story

PREWRITING *Planning Your Story*

Before you can write your story, you must identify two important elements: (1) a realistic main character and (2) a believable problem for this character to solve.

Create a Character ● Think of friends and other people you know or have read about to get ideas for your main character. You may know someone who loves animals, or someone who loves playing an instrument, or someone who is very short — like Amanda.

THINK IT OVER

Let some of these ideas play around in your brain: Could you write a story about an animal lover? What would this character be like? What might happen to this person in your story? (Don't embarrass anyone by making your character too much like a real person.)

Find a Real Problem ● Suppose your main character (we'll call her Josie) is nuts about animals. Here's the situation: Josie wants to keep a stray dog, but she knows her landlord does not allow pets. What will she do? That's her problem. Now think of a *believable* problem for your own character.

LOOKING FOR TROUBLE

This activity will help you brainstorm for problems.

STEP 1: List one or two possible problems next to the categories *schools, friends, neighbourhood,* and *family.* (Here's a definite problem: Your "best bud" may have to quit soccer because of her asthma.)

STEP 2: Decide if your main character could deal with one of these problems. Or think of other problems that might be more closely related to this person. (If you have to, you can always change your character.)

Planning Guide

To help you keep track of all of your planning ideas, you may want to use a "Collection Sheet" like the one below. You don't have to fill in all of the information before you write, and you should feel free to make changes at any time. (Sometimes a sheet like this is very helpful *after* you write your first draft. It helps you see if you have covered all of the basics in your story.)

Collection Sheet

Characters:

(List the main character first. How old are your characters and what will their names be? Think how each of your characters might look, speak, and act.)

Setting:

(Describe where and when the story will take place.)

Problem:

(What problem does the main character need to solve?)

Story Scenes:

(What are some of the things your main character may try in order to solve her or his problem?)

Purpose:

(Will your story be serious, surprising, scary, funny, or sad? One of these feelings can be a guide for your writing.)

Talk about your story ideas with your classmates before (and after) you write your first draft. As you discuss your story, at least one or two more ideas will pop into the mind.

WRITING THE FIRST DRAFT

Most writers would tell you to begin your story right in the middle of the action, but you may start your story any way you want to. Start with "One day last summer..." if that feels right to you. (You can always change it later on.)

Start Your Story ● Here are five ways to begin a story.

▓ Begin with dialogue:

> *"Put me down!" Amanda shouted.*

▓ Begin with a question:

> *How did this super athlete get stuck in such a small body?*

▓ Begin with description:

> *The gym smelled like sweat and stale popcorn.*

▓ Begin with background information:

> *All through elementary school, Amanda had been treated like a kid sister.*

▓ Begin with the main character introducing herself:

> *I might as well tell you now and get it over with. I am the shortest person in the whole class.*

Keep Your Story Going ● Try not to make things too easy for your character. You may have her involved in two or three important actions because of her problem She may do some talking, thinking, running, fighting, and so on.

End Your Story ● Your story does not have to end on a happy note. Some problems just can't be solved or completely overcome. For example, Amanda Lowe can't make herself grow taller, no matter how many bowls of Wheaties she eats. But she may be able to get her classmates to treat her with more respect.

TAKE NOTE

Most characters change in some way because of their problems. That's something to keep in mind as you write your story.

REVISING   *Improving Your Story*

As you review your first draft, make sure that all of the characters' words and actions make sense. Also make sure that your story does not move along too quickly or too slowly. The key is to keep your readers interested. If your story needs to be pumped up, try adding more details, dialogue, and action.

- *Are there any sights, sounds, smells, and feelings that you could add? Have you described the characters and the setting in your story?*

- *Would you like your story to be more active? Then include more dialogue and action scenes. Notice how the special combination of the two can build excitement:*

> *"Put me down!" Amanda shouted.*
> *"Make me!" Eric dared.*
> *"Okay, you asked for it!"*
> *Amanda twisted and kicked until Eric lost his grip. As she fell, she grabbed hold of his hair…*

EDITING & PROOFREADING

Once you have made all of the major changes in your story, read it again to make sure that it reads smoothly and clearly.

Check your work for punctuation, spelling, and grammar errors. Then complete a neat final draft of your story. Proofread this copy before you share it.

Writing Stories from History

Long Ago and Far Away...

- *Would you like to go back in time?*
- *Would you like to meet someone from the past?*
- *Would you like to relive a great event?*

You can do all of these things by writing historical stories, stories based on what *could* have happened or what did happen at a certain time or place. What's so exciting about this type of writing is that there is so much history to choose from.

A historical story should be part fact and part fiction and believable all the way through.

Writing a Historical Story

PREWRITING *Planning Your Story*

Think Historically ● When you plan and write a historical story, you may choose a historical period or event and make up characters that could have lived during that time. Or you may choose someone real, making this person your main character.

List Ideas ● The first thing you should do is make a list of different *times, events,* or *people* from history that you might like to write about. For ideas, think of history units you have studied in class and different times and people that you have always been interested in. The sample ideas that follow will help you get started. (Try to list at least five ideas of your own.)

- **Laura Secord warns the British of an American attack** (*an event*)
- **Middle Ages in Europe** (*a historical time*)
- **The Northwest Passage** (*a historical place*)
- **Ferdinand Magellan** (*a famous explorer*)
- **Tecumseh** (*a famous Native leader*)

Select a Subject ● Once you complete your list, put a check next to the idea that interests you the most. Use this idea as the starting point for your story research. (If you find that one idea doesn't work out so well, you can always try another from your list.)

Write freely for 3 to 5 minutes about your subject to help you see what you already know, and what you may need to find out.

Collect Facts ● To collect new information about your subject, start by reading about it in an encyclopedia article, in another basic reference book, or in your history text. Ask your teacher or librarian about other sources of information, too. Take careful notes as you read. (See the sample notes below.)

Sample Note-Taking Page

Listed here are facts that could have been collected for an historical story on the voyage of Ferdinand Magellan.

Facts About Ferdinand Magellan

- a Portuguese sailor who planned to sail around the world
- began his voyage on Sept. 20, 1519
- hardships began immediately (several mutinies)
- ran out of food; crew ate rats and ox hides
- stopped at the Philippines for food
- April 27, 1521, Magellan killed during a battle on the island of Mactan
- of the original 241 sailors only 110 remained
- Trinidad didn't make it back, sailors imprisoned
- Victoria under command of Juan Sebastian del Cano returned to Spain on Sept. 6, 1522
- only Juan Sebastian del Cano and 17 others survived
- Italian crew member Antonio Pigafetta kept a journal

You might find it easier to collect information by starting with a series of basic questions: *Where did Magellan's men sail? Why were they sailing? What happened to them?*

Identify Your Story Elements ● Continue your planning by identifying the basic elements for your story. You may want to use a "Collection Sheet" to help you keep track of your ideas. Use your collection sheet as you write, but feel free to make changes at any time as you go along.

Collection Sheet

Characters:

> (Decide how each of your characters might look, speak, and act. Remember to keep the time period of your story in mind.)

Setting:

> (Describe the historical time and place of your story.)

Main Action:

> (What action will your character be involved in? This action may or may not be true. But it must be believable. Within this main action, there may be some type of problem that needs to be solved.

Story Scenes:

> (What are some of the things your character might do — fighting, planning, eating, etc. — during the main action?)

Form:

> (Decide what form your story will take. You may write a basic story, or you may choose another form — a diary or a series of letters. The model on page 175 is told in diary form.)

WRITING THE FIRST DRAFT

Begin Your Story ● Start your story with some dialogue, an action scene, or a brief description. Work in background facts and introduce the main characters as soon as possible.

> *"Get down, Antonio. They will see you. Get down."*
>
> *Everything was happening so fast. Captain Magellan was dead, the crew had scattered into the woods, and now we were under attack.*
>
> *"Juan," whispered Antonio. "Since the captain is dead, you are now in charge. You must get us out of here. You must."*
>
> *Yes, Antonio was right. I, Juan Sebastian del Cano, was in charge. But get us out of here? How?*

Keep Your Story Going ● Remember that your story should be based on historical fact, and it should seem realistic. Keep these points in mind as your main character gets more involved in the story.

End Your Story ● Don't drag your story out. It should end when the main action is completed. Remember, too, that your story does not have to end on a happy note.

REVISING & EDITING   A Final Checklist

✔ Do all of the characters' words and actions make sense, considering the historical time? (John A. MacDonald wouldn't say something like, "Don't get hyper!")

✔ Does the story build in interest? (Does the main character complete the action or solve the problem in the story?)

✔ Do your sentences read smoothly? (Let a friend read it to you.)

✔ Is your final draft neat and easy to read?

Student Model

Heather Stoll's story is about a baker who lived during the Middle Ages. The story is told in the form of a diary. The introduction and two entries from the diary are shown below:

Here, you will see Genoa, Italy, through the eyes of Piero Baker, a well-to-do baker and pastry maker. Piero's shop is on Mill Road. He is a member of the guild of pastry makers. In his diary, you will find information about different shops, clothes, and products related to the Middle Ages.

Genoa, Italy, in the Middle Ages

September 3, 1348

Today I acquired four bags of flour in return for baking two loaves of bread for Widow Napoli.

Dominic and I finished Lady Sophia's order of trenchers today. She paid me well: ten bags of flour, fourteen gold coins, one yard of silk.

My wife will be pleased to see the latter. She has been awanting for a new dress.

Today I must go to the woods and cut myself a new oven spatula. Mine is sorely burnt and in need of repairs.

September 17, 1348

That clumsy excuse for a helper, Fos, spilled flour all over the floor! Now precious time must be wasted cleaning up.

The order is now more than half done. Lady Sophia is relieved. Already she is hiring minstrels and dancers, and the hall bustles with activity.

Everyone is excited! The fleet must be almost ready to go. They leave tomorrow. It is five days' voyage from the boot of my dear country to Genoa.

Writing Poems, Plays, and Songs

Writing Poems

Writing Songs

Writing Plays

Writing Riddles

Writing for Fun

Writing Poems

Words on High Wind

I write poems when I feel what I have to say needs a special shape and sound. I learned how to write my own poems by first making friends with many of the poems I found in books. Here's how you can do the same.

Ways to Make Friends with a Poem

➤ **Read the poem to yourself several times.**

➤ **Read the poem aloud; listen to what it says.**

➤ **Read it with feeling to friends or classmates.**

➤ **Talk or write about the poem.**

➤ **Copy it in a special notebook.**

Now make friends with one of my poems, following these steps.

EARTH-CLOUD-HILLTOP

WORDS

Words! said the earth.
And the cloud
bumping into the hilltop
said back, Words!
And the words
were born
on a high wind
at the tail end of June,
when the sun brights
the sky so hard
no one can stop laughing.
— Anne-Marie Oomen

What Is Poetry?

Why is poetry such a special form of writing? Let's count the ways.

1 **Poetry looks different.** It's easy to recognize poems. They are written in lines and stanzas (groups of lines), and they usually don't take up much space on a page. Some poems are short enough to fit on the inside of greeting cards. Here is a poem called "Ancestors of the Past." Notice that it is a one-stanza poem containing eight lines.

I look in the mirror
    And what do I see?
  I see an image of someone
That looks a little like me.
    Could it be the face
      Or maybe the hair?
  I know who it is now:
It's my great-great-grandma Claire.

— Phil Ryan

2 **Poetry speaks to the heart as well as to the mind.** You can like a poem for what it says (that's the mind part), and you can like it for how it makes your feel (that's the heart part). It's the "heart part" that really separates poetry from other forms of writing. (**SEE** the lyric model on page 185 for a poem that expresses deep feelings.)

3 **Poetry says a lot in a few words.** Poets create word pictures using "sensory" details that describe sights, sounds, smells, tastes, and other physical feelings.

I was standing on the street when...
The rusty old black Cadillac (**sight**)
grunted rack-a-bump-she-bang, (**sound**)
and heated up my cool spot of air, (**physical feeling**)
and spewed oily smoke (**smell**)
all over my mustard-covered foot-long hot dog. (**sight**)

— Anne-Marie Oomen

4 **Poetry says things in special ways.** Poets also create special word pictures by comparing different things. If you've ever written a *simile* ("I climbed slow as an old fly"), then you know what I'm talking about. Another special type of comparison is called a *metaphor.* Can you see what two things are being compared in the following examples?

Rain
Rain Rain
Wet Little Chicken Pox
On the Window...
        — Cassie Hoek

A gentle wind at night is
my wispy grandmother.
                — Tim Capewell

Helpful Hint For more about similes, metaphors, and other special comparisons, turn to page 182.

5 **Poetry pleases the ear.** Poets carefully arrange words so that certain sounds stand out. You already know that words sometimes rhyme in poems. But there are a lot of other ways to make poems sound pleasing.

Poets may repeat certain consonant and vowel sounds to help make their poems pleasing to the ear. You can see how this works by reading "Purple Poems." Certain consonant and vowel sounds are underlined. (**SEE** page 183 for more examples.)

Purple Poems
Quiet purple clouds rolled in.
Purple rain <u>d</u>rops <u>d</u>rip from
the clouds.
Smooth purple shells <u>w</u>ash
in <u>w</u>ith the <u>w</u>aves.
Purple <u>l</u>ightning <u>str</u>ikes a tree.
<u>P</u>urple <u>p</u>oems litter the field.
                — Katlyn McKalson

YOU DON'T SSSSAY

You will also find many of these same elements (like sensory details and similes) in regular writing. They just stand out more in poetry.

Writing a Free Verse Poem

The following guidelines will help you write a free verse poem. Free verse poetry does not follow a specific form, and it does not have to rhyme.

PREWRITING *Planning Your Poem*

Select a Subject ● Write your poem about a person, place, event, object, or idea that you find interesting. You might write about a special room, a friend, a favourite animal, music, and so on.

Collect Your Thoughts ● I decided to write a poem about my favourite animal, the dog. To get started, I wrote freely for a few minutes about one certain dog.

> I knew an alley dog. My stepmom said I was not to touch him ever, but sometimes I crawled down the fire escape and he would sit near me, but we would not touch each other. Once I took him an old sandwich and he was happy. We would watch the sun on the buildings.

WRITING A FIRST DRAFT

Create a Poem ● Here's how a free writing (like the one above) can be the start of a poem. Begin by making line breaks. At first, make these breaks where you naturally hear pauses in the sentences. Then you may try moving words (or parts) around. You may also try adding or changing words. (See how I turned my free writing into a basic poem.)

> The Alley Dog
> Never touch him! my stepmom said,
> but once I fed him an old sandwich,
> and he was happy,
> and sometimes I would
> crawl down the fire escape,
> and he would creep up near me
> and we would watch
> the sun on the buildings.

REVISING   *Improving Your Writing*

Add Word Pictures ● Does this first draft contain any specific word pictures or pleasing sounds? Yes, "crawl" and "creep" sound good and are specific. But I wanted to add more word pictures and pleasing sounds, so I thought some more and wrote this new draft.

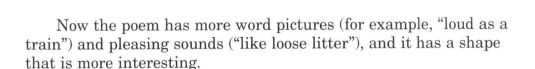

> ### The Alley Dog
>
> Never touch him! my stepmom
> shouted loud as a train. But once
> I tossed him half my butter sandwich
> and he danced like loose litter in wind.
> And once I climbed
>   slow as an
>   old fly
> down our fire escape,
> and he crept up,
>   stop
>   and go,
> like a car in bad traffic,
> and we sat near each other,
> and watched how the sun bullied
> the cracked brick wall
> into the dark.

Now the poem has more word pictures (for example, "loud as a train") and pleasing sounds ("like loose litter"), and it has a shape that is more interesting.

PROOFREADING

Some poems do not follow accepted rules of capitalization, punctuation, or spelling. If you decide to make these sorts of changes, be sure you have a clear reason for doing so. And you still need to proofread!

Poetry Checklist

The following checklist will help you edit
your poem.

- ✔ **Make sure that your poem is
  complete.** Have you left anything out?
- ✔ **Check the line breaks.** Do they add
  special meaning to your poem? Are they
  interesting or fun?
- ✔ **Make sure your poem has plenty of specific details.**
  Do the details paint interesting word pictures? Do they
  "sound" good? Have you used fresh, new comparisons?
- ✔ **Make sure your poem reads well.** Do you stumble over
  any words or lines when you read your poem? If so,
  change them.
- ✔ **Write a final copy of your poem, making all of the
  corrections.** Proofread this copy before sharing it.

FIGURES OF SPEECH

To create effective word pictures, poets often make
special comparisons. These special comparisons are often
called **figures of speech**.

- ● A **SIMILE** compares one thing to something unlike it
  using *like* or *as*. *Coat hooks hold winter hats like bare
  branches hold old nests.*
- ● A **METAPHOR** makes a comparison without using *like*
  or *as*. *The street is my heart.*
- ● **PERSONIFICATION** makes a comparison in which
  something that is not human is described with human
  qualities. *My eggs stared back like sick eyes.*
- ● **HYPERBOLE** makes exaggerated comparisons for effect.
  Sometimes these are funny. *It was so hot we fried.*

The Sounds of Poetry

Listed below are some of the devices poets use to make their poems sound pleasing to the ear. (Use some in your poems.)

Alliteration ● The repeating of the beginning consonant sounds in words like *dance*, *dare*, and *drop*.

Assonance ● The repetition of vowel sounds in words like *rain*, *makes*, *pavement*, and *wavy*.

Consonance ● The repetition of consonant sounds anywhere in the words: *The catcher wore a black jacket.*

End Rhyme ● The rhyming of words at the ends of two or more lines of poetry, as in the first two lines in Robert Frost's famous poem called "Stopping by Woods on a Snowy Evening":

> *Whose woods these are I think I know.*
> *His house is in the village though;*

Helpful Hint   Many traditional forms of poetry follow specific rhyme patterns. (**SEE** pages 184-185 for examples.)

Internal Rhyme ● The rhyming of words in the middle of lines:

> *After he had made an out,*
> *a pout rattled around his mouth.*

Onomatopoeia ● The use of words whose sounds make you think of their meanings, as in *buzz*, *thump*, and *snap*.

Repetition ● The repeating of a word or phrase to add rhythm, or to emphasize a certain idea: *The wind hissed, hissed down the alley.*

Rhythm ● The way the poem flows from one idea to the next. In free verse poetry (the type of poem used as a model on page 177), the rhythm is usually like the natural flow of spoken language. In traditional forms of poetry, words are often arranged into a definite pattern of accented and unaccented syllables. Notice in the following lines how an unaccented syllable is followed by an accented one. This is an example of patterned rhythm:

> *Becáuse I sáw no cáke,*
> *I áte a páper pláte.*

TRADITIONAL POETRY

The forms of poetry that follow have been around for a long time.

Ballad poems tell a story. The ballad is written in four-line stanzas. Often the second and fourth lines rhyme. (Here is the fist stanza of my ballad called "Ballad of Skull Rock.")

We miners long ago did find
the skull rock on the <u>lake</u>.
The silver lay in open veins,
all shining for the <u>take</u>.

Cinquain poems are five lines long with a certain number of syllables or words in each.

Syllable Cinquain

Line 1:	Title	2 syllables
Line 2:	Description of title	4 syllables
Line 3:	Action about the title	6 syllables
Line 4:	Feeling about the title	8 syllables
Line 5:	Synonym for title	2 syllables

Word Cinquain

Line 1:	Title	1 word
Line 2:	Description of title	2 words
Line 3:	Action about the title	3 words
Line 4:	Feeling about the title	4 words
Line 5:	Synonym for title	1 word

A **Couplet** is a two-line verse form that usually rhymes and expresses one thought.

Back and forth the dancer <u>whirled</u>,
A butterfly with wings un<u>furled</u>.

Some traditional poems are written totally in couplets. Other poems may use only one couplet for special effect.

Free Verse is poetry that does not include patterned rhyme or rhythm. (**SEE** the model on page 181 for an example.)

Haiku is a type of Japanese poetry about nature. It is three lines long. The first line is five syllables; the second, seven; the third, five.

> Sun moves on rubble,
> weeds grow sideways in small cracks,
> small vines cling to walls.

A **Limerick** is a funny verse in five lines. Lines one, two, and five rhyme, as do lines three and four. Lines one, two, and five have three stressed syllables; lines three and four have two.

> There once was a chef named Maurice
> Who always used way too much grease.
> His chicken was fine;
> His fries were divine,
> But his dinners just made me obese.

A **Lyric** is a song-like poem that uses sensory details to express personal feelings.

> Up! Up! Bright kites fly, ooooh,
> maroon, and yellow, and easy blue
> over the evening park.
> I like to think they pull me too,
> up into that blue, that easy blue,
> far away from the dark.

A **Quatrain** is a four-line stanza. Notice in this example that the first and third lines rhyme, and the second and fourth lines rhyme. In some quatrains the first two lines rhyme, and the second set of lines rhyme. In "Indian Summer," Wilfred Campbell wrote:

> Along the line of smoky hills
> The crimson forest stands,
> And all day long the blue-jay calls
> Throughout the autumn lands.

INVENTED POETRY

Poets have fun inventing new forms of poetry. Here are some invented forms to try.

Alphabet Poetry ● An alphabet poem uses a part of the alphabet to create a funny list poem.

Cats
Don't
Ever
Fly (willingly)

Concrete Poetry ● This is poetry in which the shape or design helps express the meaning or feeling of the poem.

The way to school is d$_{o}$$_{w}$$_{n}$

W I D E   streets
*FULLOF**BIG**PEOPLE!!!*

Definition Poetry ● This is poetry that defines a word or an idea creatively.

FRIENDSHIP
Friendship is like stars in the
sky. Like going
to fly with Peace,
and the moon shines
on us while we fly. We walk
through the sky and clouds. And we
share the future in a treasure
chest, topped with diamonds. — Jessamyn Ansary

Five Ws Poetry ● Each line in this type of poem answers one of the 5 Ws (who? what? where? when? and why?).

I
Love to 'blade
Along Venice Beach
In the middle of the day
Because people are friendly and get out of your way.

List Poetry ● This is poetry made from a list. Often the title says what the list is.

WHAT'S IN THE BOX UNDER MY BED
eight marbles and a shoestring
a cracker jack ring (I think it's magic)
my two most valuable baseball cards
the mitten that boy dropped
the letter my friend wrote

Name Poetry ● A name poem, or acrostic poem, is formed using the letters of a name or a word to begin each line in the poem.

Fierce	Calm eyes
Righteous	Oozing
Energetic	Over
Dude	Lake water

Phrase Poetry ● This form of poetry states an idea with a list of phrases.

EATING SPAGHETTI
with a twirl of a fork
and the help of a spoon
quickly up to the mouth
before it all falls off

Sensory Poetry ● Each line in this type of poem describes a subject using one of the senses. (**SEE** the bottom of page 178).

Terse Verse ● This is humorous verse made up of two words that rhyme and have the same number of syllables. The title is the subject.

Joke Books	*Kool-Aid*	*Candy*
Smile	Pink	Sweet
File	Drink	Treat

TAKE NOTE   You can try other invented forms of poetry by turning to pages 204-205.

Writing Songs

Goin' Down, Down, Ever Downstream

Have you ever wanted to write a song? Well I have, and I did! I just wrote a song called "Shanty Boar." I'll show you how I wrote it, just in case you want to follow the same steps and write a song of your own.

1 Find a First Line

One day I was thinking about *Huckleberry Finn*, a book about two friends who travel down a river on a shanty boat. I doodled this line in my notebook:

Uncle Sheb lived on a shanty boat.

Hmm. Those words had rhythm. (Say them aloud, loudest on the words in all caps.)

UNCLE Sheb LIVED on a SHANty BOAT.

Those words felt like a song. I tapped my foot to them: and ONE and TWO and THREE and FOUR. I was on my way to becoming a songwriter!

> ❝ **Good luck with your songwriting. I'll be listening for you on the radio! By the way, a version of the song "Shanty Boat" has been published as a picture book. I hope you like it.** ❞
> — Charles Temple

② Find a "Frame"

As I repeated the first line of my song out loud, a song I already knew came to mind.

FROG WENT A COURTIN'
FROG went a COURTIN' and HE did RIDE,
    Uh-huh.
FROG went a COURTIN' and HE did RIDE,
    Uh-huh.
FROG went a COURTIN', and HE did RIDE,
SWORD and BUCKLER BY his SIDE,
    Uh-huh, uh-huh, uh-huh.

The pattern of rhythm and thyme from "Frog Went a Courtin' " gave me a **frame** for writing a song about the shanty boat. It also showed me how many beats to put into each line (four beats per line, in this case). The verse from "Frog Went a Courtin' " showed me which words in my song should rhyme.

Important Note: Later, once I'd written the verses of my song, I would make up a new tune of my own.

③ Write the Verses

The words I had written —

    Uncle Sheb lived on a shanty boat —

became the first line of a verse. Now I wanted a line of words to follow each new line in my song, the way "uh-huh" does in the frog song. Lines like these are called **refrains**. Here's the refrain I though up for the shanty boat song:

    Goin' down, down, ever downstream.

The frog song repeats the words "Frog went a courtin' and he did ride," so I repeated the words "Uncle Sheb lived on a shanty boat." Next I wrote a line to rhyme with "boat," the way "side" rhymes with "ride" in the frog song:

    Uncle Sheb lived on a shanty boat,
       Goin' down, down, ever downstream.
    Uncle Sheb lived on a shanty boat,
    That sure was the shabbiest thing afloat,
       Goin' down, down, ever downstream.

4 Organize Your Verses

I wrote four or five verses before I realized that the song needed an overall **shape**. One way to shape a song is to make it like a story. You can give it a *beginning* (a couple of verses that introduce your characters and their problem), a *middle* (verses that say more about your characters), and an *end* (verses that end the story and tell how the problem was solved).

Find the Beginning

The first verse I wrote really didn't belong at the beginning; it was better for the middle. For a beginning, I wanted to introduce a man who lived on a shanty boat, in a way that would make listeners curious about him. Here's my new first verse:

> My Uncle Sheb never milked him a cow,
> > Goin' down, down, ever downstream.
> My Uncle Sheb never milked him a cow,
> Nor plucked him a chicken, nor slopped him a sow,
> > Goin' down, down, ever downstream.

Write the Middle

After a couple of verses that named all the things Uncle Sheb never did, I put in that verse about Uncle Sheb living on the shanty boat, the verse we started with. I added other verses in the middle about what the boat was like and how Uncle Sheb lived on it.

Figure Out the End

Finally, the song needed an ending. I decided to say that Uncle Sheb had died, and I wrote this line:

> They sank that shanty boat, Uncle and all...

But I wasn't willing to get rid of him entirely. I turned the shanty into a ghost boat, with someone on deck:

> And an old man stands by the steering oar,
> > Goin' down, down, every downstream.
> And an old man stands by the steering oar,
> Guess it could be Sheb, but you can't be sure,
> > Goin' down, down, ever downstream.

Songwriting Steps

1 **Find a first line.** Maybe it's a saying, or even something you just heard in the hallway. Say it over and over in different ways until it has rhythm. Tap your foot to it. Snap your fingers. Dance.

2 **Find a "frame."** A frame is a song that has rhythm and rhyme like your first line. "Borrow" that song and keep it in your head as you think up more lines.

3 **Write the verses.** Make sure that your lines or verses rhyme in the same places as the lines in your borrowed song. Be sure to consider adding a *refrain* or chorus.

4 **Organize your verses.** After you've written several verses, it's time to think of a way to organize your song. Will you have a beginning, a middle, and an end?

5 **Revise your song.**
- Consider the sound. Do the words work together to make a pleasing sound?
- Be sure you haven't put too many beats in any line — the test is to tap your foot while you say the line slowly. See if you've put the important words where they'll get the stressed beats.
- Choose the most vivid words you can — the test here is to ask others if your words make pictures in their minds.

SONGWRITER'S TOOLBOX

Rhyming Dictionary ● Many songwriters use rhyming dictionaries. These books give you gobs of words that rhyme.

Standard Dictionary ● I keep a standard dictionary handy, too, to make sure that a good rhyming word means what I think it does. Don't write something stupid just because it rhymes!

Thesaurus ● I also use a thesaurus. For instance, I couldn't find a rhyme I wanted for "pig," but the thesaurus told me that I could use "sow" instead, and that rhymed with "plough."

Writing Plays

Bringing Ideas to Life

Raise your hand if you like to do things with your friends. (Okay, good). Next, rub your fingers together if there is something you would like to get, or some problem you would like to solve. (That's right.) And lastly, tap the side of your head if you think you like to daydream or pretend. (Hey, not bad.)

Silly Questions

Why did I ask you to do these silly things? To get you thinking like a playwright. Ideas for plays come from real-life experiences as well as from a writer's lively imagination.

The models and guidelines on the following pages will help you get your fingers and mind working on your first, or next, play.

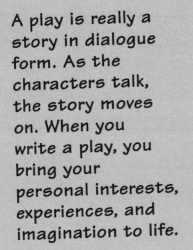

A play is really a story in dialogue form. As the characters talk, the story moves on. When you write a play, you bring your personal interests, experiences, and imagination to life.

A Model Beginning

In this model beginning, you will see that Dave and Jessica are in trouble, and they need a way out. That's how plays begin. One or more characters need to solve a problem or figure out how to get something. In between, there's *action*. How will Dave and Jessica keep their dad's mind off fishing? Will their crime be noticed? Those questions will be answered in the rest of the play.

What will We Tell Mom and Dad?

Characters: DAVE, 12 years old

JESSICA, 11 years old

DAD, their father

MOM, their mother

Place: The living room of a cabin near a river

SCENE 1

(The room is empty. Suddenly, JESSICA bursts through the door, closely followed by Dave.)

DAVE: (pushing her) It's all your fault!

JESSICA: (pushing him back) It's not! You're the one who couldn't wait till Mom and Dad got home from the store. You just had to go fishing the minute we got to this cabin. I should have never let you talk me into it.

DAVE: I just wanted to surprise them with a fish for dinner. And anyway, you're the one who borrowed Dad's new fishing rod, not me.

JESSICA: But I didn't drop it into the river, did I?

MOM: (calling from offstage) Jessica? Dave? Come help with these groceries.

DAVE: Oh, no! They're home! What are we going to do?

JESSICA: We'll just have to tell them we broke...

DAVE: (Interrupting her) Tell them? Are you kidding? This vacation will be over before it's ever begun. All we have to do is keep Dad's mind off fishing.

JESSICA: But how?

Writing a Play

Select the Main Parts ● All you really need to get started is at least two characters, a problem, and a place or a setting for the action. People you know may give you ideas for characters. Events that have made you laugh or cry may give you ideas for the problem and action in your play. Places you know may give you ideas for setting. And your dreams and imagination may give you ideas for all three parts.

Collect Details ● Use some form of a "collection sheet" or checklist to help you plan your play. (Ideas to include are listed below.) But remember that part of the fun of writing a play is seeing where your characters will take you. So don't try to plan too many details about your play before you start writing.

Collection Sheet

Main Characters #1 and #2:
   (Give each character a name and an age. Describe something about each person's appearance and personality. Decide what role he or she will "play.")

Other Characters:
   (Identify any other characters who will be part of your play. You might not know all of these until you actually start writing.)

Setting:
   (Describe where and when your play will take place.)

Main Problem:
   (What is the main problem faced by the characters?)

Action:
   (What things might they do to solve this problem?)

WRITING THE FIRST DRAFT

Before you start writing, review the model on page 193 to see how your play should be set up. Then get to work on your first draft using the suggestions below as you guide.

Start the Play ● The opening part of a play should set the scene for the main action to follow. (Remember that the characters' words and actions are the driving force in a play.)

The main characters should be introduced, the setting should be described, and the main problem should be noted. (The beginning may also describe important events that happened before the start of the play.)

Solve a Problem ● The middle of a play shows the main characters trying to solve their problem or get what they want. (This is the longest part of the play. Each new activity or event could be a different scene.)

In the model, Dave and Jessica could plan all sorts of fun activities to keep their dad from fishing.

Bright IDEA

To create excitement and maybe a little fun in your play, have your main characters get in each other's way.

End the Play ● The ending of a play shows how things finally work out. (Basically, the main characters do or don't get what they want, or they do or don't solve their problem.)

In the model, the dad may finally discover his broken fishing rod. But the kids have been so good that he probably doesn't get too mad at them. Maybe he reminds them of what they should have done instead of what they did.

REVISING *Improving Your Writing*

Read your first draft to yourself. Ask yourself if your play moves along smoothly and clearly from beginning to end. Also decide if there are parts that need to be added or cut. Then read your work out loud, paying special attention to each line. Put a check next to any lines that you want to rewrite.

Write Dialogue ● Writing dialogue is creating talk on paper. Keep this point in mind when you review and revise the first draft of your play. You want your characters to sound like they are really talking. Which of these two sounds more like a real person?

LEE: *Shar, please call me after you get home from school today.*

OR

LEE: *Shar, call me after school, okay?*

Make a Point ● Plays usually send a message or make a point about life. Readers learn this message through the characters' actions and words. By the end of *What Will We Tell Mom and Dad?*, the audience (and Dave and Jessica) would know that it is best to tell the truth. Check your play to see if it makes a point.

Ask a small group of classmates to read the different parts in your play. Listening to your play will help you find the parts that need to be changed.

EDITING & PROOFREADING

Check Your Writing ● Check the revised version of your writing for spelling, mechanics, and grammar errors. Then write a final draft of your play, following the form used for the model beginning on page 193. Proofread this draft before sharing it.

What Will We...

As you remember in the model beginning on page 193, Dave and Jessica have a problem. They've broken their dad's new fishing rod, and they don't want him to find out. How might that play continue? Student writer Faith Brawley continued the play with this scene, which adds a little more suspense to the plot.

SCENE II

(The family has just finished dinner and is chatting in the living room.)

MOM: *So, what did you guys do while we went grocery shopping?*

JESSICA: *(in a shaky voice) Well, we um...*

DAVE: *(interrupting JESSICA) We played a game of cards.*

JESSICA: *(glaring at DAVE) We also went for a swim. I pushed Dave in the water. I thought he could use a cooling off.*

DAD: *Oh, that reminds me. Do you guys want to go fishing tomorrow or would you rather go on a nature walk?*

DAVE & JESSICA: *(at the same time) NATURE WALK!*

DAD: *Okay, that settles that. We'll go on a nature walk.*

MOM: *(yawning) It's getting kind of late.*

JESSICA & DAVE: *(exiting the living room) Okay, Mom, we'll see you tomorrow.*

JESSICA: *That was a close one!*

DAVE: *(his heart skipping a beat) You're telling me!*

JESSICA: *(feeling horrible) I don't want to keep lying about this! I'm going to tell Dad!*

DAVE: *(in a panic) You can't tell him. We're already too deep in this to try and get out.*

JESSICA: *I suppose so...*

Literature
LINK

To become a good playwright, you should read a lot of plays. A good place to start is the magazine called *Plays: The Drama Magazine for Young People*, published by Plays, Inc. Most libraries have it. You can also ask your librarian to show you where plays for young people are on the shelves.

Writing Riddles

Exercising Your Mind

Question: **Why is the letter e like a question mark?**

Answer: **It's found at the end of every riddle.** *(Get it?)*

Why do so many people enjoy asking and hearing riddles? Maybe it's because there's a laugh at the end of most riddles — and because there's a surprise there, too. Can you "crack" the following riddle?

Inside an ivory box is a crystal sphere. Inside the crystal is a heart of gold. What is it?

(An egg.)

Are you ready to write a riddle or two of your own? You can start with the "Crack Up" and "What Am I" riddles.

> **66 Telling riddles is a form of mental exercise. Since so many riddles depend on puns (little jokes) and wordplay, they develop your language skills. And because many of them are crazy, they encourage your imagination to grow. 99**
> — Lorraine Sintetos

"CRACK UP" RIDDLES

Riddle #1 *Why is it hard to find a home for a gloomy whale?*
No one wants a pet that size (sighs).

Riddle #2 *Where's the best place to buy a part for a clock?*
A secondhand shop (second hand).

In each of the "crack up" riddles above, the answer contains a *pun* (a word that sounds like a word with another meaning). In the first riddle, "size" and "sighs" are pronounced the same, but have different meanings and spellings. Both, however, make sense in the answer. In the second riddle, *secondhand* has two meanings: a "secondhand" shop is a place to buy things; a "second hand" is a clock part.

Writing a "Crack Up" Riddle

1 ▶ **Brainstorm for words that sound alike.**

Example: peace (noun) piece (noun)
(Your words should be the same part of speech.)

2 ▶ **Pick a pair of words and think of a sentence (or a phrase) in which either word makes sense.**

He just wants a little peace (a little piece).

3 ▶ **Ask yourself questions.**

Who might want a little peace?
(someone around a lot of noise)

Who might want just a little piece?
(a kid being served something yucky)

4 ▶ **Create a riddle questions with this pattern:
Why is a _____ like a _____?**

Why is a teacher with noisy students like a boy being served spinach pie?

Both just want a little peace (piece).

"WHAT AM I" RIDDLES

"What Am I" riddles have been around for a long time. In this type of riddle, you try to guess what object or idea is being described. Here are two different ways to write them:

Use Metaphors

You can describe the appearance of an object as if it were something else. (By doing this, you are creating a comparison called a *metaphor*.) In the riddle on the first page in this chapter, the shell of an egg is compared to an ivory box, the white of the egg is a crystal sphere, and the yoke is compared to a heart of gold.

> *Inside an ivory box is*
> *a crystal sphere.*
> *Inside the crystal is*
> *a heart of gold.*

Use Personification

Or you can describe an object as if it were a living thing. (This is called *personification*.) In the riddle below, a shout is described as if it could fly, and we normally think of wings as belonging to living things.

> *I have no wings, but I can cross the widest*
> *street without touching the ground.*
> *What am I?*

(A shout.)

Use Surprise Endings

You can use your imagination to combine details that sound ordinary, but then take an unexpected funny twist.

> *What is grey, has big ears, and squeaks?*
> *(It sounds like a mouse. But it could be an elephant*
> *wearing new shoes!)*

Writing a "What Am I" Riddle

1 ▶ **Start by making a list of everyday objects and ideas.**

> **LIST:** flower, night, bookshelf, scissors, football, skateboard, radio

2 ▶ **Choose one noun (to be the answer to your riddle) and describe it.**

> **CHOOSE:** *night*
> **DESCRIBE:** *dark, quiet, soft, comes slowly every day, can be scary, not human*

3 ▶ **Ask yourself, "What different thing can I compare it to?" (metaphor) or "Can I describe my noun as a living thing?" (personification)**

> **COMPARE:** Study your list of descriptive words for ideas. Suppose you decide to describe the night as if it were a black cat. Both are dark and quiet.

4 ▶ **Write your riddle.**

> **WRITE:** *I'm dark and have no legs,*
> *though I sneak into your house slowly and*
> *quietly every day*
> *What am I?*
>
> (Night.)

THINK IT OVER

Try exercising your mind by creating a "What Am I" rhyming riddle. Here's an example:

> *The more times you use me,*
> *the shorter I'll grow.*
> *The more I do my work,*
> *the less yours will show.*
> *What am I?*
>
> (An eraser.)

Writing for Fun

Ideas for Friends and Family

Writing is the least expensive hobby I know. It has other advantages, too: you can write all your life, whether it's rainy or sunny, summer or winter. You can do it lying down, sitting, or standing on your head, and you can do it every day, on your own, outside of school. There are at least 700 kinds of writing besides homework. None of them are fattening, and most are very enjoyable.

Starting with Stories

Even though we listen to stories and tell stories, one thing we don't do very often is write stories down. I don't mean the kind we imagine or make up. Nearly everyone has written made-up stories from the time they were able to put words on paper. I mean the kind of stories that really happened.

> **Stories make it wonderful to be human. You won't find a horse telling a tale to another horse, or a bullfrog chuckling over a favourite joke. People do these things all the time, however.**
> — Peter Stillman

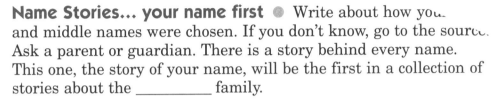

Writing Family Stories

Every family needs someone to save, or p
important people, places, and events. You ar
this job. Here are a few ideas to get you started.

Name Stories... your name first ● Write about how you
and middle names were chosen. If you don't know, go to the source.
Ask a parent or guardian. There is a story behind every name.
This one, the story of your name, will be the first in a collection of
stories about the _____ family.

... other family names ● Now check into other family names
that interest you. Are there favourite first names or middle names in
your family? How about nicknames? Last names? Tell their stories.

Birth Stories ● Find out about the day you were born. Ask your
parents. What was the weather like? What time of day did you
arrive? What important events were going on in the world that day?

Holiday Stories ● Write about the way your family celebrates
holidays — Thanksgiving, Christmas, Hanukkah, New Year's Day,
Ramadan, birthdays. Are there any special holidays that only your
family celebrates?

Recipe Stories ● Your family has favourite recipes. Write up
three or four. This way, they will always be available. (You may
even want to put together a family recipe book.)

Heirloom Stories ● Many families have special pieces of
furniture, jewellery, or paintings that have been handed down from
generation to generation. These objects are called *heirlooms*. What
are the stories behind your heirlooms? Where did they come from?
Why are they valuable to your family?

Here are some topics to get you thinking about
more family stories:

**superstitions, spooky events, disasters,
oddball relatives, rascals, pranks,
and special sayings**

Storyboards

The very first stories were recorded in picture form. We still create stories with pictures, but now we usually add a few words. Stories written in this way can be presented on a **storyboard** like the following example.

1. See Spot wait for Dick and Jane.
2. See Spot get eager.
3. See Spot get lonely.
4. See Spot get disgusted.
5. See Spot get angry.
6. See how Spot fixed them good.

It's easy to make storyboard blanks, and it's fun to fill them in. Storyboard stories can be about your family, and they can also be goofy, like the one about Spot. Make enough blanks. Not all stories will fit in six frames.

Four Kinds of Playful Poems

Found Poems ● Visit a local store that features many different products. With pencil and notepad in hand, list as many items as you care to. Later, create a poem by combining some or all of the items you have listed. Here is the start of such a poem:

> *On the shelves*
> *of our general store*
> *you can find*
> *eyebolts, stovebolts, U-bolts, and carriage bolts;*
> *bird food, cat food, dog food, and fish food...*

Dictionary Poems ● Flip to any page of a dictionary and jot down phrases that appeal to you from the definitions of at least three words. Then arrange and rearrange the phrases until they make sense. Be sure to title your work. (Can you think of a title for this one?)

> A trick of magic
> kept in motion,
> of quick movement,
> of great joy:
> writing in a journal.

Telephone Number Poems ● Telephone numbers aren't poems, but your phone number has a poem hidden inside it. You can find it by letting each number represent either syllables or whole words. Let's say your phone number is 362-4814. The first line of your poem will have three syllables (or words), the second will have six, the third will have two, and so on. Here's an example:

> *Our cat starts* (3 syllables)
> *most mornings on my lap* (6 syllables)
> *before*
> *stalking stuffed mice*
> *or dashing downstairs to explore.*
> *He*
> *likes things the same.*

Lifelong Poems ● Many poems are really lists. A long time ago, I began one with the title "Things I Love." Here are the first two lines:

> *Horse tracks in the snow*
> *Rain on my cabin roof*

It's a very long poem now, because I add to it often, sometimes just one line, sometimes more. Start your own "Things I Love" list today. Promise yourself that you will keep at it for a month, at least one line a day. You're in for some surprises.

Another good title for a lifelong poem is simple "I Am..." See where it takes you, one "I am" at a time.

> *I am... the rainbow on a soap bubble.*

Research Writing

Using the Library

Writing a Summary

Writing a Classroom Report

Using the Library

Ask the Experts!

Suppose you are asked to write a report about whales. You can use your own experience. You can talk to other people. However, if you get seasick just thinking about boats, or if the people you know don't have a whale of a tale, there are other people who can help! And, there's a place you can "meet" them and "hear" their stories and ideas —
THE LIBRARY.

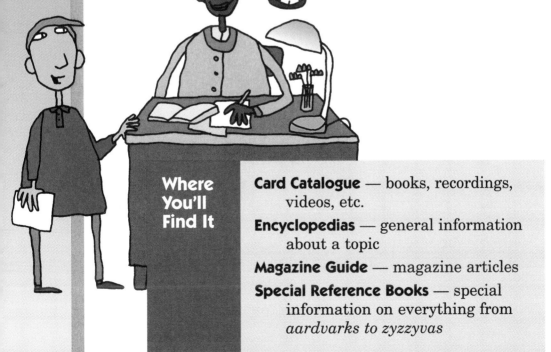

Where You'll Find It

Card Catalogue — books, recordings, videos, etc.

Encyclopedias — general information about a topic

Magazine Guide — magazine articles

Special Reference Books — special information on everything from *aardvarks to zyzzyvas*

Using the Card Catalogue

In the ocean, you need sonar and trained people to find whales. In the library, whether you're looking for giant whales or invisible atoms, you'll need the **card catalogue**. Cards in the card catalogue are placed alphabetically in drawers (or on computers). Here are some guidelines:

■ **Title Cards:** There is a **title card** for every book in the library. If a title begins with *A, An,* or *The,* skip to the next word.

Example: The title card for *The Pig-Out Blues* is in the P drawer under *Pig-Out.*

■ **Author Cards:** Every book has an author (or authors) or an editor. The name on the **author card** is listed last name first.

Example: Wilson, Eric

■ **Subject Cards:** Many books are listed on **subject cards**. They are filed alphabetically and come before title cards beginning with the same word.

Example: The subject card DINOSAUR — HISTORY comes before the title card *Dinosaur Fossils.*

Inside the Card Catalogue

To find out if your library has a certain book, look in the card catalogue (or computer) for the *title* of the book. If you don't know the title, look up the *author.* Finally, if you don't know the title or the author, look under the general *subject* of the book.

Sample Catalogue Cards

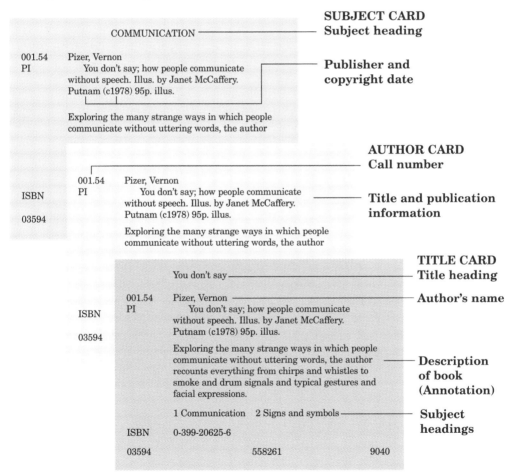

SUBJECT CARD
Subject heading

COMMUNICATION

001.54
PI   Pizer, Vernon
        You don't say; how people communicate
    without speech. Illus. by Janet McCaffery.
    Putnam (c1978) 95p. illus.

Publisher and copyright date

Exploring the many strange ways in which people communicate without uttering words, the author

AUTHOR CARD
Call number

        001.54   Pizer, Vernon
ISBN   PI   You don't say; how people communicate
                without speech. Illus. by Janet McCaffery.
03594   Putnam (c1978) 95p. illus.

                Exploring the many strange ways in which people
            communicate without uttering words, the author

Title and publication information

TITLE CARD
Title heading

            You don't say

        001.54   Pizer, Vernon
ISBN   PI   You don't say; how people communicate
                without speech. Illus. by Janet McCaffery.
03594   Putnam (c1978) 95p. illus.

            Exploring the many strange ways in which people
        communicate without uttering words, the author
        recounts everything from chirps and whistles to
        smoke and drum signals and typical gestures and
        facial expressions.

            1 Communication   2 Signs and symbols

        ISBN   0-399-20625-6

        03594   558261   9040

Author's name

Description of book (Annotation)

Subject headings

Once you have found the card in the card catalogue, copy down the call number (and the title and author) of the book. This will save you the trouble of looking it up again later if you don't find the book right away.

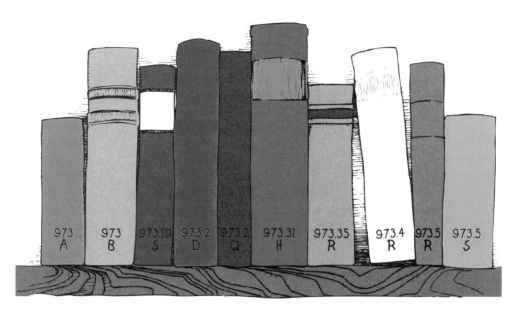

Finding a Book

Once you have found the card you want in the card catalogue, and carefully copied down the call number, you are ready to look for your book. You may find several books on the shelf with the same numbers *on the top line*. When this happens, you must look at the letters and numbers *on the second line*. See how 973 / A comes before 973 / B in the illustration above.

Using Call Numbers ➤ Some call numbers contain decimals and are longer than other call numbers. Don't let that throw you. For example, **973.19** might seem *larger* than **973.2**. In fact, it is only *longer*, not larger, because **973.2** is really **973.20**. Keep this in mind as you search for your book.

Finding Novels ➤ Fiction books (novels) are not numbered like other books. Fiction is usually kept in a separate section of the library where the books are arranged on the shelf alphabetically by the author's last name.

Finding Biographies ➤ Biographies and autobiographies are also arranged on a separate shelf by the last name of the person written about. (Ask your librarian for help locating these special shelves.)

Using a Computer Catalogue

There are different ways to tell a computer what you want. The simplest way is to use *keywords* and *logical operators*.

Using Keywords ➤ A keyword is a word related to your research topic. When you enter a keyword, the computer will look for it and list any records containing the word.

Sample Keyword: **dinosaurs**

Using Logical Operators ➤ You can combine keywords to narrow or enlarge your search. Logical operators are the words you use between your keywords. The three logical operators — *and, or,* and *not* — tell the computer what to do.

and	Use **and** to narrow your search. *And* tells the computer that *both* terms must be together before it selects them. *Sample Search:* dinosaurs **and** Jurassic
or	Use **or** to enlarge your search. *Or* tells the computer to list either *one* or *both* terms if it finds them. *Sample Search:* Tyrannosaurus rex **or** dinosaurs
not	Use **not** to narrow your search. *Not* tells the computer that the first keyword must be in the record and the second term must not be in the record. (*Not* is sometimes typed as *and not.*) *Sample Search:* dinosaurs **not** carnivores

Using the On-Line Catalogue ➤ After you've entered your keywords, a list of results (called **hits**) will appear on the screen. If you're using an on-line catalogue, you will get a list of book titles. When you select a title, the screen will show you the record for that title. You will see the same information you would find on a card-catalogue card: *title, author, copyright date,* and *call number.*

Using the Encyclopedia

An **encyclopedia** is a set of books (or a CD) with articles on every topic imaginable. The topics (or articles) are arranged alphabetically, just like a dictionary. Most encyclopedia articles begin with the basic facts. The further you read, the more details you will find. You will also find a list of related topics at the end of each article.

Using the Index

To help you find specific information about your topic, use the *Index*. (You will find it in the last volume.) The index tells you all the other places in the encyclopedia where you will find information, pictures, or other topics related to your subject. For example, here are some index entries for *Salmon* from the *Junior Encyclopedia of Canada* index:

Boldface entries for main articles

Salmon 4-350C. *See also* Atlantic salmon; Pacific salmon; sockeye salmon — **More information is available elsewhere.**

Acid Rain 1-11D
British Columbia 1-218D
Char 1-307C — **Volume number**
Columbia River 1-351A
Fishing Industry 2-159D, 2-160D, 1-161B
Grand Falls (Nfld) **2**-265B
Grayling 2-270B — **Page number**
Japanese 3-5A
Native People: Northwest Coast 3-299B, 3-299C, 3-300A, 3-302B — **This letter tells what part of the page:**

A	C
B	D

Native People: Plateau 3-310B *(with picture)*, 3-310C, 3-310D, 3-312A *(box)*
New Brunswick 3-340A, 3-340D
Trout 5-162B
No boldface means the subject is discussed under a different heading. — **Salmon Arm** 4-350D
salmon roe
Salmon 4-350A *(picture)*

Bright IDEA

Using the index may change how you decide to write about your subject. You might, for example, get a new idea for a story about the effects of acid rain on salmon, or about the importance of salmon to Native people of the Northwest Coast.

Using Other Reference Books

Reference books contain useful facts and information. You probably are most familiar with encyclopedias, dictionaries, and atlases. Other reference books can be just as helpful and are sometimes more up-to-date. Some popular titles are listed below:

- **Bartlett's Familiar Quotations** contains 20 000 quotations arranged according to when they were said, from ancient times to the present.

- **Biography Today** profiles people from around the world of interest to young readers.

- The **Oxford Children's Book of Famous People** contains important facts on more than 1000 important people from all over the world.

- The **Junior Authors** books contain information about the lives of children's and young adult authors.

 **THINK IT OVER** Many realistic fiction books contain information you might find helpful in a report. *Never Cry Wolf,* for example, contains a great deal of factual information about wolves.

- The **Illustrated Encyclopedia of Animals** includes information on more than 2000 types of animals from aardvarks to zorilles.

- The **Holidays, Festivals, and Celebrations of the World Dictionary** describes more than 1400 rituals, festivals, and celebrations throughout the world.

- **Webster's New Geographical Dictionary** lists important geographical and historical information about the world's most famous places.

- **The Canadian Global Almanac** contains facts and statistics about entertainment, sports, politics, history, religion, current events, and science and nature.

Understanding the Parts of Reference Books

When you use a nonfiction book to find information for school writing, you should know the *parts* of the book and how they can help you use that book more efficiently. Below, you will find a short description of each part of a book.

➤ The **title page** (usually the first printed page in a book) lists (1) the complete title of the book, (2) the author's name, (3) the publisher's name, and (4) the place of publication.

➤ The **copyright page** is next and gives you the year the book was published. (Remember, if the book is too old, it may no longer be a good source of information.)

➤ The **preface, foreword, introduction,** or **acknowledgment** comes before the table of contents and tells what the book is about. It may also explain why the book was written.

➤ The **table of contents** shows you the divisions of the book (units, chapters, and topics). You can use it to find major topics covered in the book.

➤ The **body** is the main section of the book.

➤ The **appendix** follows the body. Here you will find extra information such as maps, charts, tables, diagrams, letters, or copies of official documents.

➤ The **glossary** is the dictionary part of the book. It lists terms or special words used in the book and explains each of them.

➤ The **bibliography** lists books or articles used by the author to help write the book. (You can use this list to find other books on the same topic.)

➤ The **index** lists all the topics in the book alphabetically. It will tell you whether the book contains the information you need and on which page you will find it.

Using the *Children's Magazine Guide*

The *Children's Magazine Guide* is another useful guide for finding information in the library. This guide is an organized list of the latest Canadian and American magazine articles, articles you may find useful for a number of classroom reports or writing assignments.

To use the *Magazine Guide*, simply select the issue that covers the time period you are interested in. Once you have found the right issue, look for your subject. (The subjects are all listed in alphabetical order.)

If you can't find your subject, think of related topics. For example, if you are writing a report about *fossils*, you might look under *dinosaurs* or *prehistoric animals.*

Reading the Guide

When you find a magazine article you would like to read, copy down the title and date of the magazine and give it to the librarian. The librarian will get the magazine for you or show you where you can look for the article yourself. Here's a sample magazine entry from the *Children's Magazine Guide:*

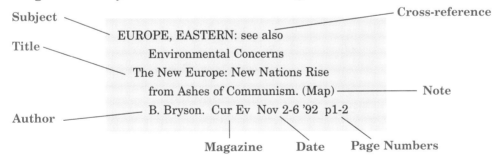

- **Subject** of the magazine article. Subjects are listed alphabetically.
- **Title** and **Author** of the magazine article.
- **Magazine** in which the article appears. A key to the abbreviations of magazine names is located on the inside front cover of the guide.
- **Date** (month, week, and year) the magazine was published.
- **Page Numbers** where the article can be found in the magazine.
- **Notes** give you more information about what's included in the article.
- **Cross-references** tell where more information can be found.

Writing a Summary

Learning and Remembering

Think of all the reading you do in school. For daily assignments, you are asked to read handouts, chapters, and stories. Then on your own, you are expected to do additional reading for special reports and projects. That's a lot of reading. You need a strategy or method to help you understand and remember the important ideas in these assignments. One such strategy is **summary writing**.

The process of writing a summary is a little like squeezing out toothpaste. You squeeze out just what you need and leave the rest in the tube.

The Big Squeeze

When you write a summary, you select only the most important ideas from something you have read. You then combine these ideas into a clear and simple mini-report. Writing a summary tests how well you understand something you have read. It is a very effective learning tool, one that you will use again and again as a student. To see how a summary is written, refer to the model and guidelines that follow.

Original

This article form *The Junior Encyclopedia of Canada* describes the way paper is made.

How Paper is Made

The first step in the process of converting a tree into paper is to harvest the tree. It is then cut into logs and hauled to the mill. At most pulp and paper mills, whole logs are stripped of their bark and broken up into chips. Complex machinery turns these wood chips first into pulp and then into paper.

Wood is made of cellulose fibres, which are held together by a substance called lignin. The purpose of pulping is to separate the fibres. One way to turn wood into pulp is to grind it. Another way is to cook it with chemicals in a kind of huge pressure cooker. The two main kinds of chemical pulp are sulphate and sulphite.

To make paper, the pulp is mixed with water and poured evenly on a paper-making machine as long as a football field. The water is removed by gravity, vacuum action, and heat as the sheet of paper speeds down the length of the machine. The fibres bond to one another, forming a web of paper at the dry end of the machine. Researchers perform tests at each stage.

Model Summary

To make paper, trees are harvested, cut into logs, and taken to a mill. There, the bark is removed, and the logs are chipped. The chips are either ground or cooked with chemicals to form wood pulp. When the pulp, mixed with water, is poured onto a huge machine, the fibres bond, creating a long sheet of paper. As the paper moves along the machine, the water is removed, and the paper dries.

Writing a Summary

PREWRITING *Planning Your Summary*

Skim and List ● Learn as much as you can about a
reading selection before you try to summarize it.

➤ Skim it once to get the general meaning. Then read the
selection carefully, paying special attention to key words
that are **boldfaced** and *italicized*.

➤ Next, list the main points on your paper.

➤ Check your list against the reading selection to make sure
you haven't missed anything.

WRITING THE FIRST DRAFT

Use Your Own Words ● Write your summary in clear and
complete sentences. Use your own words, except for key words.

➤ The first sentence should state the main idea of the
selection. (**SEE** the next page for help.)

➤ Include only the most important information in the rest of
your summary. Do not get too detailed.

➤ Arrange your ideas in the most logical order.

➤ Add a concluding sentence, if one seems to be needed.

 Writing a summary is really a lot like writing
a paragraph. The first sentence in a summary
is the topic sentence. The sentences that
follow must support the topic sentence.

REVISING *Improving Your Work*

Review It Carefully ● Ask yourself the following questions:

➤ Have I included all of the important ideas?

➤ Have I stated these ideas clearly and in my own words?

➤ Could another person get the main idea of the selection by
reading my summary?

Finding the Main Idea
A Closer Look at Summarizing

The main idea in the model reading selection is stated right in the title: "How Paper is Made." That's easy. But what happens when you can't figure out or find the main idea? Try one or more of the following activities.

Self Check ● Make sure you have followed all of the steps listed under "Planning Your Summary" on page 218.

Big Questions ● Ask yourself some important questions. What is the biggest, largest, or most important idea in this reading material? What do I want to remember about this material a month from now? (How much do I have to squeeze out?)

Sharing Session ● Talk about the selection with a classmate. What do each of you think the reading is about? Work out any differences in your thinking until both of you agree on the main idea.

Reading Strategies ● Use a reading strategy like KWL (**K**now, **W**ant, **L**earn) to help you focus your attention on the important points in the reading material. (**SEE** pages 237-243 for more on these strategies.) Once you discover the main idea of a reading selection, all of the other parts of your summary should naturally fall into place.

Summarizing is an important part of other longer forms of writing, especially book reviews, classroom reports, and news stories. Look at the guidelines for writing a summary when using these other forms of writing.

Writing a Classroom Report

Sled Dogs: Canine Athletes

Your teacher says, "Today, students, we're going to begin our reports on dogs."

"Oh, no! Not another report," you think. "Sometimes they can be so *boring*." But wait a second. Your teacher is now saying this report should be on something different about dogs, not the same old stuff. Maybe you've seen a story about a dog on television, or in a magazine or a movie. Or maybe you have a personal story to tell.

No *Boring* Topics!

When you write a report, you should find a topic that you would like to know more about, a topic that is truly interesting — one that you would enjoy reading about, writing about, and sharing with others.

> **66 Just as we've helped many of our students write reports, we'll show you how the whole process of researching, organizing, and writing your report might go. You can begin by turning to the next page and reading the report we wrote. Then, on the pages which follow, we will show you the process we used to write it. 99 We hope it helps.**
> — *Peter & Connie Roop*

SLED DOGS: CANINE ATHLETES

BEGINNING
The report
begins by
setting the
scene.

In the crisp morning air, at 30 degrees below zero, the dogs are barking and frisking, anxious to be gone. As the official begins the countdown, the mushers stand ready on the sleds. "Three… two… one… Go, driver!" The dogs are off, racing along the trail at about 40 kilometres an hour. "Mush! Mush!" yells the driver — as if the team needed such encouragement. The race has begun.

The driver's only way of controlling the team is by voice signals. For this reason, the dogs must be well trained, or chaos could easily ensue. In the excitement of a race, it can be quite an art to control the teams, which may have anywhere from 3 to 16 dogs, all eager to run and run and run.

Dogsledding was used for thousands of years by Arctic people, as a practical way of travelling over the snow. When Europeans came to the North, they too adopted this means of transportation. It was not until the invention of the snowmobile in this century that dogsledding became a largely recreational pursuit. (The Inuit word for snowmobile means "mechanical dog.")

MIDDLE
A number of
fascinating
facts are
included in
the body.

The dogs used in races are usually a mix of several breeds, although most contain some Siberian Husky and some Alaskan Malamute blood. The Canadian Eskimo dog, bred by Arctic people over thousands of years, almost became extinct when the snowmobile arrived. Today, thanks to breeders, they have survived, although they are rarely used in races.

The bond between driver and dog can be intense. One musher recalls her dog's concern after she fell in a frozen lake: "I built a fire and changed out of my wet clothes right away, but I was still shivering. So I decided to unhitch one of the dogs, and hope he wouldn't take off. Sandro seemed to understand what I wanted. Instead of bolting, which is what sled dogs instinctively do, he came and lay down right next to me, warming me up with his body heat. He probably saved my life."

END
A final
thought
is added
to keep the
readers
thinking.

Sled dog racing is a fast-growing sport. Almost any weekend in the winter, a race is being held somewhere in North America. Mushers are dedicated to their sport — and to their dogs. They have to be: preparing for a big race, like the 1760-kilometre (1100-mile) Iditarod in Alaska, can cost thousands of dollars. But the thrill of racing seems to be enough to keep them coming back for more

As Simple As A B C

There are three major steps to follow when you write a classroom report. This chapter will help you understand and follow this three-step plan:

A. Select a good topic.
B. Collect information about that topic.
C. Connect that information into a well-written report.

A SELECT A GOOD TOPIC

The first thing you have to do when you write a report is to find a good topic. A good topic is one that is interesting and *specific*. (*Dogs* is a general topic; *huskies* is more specific. More about that later.) You also have to find a topic that works well for your assignment. To do that, you need to explore all the possibilities.

1 **Create a web, list, or cluster.** Start with the general topic assigned by your teacher, or one you've chosen, and jot down as many ideas about that topic as you can. We needed to write a report on dogs for a local magazine, but the specific topic was up to us. Below is the web we created to help us find a specific topic.

General Topic Web

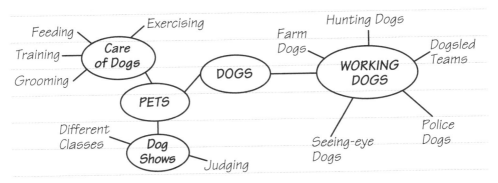

 Notice that we began our web by dividing it into the two biggest dog topics or categories we could think of: **pets** and **working dogs**.

2 **Let your web (list, cluster) sit.** After a couple of hours (or even a full day), go back to your web and find an item or two that interests you the most.

After looking closely at our web, we felt we wanted to write about working dogs. This became our chosen subtopic. We were now one step closer to our specific topic.

3 **Ask general questions.** Once you've decided upon your subtopic, begin another web. This web will hold all the questions you'd like answered about your topic. Knowing we were headed for the ocean depths, we drew the one below.

Subtopic Web

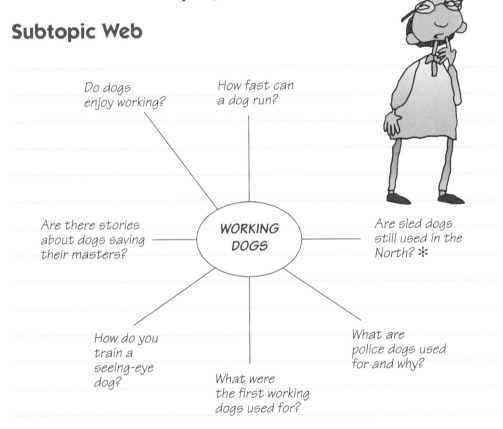

Do dogs
enjoy working?

How fast can
a dog run?

Are there stories
about dogs saving
their masters?

WORKING
DOGS

Are sled dogs
still used in the
North? ✳

How do you
train a
seeing-eye
dog?

What were
the first working
dogs used for?

What are
police dogs used
for and why?

✳ As we worked on our second web, we began to think about doing our report on sled dogs. So we starred this question. We were beginning to find out what really interested us.

4 **Ask specific questions.** By the time we finished our second web, we knew that we wanted to do our report on sled dogs. To help us decide what we would include in our report, we made a list of questions that we wondered about. We figured our readers would wonder about the same things.

Specific Topic List

SLED DOGS

Are they still used for transportation?
Where are dogsled races held?
How many dogs in a team?
Can we interview someone who has taken part in
    a dogsled race?
Are there any good stories about them?
How fast do they go?
What breed is best for dogsledding?
How does the driver control the team?

B COLLECT INFORMATION

Once you've decided on your specific topic and collected your questions, it's time to start doing your research. Here are some suggestions for helping you gather information.

1 Use a gathering grid. This activity will help you to organize your information. Because you'll need to make a huge grid, it's best to use a big piece of paper (or two standard-size pieces taped together). Then draw lines like the ones shown on our sample grid on the next page, and do the following:

➤ Write your topic in the upper left-hand corner.

➤ List your questions down the left side of your grid.

➤ List all the sources of information across the top. (See number 3 below for more on *sources*.)

2 Ask open-ended questions. As you list your questions on your grid, try to make them open-ended. An open-ended question is one that requires more than a "yes" or "no" answer. For example, the question "Can sled dogs go fast?" will not give you as much information as "How fast can sled dogs go?"

3 Find good sources of information. As you know, it's impossible to write a *good* report without a *good* topic and *good* information. Here are some sources you can use.

● **Use your school and public libraries.** (***SEE*** the chapter in this handbook about using libraries, pages 207-215.)

● **Find experts on your topic to write or talk to.** (***SEE*** page 125 for interview techniques and pages 142-147 for writing business letters.)

● **Ask your teacher, a parent, or your friends what they know.** (You might be surprised! Take your notebook and ask away.)

Some schools have a computer information service that you can use to find all kinds of material. Ask your teacher if your school has this service.

Gathering Grid

Sources of Information

Sled Dog Racing	Books	Encyclopedias	Interviews	Magazine Articles
How long have dogsleds been used?		Were used for thousands of years by Inuit and their predecessors. Cdn. Encyc.		
Are they still used for transportation?		Not much since invention of snowmobile in 20th c Cdn. Encyc.		
How fast do they go?	Up to 30 km/h Racing, p. 13			
Where are races held?				
What breed is best?	See index card, "Breeds"			
How many dogs in a team?	3 to 16 Racing, p. 61			
Any good stories?			Interview with A. Klein in writer's notebook	
How do drivers care for their dog teams?	Diet with lots of meat, health watched carefully, lots of training Racing, p. 43			
How does driver control the team?	team can easily get out of control Puppies, p. 48			Voice commands, e.g. "Mush, Gee, Haw." World, p. 4.

Your Questions

4 **Answer your questions.** Fill in the answers to your questions, as we have, right on your grid. At times you'll have more information than the grid will hold. Note cards can then prove very useful.

5 **Use note cards, if needed.** Books, encyclopedias, interviews, magazines! There can be a lot of information to write down for a report. Your grid will help you keep track of all your facts, but you may find that some of the facts just won't fit. That's when you may need to use note cards. Simply write the questions across the top of an index card and list all your answers on the card.

Quotes: When you read something in a book or magazine that you want to use word for word, copy down the quote just as it was written. Do the same for what is said in interviews. (Remember to use quotation marks before and after a quote.)

Sample Note Cards

Are they still used for transportation? Canadian Encyclopedia
- Snowmobile mostly took over transportation role in 20th c.
- Many breeds of northern working dogs died out.
- Snowmobile called "mechanical dog" in Inuktitut.

Encyclopedia Card

Any good stories?
— A. Klein falling in the lake
"I built a fire and changed out of my wet clothes right away, but I was still shivering. So I decided to unhitch one of the dogs, and hope he wouldn't take off. Sandro seemed to understand what I wanted. Instead of bolting, which is what sled dogs instinctively do, he came and lay down right next to me, warming me up with his body heat. He probably saved my life."

Interview Card

What breeds are best? Racing Sled Dogs — book
- Most popular breed today Alaskan husky
- Usually a mixture of Siberian husky, malamute, and other dogs
- Hounds and others also sometimes used for breeding sled dogs
- Purebred malamutes, Siberian huskies, and other northern breeds are rarely used for races; good for pulling loads, but not fast enough

Magazine or Book Card

6 **Check your information.** It is important that you take time to look over all your information before you start writing your report. By using different kinds of information, you will keep your readers interested. Try to include some of the following:

■ quotes from experts or people with experience

■ stories that sound as if you were an eyewitness

■ colourful or powerful words that fit your topic

■ interesting diagrams and drawings

■ humorous or surprising information about the topic

C CONNECT YOUR IDEAS

Once you have answered all your questions and organized all your information, it's time to begin writing your report. Here are some tips to help you make your report clear and interesting.

1 **Begin your report with a hook.** Most writing needs a good hook, something that will start it off with a bang. Starting with a *short story* is one way to begin. The race description at the beginning of our report is our *hook*.

SLED DOGS: CANINE ATHLETES

In the crisp morning air, at 30 degrees below zero, the dogs are barking and frisking, anxious to be gone. As the official begins the countdown, the mushers stand ready on the sleds. "Three... two... one... Go, driver!" The dogs are off, racing along the trail at about 40 kilometres an hour. "Mush! Mush!" yells the driver — as if the team needed such encouragement. The race has begun.

Other Ways to Begin...

- with a quote from an interview *("Sometimes I wonder who is in control: the dogs or me!")*

- with a dramatic statement. *(For as long as there have been people in the Arctic, there have been sled dogs.)*

- with a character or subject introduction *(Strong, tough, and built for speed, sled dogs are made to survive — and thrive — in the harsh conditions of the far north.)*

- with description *(In the crisp morning air, at 30 degrees below zero, the dogs are barking and frisking...)*

2 **Tie your facts together**. Now it's time to tie your facts together in an interesting way. Simply listing the facts you've gathered would turn out like a shopping list: useful, but boring! But linking your facts together from beginning to end can change a list into an interesting report.

THINK IT OVER

Our second, third, and fourth paragraphs report fascinating facts about sled dogs. By linking them to the hook (the first story in our report) and to what comes next (the quote from our interview), we have created an interesting "body" for our report.

The driver's only way of controlling the team is by voice signals. For this reason, the dogs must be well trained. In the excitement of a race, it can be quite an art to control the teams, which may have anywhere from 3 to 16 dogs, all eager to run and run and run.

Dogsledding was used for thousands of years by Arctic people, as a practical way of travelling over the snow. But with the invention of the snowmobile in this century, dogsledding became a largely recreational pursuit. (The Inuit words for snowmobile means "mechanical dog.")

The dogs most used in races are Alaskan huskies — usually a mix of Siberian husky, Alaskan malamute, and a variety of other breeds. The Canadian Eskimo dog, bred by Arctic people over thousands of years, almost became extinct when the snowmobile arrived. Today, thanks to breeders, they have survived, although they are rarely used in races.

3 **Use quotes and charts.** In your report, include someone's actual words. That's a **quote**. A person's real words are almost always interesting. A strong quote from a real person brings your report to life. Our quote was one of many we could have picked from, but it said so much and was so exciting, we chose it over all the others.

Helpful Hint
Use charts or diagrams if you think they would make your report more interesting or easier to understand.

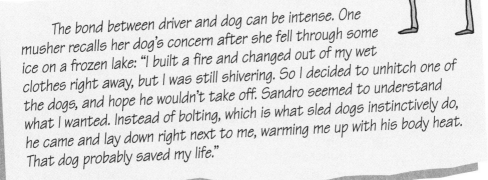

> The bond between driver and dog can be intense. One musher recalls her dog's concern after she fell through some ice on a frozen lake: "I built a fire and changed out of my wet clothes right away, but I was still shivering. So I decided to unhitch one of the dogs, and hope he wouldn't take off. Sandro seemed to understand what I wanted. Instead of bolting, which is what sled dogs instinctively do, he came and lay down right next to me, warming me up with his body heat. That dog probably saved my life."

4 **End with a strong point.** End your report with another story (a short one) or a strong point. We ended our report by mentioning the sport's rising popularity and describing the dedication and enthusiasm of those involved in it.

> Sled dog racing is a fast-growing sport. Almost any weekend in the winter, a race is being held somewhere in North America. Mushers are dedicated to their sport — and to their dogs. They have to be preparing for a big race, like the 1760-kilometre (1100-mile) Iditarod in Alaska, can cost thousands of dollars. But the thrill of racing seems to be enough to keep them coming back for more.

5 **List your sources.** Your teacher may ask you to make a list of the materials (sources) you used to write your report. In that case, you will need to include a **bibliography** page at the end of your report. To make a bibliography page, simply list your sources alphabetically by the author's last name, or by the title if there is no author given. Follow the example listed below.

Bibliography

BOOKS Author (last name first). <u>Title</u> (underlined). City where the book is published: Publisher, copyright date.

> *Paulsen, Gary. <u>Puppies, Dogs, and Blue Northers: Reflections on Being Raised by a Pack of Sled Dogs</u>. New York: Harcourt, Brace & Company, 1996.*

MAGAZINES Author (last name first). "Title of the article" (in quotation marks). <u>Title of the magazine</u> (underlined). Date (day month year): Page numbers of the article.

> *Rinard, Judith E. "Go, Team, Go!" <u>National Geographic World</u>. December 1996: 2–5.*

Note: If your entry runs more than one line, indent the second and third lines five spaces.

ENCYCLOPEDIAS "Article title" (in quotation marks). <u>Title of the reference book</u> (underlined). Edition. Date published.

> *"Dog Sledding." <u>Canadian Encyclopedia</u>. 2nd ed. 1988.*

FILMS, SLIDES, VIDEOTAPES <u>Title</u> (underlined). Medium (film, videocassette, etc.). Production company, date. Time length.

> *<u>Qimmiq: Canada's Arctic Dog</u>. Videocassette. National Film Board, 1979. 24 min.*

INTERVIEWS Author (last name first). Type of interview. Date (day month year).

> *Klein, Adrian. Personal interview. 20 January 1997.*

PAMPHLETS Author (last name first). <u>Title</u> (underlined). City where pamphlet is published: Publisher, copyright date.

> *Wang, C. <u>Sled Dog Competitions</u>. Edmonton: Canadian Sled Dog Club, 1997.*

Writing a Report: A Summary Checklist

SELECT A GOOD TOPIC

1. Create a web (list, cluster).
2. Let your web sit.
3. Ask general questions.
4. Ask specific questions.

COLLECT INFORMATION

1. Use a gathering grid.
2. Ask open-ended questions.
3. Find good sources of information.
4. Answer your questions.
5. Use note cards, if needed.
6. Check your information.

CONNECT YOUR IDEAS

1. Begin with a hook.
2. Tie your facts together.
3. Use quotes and charts.
4. End with a strong point.
5. List your sources.

CHECK YOUR REPORT

1. Have you used clear, complete sentences?
2. Are your paragraphs well organized?
3. Have you covered the topic completely?
4. Have you used quotation marks correctly?
5. Have you checked your spelling, usage, and punctuation?
6. Is your report written or typed neatly?

Other Ways to Present a Report

Ask your teacher if you can try a different format for sharing what you've learned about your topic. Here are some other ways to do a report:

➤ **Write a poem.** (***SEE*** the "Writing Poems" chapter.)

➤ **Perform a play.** (***SEE*** the "Writing Plays" chapter.)

➤ **Write a song.** (***SEE*** the "Writing Songs" chapter.)

➤ **Do and describe an experiment.** (***SEE*** the "Writing Explanations" section.)

➤ **Draw a cartoon or series of cartoons.** (Include information in bubbles or as captions.)

➤ **Give a speech.** (***SEE*** the "Giving Speeches" chapter.)

➤ **Write a historical story.** (***SEE*** the "Writing Stories from History" chapter.)

➤ **Take pictures and make a photo essay.**

MINI LESSON To give you an idea of how different forms of writing can work for a report, practise converting our report, "Sled Dogs: Canine Athletes," into one of the forms listed above.

The Tools of Learning

Improving Your Reading

Using Reading Strategies

Reading Pictures

Using Reading Strategies

A Plan of Action

When you read, you want the ideas on the page to make sense. You want to enjoy what you read. You also want to be able to remember and use the information. So how can you become a better reader? One way is to follow the simple plan we've suggested below:

- **Read often.**
- **Read everything.** (stories, books, newspapers, magazines, even computer screens)
- **Change your speed as you read.**
- **Use reading strategies.**

When you re-read something or take notes, or talk about what you have read, you are using reading strategies. That's what we are going to talk more about in this chapter: how to use reading strategies to make you a better student. We hope you find it helpful.

What Are Reading Strategies?

A **strategy** is a plan or way of doing something. There are many strategies readers can use, and good readers use them often. They use them *before, during,* and *after* reading. Here are some strategies to help you read your textbook materials.

➤ Before Reading

Before you begin reading, try to get "the big picture," or overall point, of the material. Here are some strategies to help you preview what you are about to read:

- Think about the title and then ask yourself some questions:
  1. *What do I know about this topic?*
  2. *What would I like to know?*
  3. *What is this chapter or article probably going to be about?*
- Next, preview the pages by looking at the major headings, **boldfaced words**, *italicized words*, and picture captions.
- Look for a summary at the end of the chapter and read it carefully.
- Also look for charts, graphs, pictures, and diagrams, and think about what each is "saying" about the topic.

➤ During Reading

As you read, try to be an alert, active thinker!

- Look for the answers to any questions you may have.
- Stop every so often and ask yourself, "What did I just read?" Then answer your own question.
- Make a list of key words, phrases, or summary sentences.

 **TAKE NOTE**   Try to figure out the author's purpose or pattern of organization. (Read "Purpose Patterns" on the next page.)

PURPOSE PATTERNS

Picking out the author's purpose as you read is another helpful reading strategy. Here are four common "purpose patterns" you can look for when you read:

The Sharing-Experience Pattern ● Writers often share their personal experiences with their readers. Watch for words like "I" or "us." You can usually read this material quickly. As you are reading, ask yourself, "Why is the writer telling this story?"

The Question/Answer Pattern ● Look for questions as you read, especially at the beginning of chapters or paragraphs. Remember, the author's purpose is to give you the answer to each question. Don't stop until you find it.

The Opinion/Reason Pattern ● Watch for "I believe..." or "In my opinion..." A reason should follow the opinion. Find it.

The Fact/Proof Pattern ● Watch for a factual statement followed by evidence or "proof." The proof might be a list of facts, a series of examples, or a chart. Read slowly. (If you don't understand the factual statement, look up individual words you don't know or ask someone for help.)

➤ *After Reading*

After you have finished reading — but before you close the book or put the materials away — look over the pages again. Here are some reviewing tips:

■ Ask yourself some questions:

  1. *What do I know now that I didn't know before I read this?*

  2. *If I had to tell someone what I just read, what would I say?*

■ Talk about what you have just read with anyone who will listen.

■ Write a summary of what you've read. (**SEE** pages 216-219.)

Reading Strategies You Can Use

SRN (Survey, Read, Note)

SRN is an easy strategy to use when you read non-fiction. Simply divide your notebook paper into two columns and *survey, read,* and *take notes.*

1 **Survey.** Read the title, major headings, subheadings, **boldfaced** and *italicized* words, picture captions, and the summary.

2 **Read.** Before you read each section, write the heading or subheading in the left-hand column of your paper.

3 **Note.** When you finished reading a section, write the key words, phrases, or ideas in the right-hand column next to each heading.

Geography

A Land of Many Climates — pages 46–47

Introduction	Climate has two main parts: temperature and precipitation
Temperature	= how cold or warm a place is
	In Canada, the Arctic Islands are the coldest places because they are near the North Pole. British Columbia is one of the warmest places because it's near the Pacific Ocean. High places, like the mountains, are cooler than the land level with the ocean.
Precipitation	= rain and snow
	Plants need precipitation and warm weather to grow. When a place has cold winters and warm summers, plants will grow during the summer, known as the growing season.

MAPPING

Mapping is another good reading strategy, especially when you read textbooks. All you have to do is write the subject in the centre of the page and draw a map of what you're reading. Mapping helps you do several important things:

■ pick out the main topic *before* you begin reading

■ focus on the subject and remain alert *during* reading

■ review, summarize, and use the information *after* reading

Sample Reading Map

Below is a sample reading map drawn during a reading assignment in math. Notice how easy it is to understand this information about triangles when you are able to "see" it.

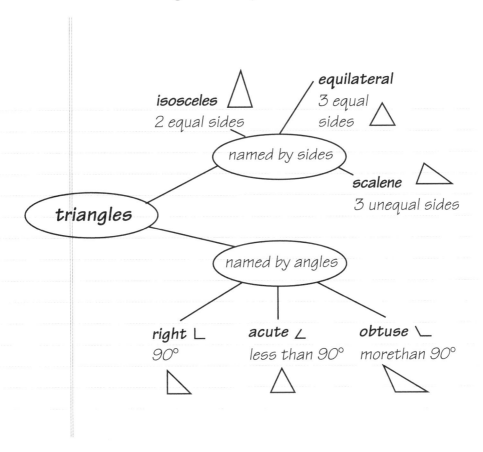

KWL (Know, Want, Learn)

KWL is a good strategy to use by yourself or with a partner. Simply divide your page into three columns and put a **K**, a **W**, and an **L** above each.

Famous Walls Around the World		
(K) What do I **know**?	**(W)** What do I **want** to learn?	**(L)** What did I **learn**?
1. There are lots of them: Great Wall of China, The Vietnam Memorial, etc. 2. Each was built for a different reason.	1. How long is the Great Wall of China? 2. When was it built? 3. Who built it? Why? 4. How many walls are there?	1. The Great Wall was built more than 2000 years ago. 2. East and west sections were made of different materials. 3. There are lots of walls! Hadrian's Wall, the Wailing Wall...

How to Use the KWL Chart

■ Write what you **know** in the "K" column. This will start you thinking about the topic. Questions will begin popping into your head. This will lead you into the second column, "What do I **want** to learn?"

■ Fill in the "W" column with what you **want** to learn. This will give you many things to look for as you read. (Your teacher may also suggest what you should be looking for as you read.)

■ Once you have finished reading, fill in the "L" column: "What did I **learn**?" Then check to see which questions from column "W" were answered. Which questions were not answered? Were any of the facts you thought you knew incorrect or only partially true?

Bright IDEA

You might make a separate chart showing what you learned. You might even write a report, poem, news story, etc. (**SEE** page 233 for more ideas.)

WRITING TO LEARN

Listed here are many of the common writing-to-learn strategies you can use before, during, and after you read. Experiment with a number of them until you find the ones that work best for you.

First Thoughts ● Write down your first impressions of the reading material — either before you read or soon after you start reading. This will help you focus your thoughts.

Stop 'n' Write ● Whenever you feel the need, stop and write down your thoughts and feelings about interesting (or confusing) ideas in your reading. Write freely in brief bursts of 2–3 minutes.

Clustering ● In the centre of a page, write a word that relates to an important idea in the reading. Circle that word. Then think of other related words or ideas and write them around your key word. (**SEE** page 26 for a sample.)

Dialogues ● Have two people discuss an idea from your reading. (You can be one of the speakers.) Then write a short summary of this discussion. This will bring your reading to life.

Pointed Questions ● Keep asking yourself why… why… why in your writing. Keep asking until you reach a dead end or a natural stopping point.

Retelling ● Pretend your friends did not read what you did, but they need to know the information. Think about what you would tell them and write it down. Then practise retelling it out loud.

Many teachers will tell you that writing is the best strategy you can use to understand and remember what you've read. Try it and see for yourself.

Elements of Literature

Like most people, you know a good story or book when you read one. But can you put into words why you liked it? The following glossary of what "goes into" a story (the elements) will help you understand and write about what you've read.

Action is everything that happens in a story.

The **antagonist**, or villain, is the person or thing fighting against the hero of a story. *Example:* The Joker is Batman's antagonist.

An **autobiography** is a story the writer tells about her or his own life.

A **biography** is a story the writer tells about another person's life.

A **character** is a person in a story.

A **comedy** is a story that makes you smile, or even laugh.

Conflict is the "problem" in a story. There are five basic types of conflict.

➤ *Man vs. Man:* A character has a problem with one or more of the other characters.

➤ *Man vs. Society:* A character has a problem with society — the school, the law, tradition.

➤ *Man vs. Himself:* A character struggles with himself, trying to decide what to do about some problem.

➤ *Man vs. Nature:* A character is in conflict with some element of nature — bitter cold, extreme heat, a tornado.

➤ *Man vs Fate (Destiny):* A character fights against a problem that seems too big to control.

Dialogue is the talking between characters in a story.

Drama is the form of literature commonly known as plays.

Mood is the feeling a reader gets from a story: happy, sad, peaceful.

The **moral** is the lesson a writer is trying to teach in his or her story. A children's story might have a moral such as "Treat others as you would like to be treated."

A **myth** is a story created to explain a mystery of nature.

The **narrator** is the person or character who is telling the story. For example, Harold the dog tells the story of the family he lives with in the book *Bunnicula;* so the narrator is actually a dog.

A **novel** is a book-length story created from the author's imagination.

The **plot** is the action of the story. The plot is usually a series of incidents which build on one another from the beginning to the end of the story.

The **plot line** shows the action in a story. It has five parts: *exposition, rising action, climax, falling action,* and *resolution.*

➤ The *exposition* (usually at the beginning of the story) explains what happened before the story starts and the setting of the story, and often introduces the characters.

➤ The *rising action* is the central part of a story during which various problems arise, and it leads up to the climax.

➤ The *climax* is the turning point in the action of a story.

➤ *Falling action* is the part of a story that follows the climax, or turning point; it has the action or dialogue needed to bring the story to an end.

➤ The *resolution* is the end of a play or story when the problems are solved.

The **point of view** is the angle from which a story is told. This depends upon who is telling the story.

➤ A *first-person* point of view means that one of the characters is telling the story:
    *Yes, **I'd** been told that dragonflies could not sew **my** mouth shut, but Mom didn't know everything.*

➤ A *third-person* point of view means that someone outside of the story is telling it:
    *Yes, **she'd** been told that dragonflies could not sew **her** mouth shut, but her mom didn't know everything.*

The **protagonist** is the hero of the story.

Romance is writing that shows life as the author or reader might like it to be rather than as it really is. Often, a romance is full of evil spies, adventure, and superheroes.

The **setting** is the time and place of a story.

The **theme** is the *subject* or *message* being written about.

The **tone** is the author's feeling about a piece of writing. The author's tone may be *serious, funny, angry, sad,* or...

The **total effect** of a piece of writing is the overall influence it has on you, the reader — the way it makes you feel and the ideas it gives you.

A **tragedy** is a story about a hero or heroine who is destroyed by a personal weakness, or flaw: envy, jealousy, greed, etc.

Turn to *Writing Poems* on pages 182–187 for additional information on the "elements" of poetry.

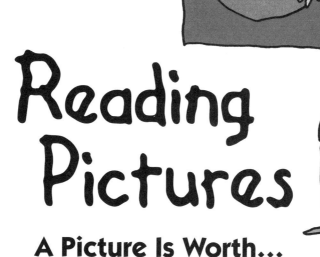

Reading Pictures

A Picture Is Worth...

Did you know that the first writing ever invented didn't have any words? It used pictures instead. Egyptian kids who lived about 5000 years ago learned by "reading" a kind of picture writing called *hieroglyphics:*

KLEOPATRA

Aboriginal peoples also used picture writing to "talk" to other tribes that didn't speak their language. That's one useful thing about pictures — they mean the same thing to everybody. "Bear" is **oso** in Spanish, **ours** in French, and **makoons** in Anishinaabe, but everybody understands ➤

➤ Symbols

The pictures used in picture writing are called "symbols." A symbol is just a simple picture or drawing that stands for something. Sometimes it's easy to tell what a symbol means, because it looks just like the thing it stands for.

Signs and Symbols ● But sometimes symbols stand for things that you can't really draw a picture of — like the equals sign. Nobody knows what "equals" looks like, but everybody who knows basic math knows that = means "equals."

There are lots of different symbols. Some are used by just about everybody. Some are used only in certain subjects. When you study a new subject, you have to learn the symbols used in that subject.

Here are a few examples of signs and symbols used in different subjects. How many do you know?

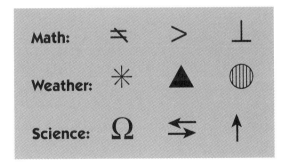

If you see a symbol, and you don't know what it means, look in the appendix or glossary of the book. You may also look under "Signs and Symbols" in the table of contents of your dictionary.

➤ **Diagrams**

A **diagram** is like a map, but instead of a place, it shows... almost anything! You could draw a diagram of a bicycle, a computer, or the bones in the human hand.

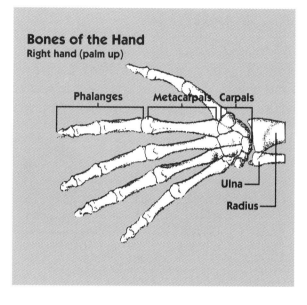

Bones of the Hand
Right hand (palm up)

Phalanges   Metacarpals Carpals

Ulna
Radius

Picture Diagram ●

A picture diagram is a drawing that shows how something is put together, how the parts relate to one another, or how the thing works. Diagrams may leave out some parts, showing only what you need to learn. This diagram of a hand leaves out the skin and muscles so that you can see the bones.

Line Diagram ●

In a way, line diagrams are like symbols: They can show something that you can't really see. For example, a family tree is a diagram of how your relatives are related. It helps you get a picture of where everybody fits, but your parents aren't really hanging over your head! (Are they?)

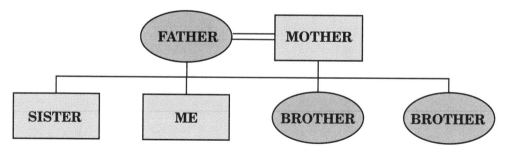

FATHER — MOTHER

SISTER   ME   BROTHER   BROTHER

THINK IT OVER

If a diagram is picturing motion, it usually shows things moving from left to right. A diagram that picture time usually shows it moving from top to bottom (like in the family tree). Look for clues like this to help you "read" diagrams.

➤ Graphs

Graphs are pictures that help us see how two things are related. They are pictures of information — information about how things changed over time, or information about how things compare to one another.

There are different kinds of graphs for different kinds of information. The most common kinds of graphs are **bar graphs**, **line graphs**, and **pie graphs**.

Bar Graph ● A bar graph shows how two or more things compare to one another at the same time. When you read a bar graph, it's important to remember that it's like a snapshot taken at one point in time.

The bars of a bar graph can go up and down or sideways. Either way, the graph pictures exactly the same information.

Both bar graphs below show the number of guppies in the grade 6 aquarium compared to the number in the grade 7 aquarium at the end of the school year.

Model Bar Graph

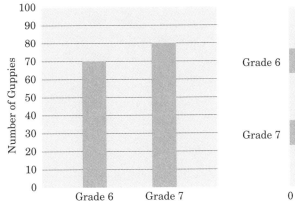

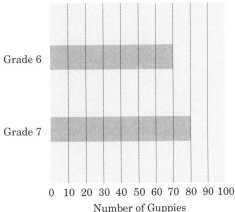

**Number of Guppies
in Grade 6 and 7
Aquariums at End
of School Year**

**Number of Guppies
in Grade 6 and 7
Aquariums at End
of School Year**

Line Graph ● A line graph always begins with a "grid." The horizontal (left-to-right) side of the grid stands for **passing time**. The vertical (top-to-bottom) side stands for the **subject** of the graph (whatever is passing through time). The line which passes through the grid allows you to study the subject as it passes through time.

The line graph below shows how many guppies were in the grade 7 aquarium in each month of the school year so far. Guppies are the *subject* of this graph, and *time* is measured in months (September through June).

Model Line Graph

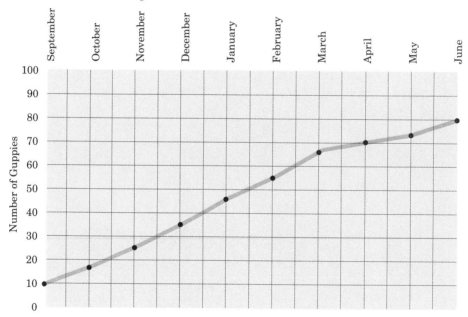

**Number of Guppies
in the Grade 7 Aquarium Each Month**

Sometimes a line graph will contain dots or points on the line to help make it easier to read. (See the dots in the graph above.) Other times, the line will have no markings on it. You have to picture the points in your mind's eye.

Pie Graph ● A pie graph shows how each part of something compares to the other parts and to the whole "pie." This pie graph shows what part (or percentage) of the total number of guppies is contained in each grade or classroom aquarium. You can see at a glance which classrooms have lots of guppies, and which have few. (If there are 100 guppies in the whole school, the grade 7 class would have 28 guppies, because 28% of 100 is 28.)

Model Pie Graph

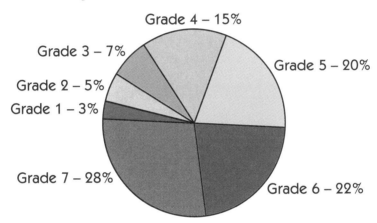

**Part (or Percentage)
of the Total Number
of Guppies in Each Grade**

 If you have trouble understanding a graph, remember the following hints. They should help you see things more clearly:

■ A **line graph** tells you how things changed over time.

■ A **bar graph** compares things at the same time.

■ A **pie graph** shows how things compare to one another; it also shows what percentage of the whole thing each part takes up.

■ Every graph has a subject (just like a paragraph): figure out what the subject is.

■ Some graphs simply repeat information that's already spelled out in words; other graphs tell you more about a topic.

➤ Tables

Like diagrams and graphs, tables try to "show" how certain things are related. Tables have *rows* (going across) and *columns* (going down). Rows contain one kind of information, while columns contain another kind of information. The table makes it easy to see how the different kinds of information fit together.

Schedule ● The table below is a bus schedule. The rows show days of the week; the columns show times of day. A check mark means a bus leaves on that day, at that time.

	8 a.m.	Noon	6 p.m.
Mon. - Fri.	✔	✔	✔
Saturday	✔	✔	
Sunday		✔	
Holidays	✔	✔	✔

Distance Table ● Another common kind of table is a distance on kilometre table. To read a distance table, find the place you're starting from. Then, find the place you're going to in the opposite part of the table. Finally, find the place where the row and the column meet — that's how far it is from one place to the other.

	Calgary	Ottawa	St. John's
Vancouver	1057	4611	7403
Winnipeg	1336	2218	5010
Fredericton	4558	1024	1777

MINI LESSON Read the two tables above and answer the following questions:

■ If you wanted to take a bus on Canada Day to visit your grandmother, what time of the day could you leave?

■ If you live in Ottawa, and your grandmother lives in Winnipeg, how many kilometres will you travel on that bus?

Conversion Table ● Another very useful table is a conversion table. This is a table that converts (changes) information from one form to another. Some popular conversion tables show how to change metric measurements to imperial measurements and dollars to foreign money.

Metric	Imperial Measurements	
2.54 centimetres	1 inch	
0.3048 metre	1 foot	12 inches
0.9144 metre	1 yard	3 feet
0.4732 litre	1 pint	
0.9463 litre	1 quart	2 pints

Custom-Made Tables ● Tables show more than schedules, distances, and conversions. They can show all kinds of information. Imagine that for a science project you needed to guess how much some things weigh, and then weigh them to find out how well you guessed. You could make a table like this:

Things I weighed	estimated weight	actual weight	difference
my hamster	450 g	210 g	240 g
my cat	4.5 kg	3.6 kg	.9 kg
my dog	45 kg	31 kg	14 kg
my friend	45 kg	34 kg	11 kg
my mom	113 kg	53 kg	60 kg
me	41 kg	34 kg	7 kg

Bright
IDEA

For more practice reading tables, turn to the "Useful Tables and Lists" section. Make sure you look at the entire table first to get the "big picture." Then look closely at the labels so you understand how each table works.

Improving Your Spelling and Vocabulary

Building Vocabulary Skills

Becoming a Better Speller

Building Vocabulary Skills

Becoming More Wordwise

Think of your vocabulary as all the words you are able to use. These are the words you use when you are reading, writing, and talking. They are the tools in your language tool kit. The more tools you have, the better you will be able to think and communicate.

Smarten Up!

Having more words at your command also helps you become a better listener and reader. Let's say you hear this comment: "Jim *donated* $10 to the group." By knowing what "donated" means, you would know that Jim does not expect to get his money back. Then you hear, "Carlos *lent* $10 to the group." By knowing what "lent" means, you would know Carlos expects to get his money back.

So how can you "smarten up" and become a better listener and reader? Just read (and follow) the suggestions given in this chapter.

Strategies for Building Your Vocabulary

1 **Read, read, read!** Books, magazines, and newspapers contain many more new words than you will ever encounter in conversations or on television. So spend time reading.

2 **Use context clues.** When you are reading and come across a word you don't know, you can use the other words in the sentence (the *context*) to figure it out. The tips that follow will help you use context clues.

- Study the sentence containing the word as well as the sentences that come **before and after**.

- Search for clues that tell you what part of speech the word is (*noun, verb, adjective*, etc.).

- See if a **synonym** or an **antonym** is given:

  *Carmen thought the field trip was **tedious — not interesting**, as they said it would be.* (If the trip was "not interesting," what could "tedious" mean? Does this meaning fit the sentence?)

- Search for clues that appear in a **series of words**:

  *Luis loaded the group's equipment into the van. He put the **amplifiers and speakers** in first, and then loaded the **guitars and synthesizers**.* (If you know what speakers and guitars are, can you guess what the other equipment might be?)

3 **Keep a vocabulary notebook.** Keep a special place in your writer's notebook for new words. Divide the page into three columns and label them as shown below:

Vocabulary		
Words chuck (verb)	**Definitions** 1. To toss or throw 2. To pat or tap	**Sentence** He chucked his old shirt.

4 **Turn to a thesaurus.** A thesaurus is a book of words and their synonyms — words that mean pretty much the same thing. It will help you find the best way to say something. Here are just some of the words (synonyms) you'll find listed under *happy* in the thesaurus.

happy: **joyful, elated, glad, cheerful, radiant**

As you can see, a **thesaurus** helps you find just the right word. It is a "backward" dictionary. You go to a dictionary when you know the word but need to find its meaning. You go to a thesaurus when you know the meaning but need a different word.

Look Up the Right Word ● For example, you can use a thesaurus to find just the right word for *scare* in the following sentence:

*Jose wanted to _____ his classmate
with the rubber spider.*

Simply look up the word *scare* as you would in a dictionary. You will find a long list of words that mean something similar to *scare.* (As you can see below, it is located between *scarce* and *scatter.*)

Entry words

*Another form of
the entry word*

scarce	scanty, sparse, rare *plentiful* SCARCITY	
scare	frighten, alarm, startle, unnerve, terrify, horrify, appall	*Synonyms*
scatter	disperse, distribute, spread, separate, part, split up, squander, stew *gather, collect*	*Antonyms*

Choose the Right Word ● Look over the list of synonyms and choose the word that works best for your sentence. In the example, the best word is *startle:*

*Jose wanted to   __startle__   his classmate
with the rubber spider.*

5 **Use a dictionary.** Use your dictionary to look up each new word you discover. (The guide words at the top of each page will help you find it.) In addition to helping you understand the meanings of words, here are some of the things a dictionary can help you with.

Spelling ● If you don't know how to spell a word, try looking it up by how it sounds.

Capital Letters ● A dictionary shows if a word needs to be capitalized.

Syllable Division ● Some dictionaries show where you can divide a word. Spaces or heavy black dots divide a word into syllables. A (-) shows where hyphens are needed.

Accent Marks ● An accent mark (´) shows which syllable should be stressed when you say a word.

Pronunciation ● To remember a word and its meaning, you must know how to say it. A dictionary will spell each word phonetically. A pronunciation key is usually given at the front or back of the book.

Parts of Speech ● A word can be used in different ways. The dictionary will tell you the part of speech of each word you look up.

Word History ● Some dictionaries have stories about where words came from or how their meanings have changed through the years.

Synonyms and Antonyms ● Synonyms (words with similar meanings) are sometimes listed with sample sentences. Antonyms (words with opposite meanings) may be listed last.

Meaning ● Some words have only one meaning. Some words have several meanings, and you will have to choose the best one.

A dictionary can also help you use *old* familiar words in *new* ways. If you read all of the different meanings for a word, you may discover another way to use it. (For example, the word *set* has over 100 different meanings!)

Sample Dictionary Page

Guide word —— **pinch**

pinch (pinch) *n.* 1. a sharp, quick squeeze with the thumb and a finger. 2. a small amount: *a pinch of salt.* *pl.* **pinches.** —*v.* to squeeze between the thumb and a finger.

—— Plural spelling

Verb forms ——— **pinching, pinched.**

pine (pīn) *n.* a tall tree with cones and very thin, sharp, green leaves that are called needles: *Pines do not lose their needles in winter.*

Accent marks ———

pineapple (pin´ ap´ el) *n.* a large, sweet, yellow fruit that grows in hot places: *A pineapple has a rough, prickly skin*

The old English word "pineapple" was first used for what we now call a "pine cone." The fruit we now call **pineapple** got its name because its shape and skin made it look like a large prickly pine cone.

—— Word history

Capital letters — **Ping-Pong** (ping´ pong´) *n.* a trademark name for table tennis.

pink (pingk) *n.* a very light red colour. —*adj.* having this colour.

—— Pronunciation

pitch (pich) *n.* in baseball, a throw of the ball to the batter. *pl.* **pitches.** —*v.* **1.** to throw: *to pitch a ball.* 2 to set up; *to pitch a tent.* **pitching, pitched.**

Different meanings ———

pitcher (pich´ er) *n.* **1.** a large jug: *a pitcher of milk.* **2.** the baseball player who pitches the ball: *The pitcher struck out the batter.*

—— Example

pitchfork (pich´ fork´) *n.* a long, large fork, used for tossing hay.

Illustration ———

pleasant (plez´ ant) *adj.* nice, friendly; pleasing: *Raju is a pleasant person.*

Antonym ——— (*opp.* **unpleasant.**) —pleasantly *adv.*—— Related adverb

6 Study words parts and forms.

You can figure out the meanings of new words by learning about the three word parts:

- ■ **prefixes** (common word beginnings)
- ■ **suffixes** (common word endings)
- ■ **roots** (common word bases)

For example, knowing that the prefix "non" means "not" helps you figure out the meaning of the word "nonsense": something that does *not* make sense. Knowing that the suffix "less" means "without" helps you figure out the meaning of "senseless": without sense.

Use Word Parts ● Before you can use word parts well, however, you must learn the meanings of some of the most widely used prefixes, suffixes, and roots in our language. For instance, the prefix *astro* is found in the word *astronomy* where it means *star*; it is also found in the words *astrodome* and *astronaut*, where it also means *star*.

Use Word Forms ● Look for other forms of words you already know. Suppose you know that the word "judge" means "to decide or settle something." When you see or hear the words *judgment, judgmental,* and *judicial,* you'll already have some idea of what they mean.

On the next nine pages, you will find a list of the most common prefixes, suffixes, and roots in the English language. Look them over and see if you recognize any. Then learn as many as you can — a few at a time.

PREFIXES

Prefixes are those word parts that come *before* the root word (pre = before). Prefixes often change the meaning of a word.

ambi, amphi *[both]*

ambidextrous (*skilled with both hands*)
amphibious (*living on both land and water*)

anti *[against]*

antifreeze (*a liquid that works against freezing*)
antipollutant (*designed to work against pollution*)

astro *[star]*

astronomy (*study of the stars*)
astronaut (*star traveller, space traveller*)

auto *[self]*

autobiography (*writing about yourself*)
autonomy (*self-government*)

bi, bin *[two]*

binocular (*having to do with both eyes*)
biweekly (*every two weeks*)

cent *[hundred]*

centimetre (*1/100 of a metre*)
century (*a period of 100 years*)

circum *[around]*

circumference (*the line that goes around a circle*)
circumnavigate (*to travel completely around*)

co *[together, with]*

coauthor (*one who writes with at least one other person*)
copilot (*one who flies with and assists the main pilot*)

ex *[out]*

exit (*the act of going out*)
expel (*drive out*)

for *[before, earlier]*

forecast (*predicting something before it happens*)
forefather (*a related person who lived at an earlier time*)

hemi, semi *[half]*

hemisphere (*half of a sphere*)
semicircle (*half of a circle*)

hyper *[over]*

hyperactive (*overly active*)
hypersensitive (*overly sensitive*)

inter *[among, between]*

intermission (*a pause between the acts of a play*)
international (*of or between two or more nations*)

macro *[large]*

macrocosm (*the world as a whole*)
macrodent (*having large teeth*)

mal *[badly, poorly]*

maladjusted (*poorly adjusted*)
malnutrition (*poor nutrition due to improper diet*)

micro *[small]*

microfilm (*a very small film*)
microscopic (*so small it can be seen only under a microscope*)

mono *[one]*

monochrome (*one colour*)
monorail (*a vehicle that runs on one track*)

non *[absence of, not]*

nonfat (absence of fat)
nonfiction (not fiction)

oct *[eight]*

octagon (a shape with eight sides)
octopus (a sea animal having eight armlike tentacles)

penta *[five]*

pentagon (a figure having five angles or sides)
pentameter (a line of verse composed of five metrical lines)

poly *[many]*

polychrome (many colours)
polygon (a figure having many angles or sides)

post *[after]*

postscript (a note added after the end of a letter)
postwar (after a war)

pre *[before]*

predict (to tell about something before it takes place)
preview (showing something before the regular showing)

pseudo *[false]*

pseudonym (false or assumed name)
pseudopod (false foot)

quad *[four]*

quadrant (one quarter of a circle)
quadruple (four times as much)

quint *[five]*

quintet (a group of five musicians)
quintuplet (one of five children born in a single birth)

re *[again, back]*

return (to come back)
rewrite (to write over again)

sub *[under]*

submerge (put under)
subsoil (layer of weathered material under the surface soil)

trans *[across, beyond]*

transoceanic (crossing the ocean)
transplant (to move something from one place to another)

tri *[three]*

triangle (a figure that has three sides and three angles)
tricycle (a three-wheeled vehicle)

un *[not]*

uncomfortable (not comfortable)
unhappy (not happy)

uni *[one]*

unicycle (a one-wheeled vehicle)
unique (one of a kind)

NUMERICAL PREFIXES

Prefix	Symbol	Equivalent	Prefix	Symbol	Equivalent
tera	T	trillionfold	**deci**	d	tenth part
giga	G	billionfold	**centi**	c	hundredth part
mega	M	millionfold	**milli**	m	thousandth part
kilo	k	thousandfold	**micro**	u	millionth part
hecto	h	hundredfold	**nano**	n	billionth part
deca	da	tenfold	**pico**	p	trillionth part

SUFFIXES

Suffixes come at the end of a word. Sometimes a suffix will tell you what part of speech a word is. For example, many adverbs end in the suffix *ly*.

able *[able, can do]*

agreeable *(able or willing to agree)*
capable *(able to do something)*

al *[relating to]*

gradual *(relating to "grades" or degrees)*
manual *(relating to the hands)*

ed *[past tense]*

called *(past tense of call)*
learned *(past tense of learn)*

er *[one who]*

baker *(one who bakes)*
teacher *(one who teaches)*

er *[used to compare things]*

neater *(more likely to be neat than another)*
tougher *(more likely to be tough)*

ess *[female]*

actress *(a female actor)*
lioness *(a female lion)*

est *[used to show superiority]*

fastest *(most able to move rapidly)*
hottest *(highest of all temperatures)*

ful *[full of]*

careful *(full of care)*
helpful *(full of help)*

ic *[like]*

metallic *(like metal)*
poetic *(like poetry)*

ily *[in some manner]*

happily *(in a happy manner)*
steadily *(in a steady manner)*

ing *[an action or process]*

talking *(to talk)*
writing *(to write)*

ist *[one who]*

artist *(one who does art)*
chemist *(one who specializes in chemistry)*

less *[without]*

careless *(without care)*
hopeless *(without hope)*

ly *[in some manner]*

bashfully *(in a bashful manner)*
quickly *(in a quick manner)*

ment *[act of, result]*

achievement *(result of achieving)*
movement *(act of moving)*

ness *[state of]*

carelessness *(state of being careless)*
restlessness *(state of being restless)*

ology *[study, science]*

biology *(study of living things)*
geology *(study of earth, rocks)*

s *[plural, more than one]*

books *(more than one book)*
trees *(more than one tree)*

sion, tion *[state of]*

action *(state of doing something)*
infection *(state of being infected)*

y *[inclined to]*

cheery *(inclined to be cheerful)*
itchy *(inclined to itch)*

ROOTS

Knowing the **root** of a word — especially a difficult word — can help you understand and remember it much better. This can be very useful when learning new words in all your classes.

acid, acri *[bitter, sour]*

acrid *(bitter or sour taste or odour)*
antacid *(works against stomach acid)*

ag, act *[do, move]*

agent *(someone who acts for another)*
agitate *(to cause to do something)*

ali, alter *[other]*

alias *(a person's other name)*
alternative *(another choice)*

am, amor *[love, liking]*

amiable *(friendly)*
amorous *(loving)*

anni, annu, enni *[year]*

anniversary *(happening at the same time every year)*
annually *(yearly)*
centennial *(once every 100 years)*

anthrop *[human]*

anthropoid *(humanlike)*
anthropology *(study of humankind)*

aster *[star]*

aster *(star flower)*
asterisk *(starlike symbol)*

aud *[hear, listen]*

audible *(can be heard)*
auditorium *(a place to listen)*

bibl *[book]*

Bible *(sacred book of Christianity)*
bibliography *(list of books)*
bibliophile *(a book lover)*

bio *[life]*

biography *(writing about a person's life)*
biology *(study of life)*

centri *[centre]*

centrifugal *(moving away from the centre)*
concentric *(having a common centre)*

chrom *[colour]*

chromosome *(colour body in genetics)*
monochrome *(one colour)*

chron *[time]*

chronological *(in order of time)*
synchronize *(together in time)*

cide *[kill]*

genocide *(killing a race)*
homicide *(killing a human)*

cise *[cut]*

incision *(a thin, clean cut)*
precise *(cut exactly right)*
incisors *(the teeth that cut or tear your food)*

cord, cor *[heart]*

cordial *(heartfelt)*
coronary *(relating to the heart)*

corp *[body]*

corporation *(a legal body)*
corpulent *(having a large body)*

cosm *[universe, world]*

cosmos *(the universe*
microcosm *(a small world)*

cred *[believe]*

credit *(belief, trust)*
incredible *(unbelievable)*

cycl, cyclo *[wheel, circular]*

bicycle *(a cycle with two wheels)*
cyclone *(a circular wind)*

dem *[people]*

democracy *(people rule)*
epidemic *(on or among the people)*

dent, dont *[tooth]*

denture *(false teeth)*
orthodontist *(someone who straightens teeth)*

derm *[skin]*

dermatology *(the study of skin)*
epidermis *(outer layer of skin)*

dic, dict *[say, speak]*

dictionary *(a book of words people use or say)*
predict *(to tell about something in advance)*

dynam *[power]*

dynamite *(powerful explosive)*
dynamo *(power producer)*

equi *[equal]*

equilibrium *(a state of balance; equally divided)*
equinox *(day and night of equal length)*

fac, fact *[do, make]*

factory *(a place where people make things)*
manufacture *(to make by hand)*

fer *[bear, carry]*

conifer *(a cone-bearing tree)*
ferry *(carry from place to place)*

fide *[faith, trust]*

confident *(trusting oneself)*
fidelity *(faithfulness to a person or cause)*

fin *[end]*

final *(the last or end of something)*
infinite *(having no end)*

flex *[bend]*

flexible *(able to bend)*
reflex *(bending or springing back)*

flu *[flowing]*

fluid *(waterlike, flowing substance)*
influence *(to flow in)*

forc, fort *[strong]*

force *(strength or power)*
fortify *(to make strong)*

fract, frag *[break]*

fracture *(break)*
fragment *(a piece broken from the whole)*

gastr *[stomach]*

gastric *(relating to the stomach)*
gastritis *(inflammation of the stomach)*

gen *[birth, produce]*

congenital *(existing at birth)*
genetics *(study of inborn traits)*

geo *[earth]*

geometry *(measuring the earth)*
geography *(study of the earth)*

grad *[step, go]*

gradual *(step-by-step)*
graduation *(taking the next step)*

graph *[write]*

autograph *(self-writing)*
photograph *(light-writing)*

greg *[herd, group]*

congregation *(a group functioning together)*
segregate *(tending to separate one group from another)*

hab, habit *[live]*

habitat *(the place in which one lives)*
inhabit *(to live in)*

hetero *[different]*

heterogeneous *(different in birth or kind)*
heteronym *(words spelled the same but pronounced differently)*

homo *[same]*

homogeneous *(of the same kind)*
homogenize *(to blend into a uniform mixture)*

hum *[earth]*

exhume *(to take out of the earth)*
humus *(earth; dirt)*

hydr *[water]*

dehydrate *(take water out of)*
hydrophobia *(fear of water)*

jest *[throw]*

eject *(to throw out)*
project *(throw forward)*

leg *[law]*

legal *(related to the law)*
legislature *(the group of people who make laws)*

log, ology *[word, study]*

psychology *(the study of mind)*
zoology *(the study of animals)*

luc, lum *[light]*

lumen *(a unit of light)*
translucent *(letting light come through)*

magn *[great]*

magnificent *(great)*
magnify *(increase to a greater size)*

man *[hand]*

manicure *(to fix the hands)*
manufacture *(to make by hand)*

maniac *[madness]*

kleptomania *(abnormal tendency to steal)*
maniac *(a mad person)*

mar *[sea, pool]*

marine *(related to the sea)*
marsh *(a wet, grassy area)*

medi *[middle, between]*

Mediterranean *(lying between lands)*
medium *(in the middle)*

mega *[great]*

megalopolis *(great city or an urban region)*
megaphone *(makes a great sound)*

mem *[remember]*

memo *(a note; a reminder)*
memorial *(a remembrance of someone)*

metre/meter *[measure]*

metre *(a unit of measure)*
voltameter *(instrument to measure volts)*

migra *[wander]*

emigrant *(one who leaves a country)*
migrant *(someone who wanders from place to place)*

mit, miss *[send]*

emit *(send out; give off)*
missile *(an object sent flying)*

mob, mot *[move]*

mobile *(capable of moving)*
promotion *(to move forward)*

mon *[warn, remind]*

admonish *(warn)*
monument *(a reminder of a person or an event)*

morph *[form]*

amorphous *(with no form or shape)*
metamorphosis *(change of form)*

mort *[death]*

immortal *(something that never dies)*
mortuary *(a place for the dead)*

multi *[many, much]*

multicultural *(including many cultures)*
multiped *(an organism with many feet)*

nat *[to be born]*

innate *(inborn)*
nativity *(birth)*

neur *[nerve]*

neuritis *(inflammation of a nerve)*
neurologist *(a physician who treats the nervous system)*

nov *[new]*

innovation *(something newly introduced)*
renovate *(to make like new again)*

numer *[number]*

enumerate *(to find out the number)*
innumerable *(too many to count)*

omni *[all, every]*

omnipresent *(present everywhere)*
omnivorous *(all-eating)*

onym *[name]*

anonymous *(without a name)*
pseudonym *(false name)*

ortho *[straight]*

orthodontist *(someone who straightens teeth)*
orthodox *(straight or usual belief)*

pac *[peace]*

Pacific Ocean *(peaceful ocean)*
pacify *(make peace)*

patr *[father]*

patriarch *(the father of the family)*
patron *(special guardian or father figure)*

path, pathy *[feeling, suffering]*

empathy *(feeling with another)*
telepathy *(feeling from a distance)*

ped *[foot]*

pedal *(lever for a foot)*
pedestrian *(one who travels by foot)*

pend *[hang, weigh]*

pendant *(a hanging object)*
pendulum *(a weight hung by a cord)*

phil *[love]*

Philadelphia *(city of brotherly love)*
philosophy *(love or study of wisdom)*

phobia *[fear]*

acrophobia *(fear of high places)*
agoraphobia *(fear of public, open places)*

phon *[sound]*

phonics *(related to sounds)*
symphony *(sounds made together)*

photo *[light]*

photograph *(light-writing)*
photosynthesis *(action of light on chlorophyll)*

pop *[people]*

population *(the number of people in an area)*
populous *(full of people)*

port *[carry]*

export *(carry out)*
portable *(able to be carried)*

proto *[first]*

protagonist *(the first or leading character)*
prototype *(the first model made)*

psych *[mind, soul]*

psychiatry *(healing of the mind)*
psychology *(study of the mind)*

rupt *[break]*

interrupt *(break into)*
rupture *(break)*

sci *[know]*

conscious *(knowing or being aware of things)*
omniscient *(knowing everything)*

scope *[see, watch]*

kaleidoscope *(instrument for viewing beautiful forms)*
stethoscope *(instrument for listening to sounds in the body)*

scrib, script *[write]*

manuscript *(written by hand)*
scribble *(write quickly)*

sen *[old]*

senile *(showing the weakness of old age)*
senior *(an older person)*

sequ, secu *[follow]*

consecutive *(following in order, one after another)*
sequence *(one thing following another)*

spec *[look]*

inspect *(look at carefully)*
specimen *(an example to look at)*

sphere *[ball, sphere]*

hemisphere *(half of a sphere)*
stratosphere *(the upper portion of a sphere)*

spir *[breath]*

expire *(breathe out; die)*
inspire *(breathe into; give life to)*

strict *[draw tight]*

boa constrictor *(snake that constricts its prey)*
constrict *(draw tightly together)*

tact, tag *[touch]*

contact *(touch)*
contagious *(transmittable by touching)*

tele *[far]*

    telephone *(a device for far sounds)*
    telescope *(a device for far looks)*

tempo *[time]*

    contemporary *(those who live at the same time)*
    tempo *(rate of speed)*

tend, tens *[stretch, strain]*

    extend *(to make longer)*
    tension *(tightness caused by stretching)*

terra *[earth]*

    terrain *(the surrounding earth or ground)*
    terrestrial *(relating to the earth)*

therm *[heat]*

    thermal *(related to heat)*
    thermostat *(a device for controlling heat)*

tom *[cut]*

    anatomy *(cutting apart a plant or animal to study it)*
    atom *(cannot be cut or divided)*

tox *[poison]*

    intoxicated *(poisoned inside)*
    toxic *(poisonous)*

tract *[draw, pull]*

    traction *(the act of pulling or gripping)*
    tractor *(a machine for pulling)*

typ *[print]*

    prototype *(a first print)*
    typo *(a printing error)*

vac *[empty]*

    vacant *(empty)*
    vacuum *(a space empty or devoid of matter)*

val *[strength, worth]*

    equivalent *(of equal worth)*
    evaluate *(find out the worth)*

vert, vers *[turn]*

    divert *(turn aside)*
    reverse *(turn back)*

vid, vis *[see]*

    supervise *(oversee or watch over)*
    video *(what we see)*

viv *[alive, life]*

    revive *(bring back to life)*
    vivacious *(full of life)*

voc *[call]*

    vocal *(calling with your voice)*
    vocation *(a calling)*

vor *[eat greedily]*

    carnivorous *(flesh-eating)*
    herbivorous *(plant-eating)*

zo *[animals]*

    zodiac *(circle of animals; the constellations)*
    zoology *(study of animal life)*

Becoming a Better S-p-e-l-l-e-r

A Self-Help Guide

You write about good ideas. You use vivid words. You make **sure** the words in your final drafts are spelled correctly.

Why? *Beecus speling erers ar harrd tu rede. And besides, people won't know how smart you really are ef yew spel lyck thes.*

So you want to spell correctly. But how do you do that? Here are four things you can do:

1 Make a spelling dictionary.

2 Use strategies for remembering spellings.

3 Learn to proofread for spelling.

4 Learn some basic spelling rules.

1 Make a spelling dictionary.

Use a Notebook ● To make a spelling dictionary, take a small notebook and label the pages with the letters of the alphabet. (Put one letter on the top of each page.) Then, each time you have to look up a spelling word in the regular dictionary, write that word in your spelling dictionary. Next time you can look it up in your spelling dictionary.

 Study the words in your spelling dictionary whenever you can. Before long you will be able to spell these words without looking them up.

2 Use strategies for remembering spellings.

Use Your Senses ● Experts say one of the best ways to remember spellings is to use your senses: seeing, hearing, and feeling. Here's a *sensory system* you can use to study for spelling tests:

➤ **Look at the word as you say it aloud.**

➤ **Write the word. Name each letter as you write it.**

➤ **Read the word aloud again.**

➤ **Check to make sure you spelled the word correctly.**

➤ **Cover the word and write it again. Name each letter as you write it. Check your spelling.**

Use Sayings ● By remembering (and making up!) a few sayings, you can avoid some very common spelling errors.

You have a PAL in your princiPAL.   People say BRrrr in February.
I always want SecondS of dessert.   Writing papER is stationERy.

Use Acrostics ● You can also use acrostics to help you spell better by making up sentences for difficult words.

GEOGRAPHY — Giraffes eat old, greasy rugs and paint houses yellow
ARITHMETIC — A rat in the house might eat the ice cream.

3   Learn to proofread for spelling.

After you have revised your writing assignments so that they make sense, you must edit them for punctuation, grammar, and spelling errors. We suggest that you check spelling last. Here are some suggestions for you to use.

Read from Bottom to Top ● Start with the last line of your draft and read from bottom to top. This will force you to concentrate on each individual word.

Use an index card or a half sheet of paper right beneath the line you are studying. Once you finish checking one line, move the index card up to the next one.

Correct the Misspellings ● Put a line through any misspelled word and make the correction right above it. (*Remember:* If you skip every other line when you write your draft, it is much easier to make corrections.)

Circle the Puzzlers ● If you are not sure about a spelling, circle it. Go back to the circled words when you have finished checking your entire paper. (For help, use your own spelling dictionary, the spelling list in this handbook, or a regular classroom dictionary.)

Ask for Help ● Finally, have a friend or classmate check your corrections and look for other spelling errors in your writing.

Special Note: If you used a computer, make sure to run your work through the spell checker. Also check it yourself for names, homonyms (*inn* instead of *in*), wrong words, and so on. Your spell checker will not find these kinds of errors for you.

Turn to the following pages for help:

4 Learn some basic spelling rules.

You can avoid some spelling errors by learning a few basic spelling rules. As you will see, most of these rules deal with adding endings to words.

➤ **Words Ending in Y** ● When you write the plurals of words that end in **y**, change the **y** to **i** and add **es**. If the word ends in **ey**, just add **s**.

bully, bullies   monkey, monkeys

➤ **Consonant Ending** ● When a one-syllable word with a short vowel needs an ending like **-ed** or **-ing**, the final consonant is usually doubled.

bat, batted   get, getting

➤ **I Before E** ● For words spelled with **i** and **e**, remember this: "**i** before **e**, except after **c**, or when rhyming with say, as in neighbour and weigh."

believe, receive, sleigh

EXCEPT Here are some exceptions: ***either, neither, their, height, weird,*** and ***seize.***

➤ **Silent E** ● If a word ends with a silent **e**, drop the **e** before adding an ending (suffix) that begins with a vowel.

use, using, useful
believe, believing, believable
nine, ninety, nineteen

EXCEPT Notice that you do ***not*** drop the e when the suffix begins with a consonant (*-ful, -ty, -teen*).

Improving Your Speaking and Listening

Giving Speeches

Performing Poems

Improving Viewing Skills

Improving Listening Skills

Giving Speeches

Speak to the Clouds

When I was about your age, I loved to swing.
But we didn't have a swing, so I went to Angie's
place. Not only could I swing at Angie's, I could also
sing at her house because no one could hear me.
I sang songs that seem corny now, and even though
I was alone, I pretended I was a star on a TV show!
I still love to swing and sing. What has changed is
that I now love to have an
audience, not just when I
sing, but also when I talk.

> **Like you, I talk to express
> my ideas and opinions.
> I also speak to groups as
> part of my job, and
> every time I give a
> speech, I feel like the
> young girl I used to
> be. I get excited. My
> heart pounds. It's as
> if I were swinging
> up into the clouds.**
> — Gloria Nixon-John

Writing a Speech

How do you feel when you are asked to speak in front of others? Do you get a little nervous or excited? Do you enjoy sharing your feelings and ideas with others, especially your classmates? If you're like most people, you enjoy talking about things you're interested in or know a lot about. (You probably don't enjoy talking about topics that don't interest you or topics you don't know much about.) That's why it's so important to select the right topic whenever you are asked to give a report or speech in class.

Types of Speeches

The first question you have to ask yourself when you begin searching for a good topic is "Why am I giving this speech?" Is it to share information, to demonstrate something, or to change people's minds?

➤ **Speech to Inform:** Give information (facts, figures, history, etc.).

➤ **Speech to Demonstrate:** Show others how to do something.

➤ **Speech to Persuade:** Present facts to change people's minds.

The Steps in the Process

No matter what type of speech you choose to write, you should follow these eight steps from start to finish. That's why I wrote this chapter — to help you through each step in the process.

1	**PICK THE TOPIC CAREFULLY.**
2	**NARROW YOUR TOPIC.**
3	**GATHER ENOUGH INFORMATION.**
4	**PREPARE AN EXCITING INTRODUCTION.**
5	**WRITE AN OUTLINE.**
6	**WRITE YOUR SPEECH.** *(OPTIONAL)*
7	**PRACTISE YOUR DELIVERY.**
8	**PRESENT YOUR SPEECH.**

1 PICK THE TOPIC CAREFULLY.

When you are asked to write and give a speech, you should begin by picking a good topic. Here are some questions you can ask:

- ■ **What do I know a lot about?**
- ■ **What would I like to know more about?**
- ■ **What do I do for fun?**
- ■ **What do I read about?**
- ■ **What do I talk about with my friends?**

(**SEE** "Selecting a Subject" on pages 26–27 for more help.)

2 NARROW YOUR TOPIC.

Let's suppose that my teacher asked me to give a **demonstration speech** for my class. I own and love horses, so "horses" is a natural choice. Horses… now that's a big topic. Too big for one speech. SO I decide, since I can bring props with me, I'll bring in my saddle and demonstrate how to put a saddle on a horse.

If my teacher had asked me to give an **information speech**, I could have informed my audience about the care and costs of keeping a horse. Or, if my teacher has asked me to give a **persuasive speech**, I could have tried to convince my audience that anyone can enjoy riding horse.

About It

Pick your topic the way you would pick the food and music for a party. Who will be present? If you were inviting grandparents, would you play rap music? If all of the guests were 11 or 12, would you serve lima beans and brussels sprouts? Of course not!

3 GATHER INFORMATION.

Remember, books and magazines are not the only sources of information!

- **Talk or write to experts in your school, family, or neighbourhood.**
- **Observe and take notes on people, places, and events.**
- **Watch videos, movies, and TV programs.**
- **Scan the newspaper.**
- **Remember things from your own experience.**

To make your ideas clearer, you might look for drawings, photos, videotapes, or props you can use during your speech.

4 PREPARE AN EXCITING INTRODUCTION.

Now that you have chosen and narrowed your topic and gathered information, it's time to prepare an introduction. Writing an introduction will help you think about *what* you want to say and *how* you're going to say it. Here are some tips:

➤ *Use a famous quote.*
"Any election is like a horse race, in that you can tell more about it the next day."   — Sir John A. Macdonald

➤ *Ask an interesting question.*
Did you know that horses have a language of their own?

➤ *Tell a story.*
One day two summers ago, I was riding my horse in the field down the road from our house when suddenly...

➤ *Make a striking statement.*
Horses understand body language better than people do. The slightest twitch of your body can tell a horse to move.

➤ *Refer to a recent incident.*
Recently, over 1200 wild horses were removed from Canadian Forces Base, Suffield, in southern Alberta.

5 WRITE AN OUTLINE.

After you've written an introduction, you should write an outline of what you plan to say in your speech. You can do this on index cards or on a sheet of paper. As you'll see, I used only short phrases to remind me of what I wanted to say.

TAKE NOTE

I wrote out my introduction and conclusion word for word so that I could learn them so well I wouldn't stumble.

Introduction   #1

The average horse weighs between 450 and 720 kg. When you consider I weigh just a small fraction of that, it seems amazing that I can get on the back of such a large animal and convince him to take me where I want to go. The things I know about the personality of each horse help, but I also depend on other things, including the equipment: the bridle, bit, reins, and saddle. And since the saddle goes on first, let's start there.

Equipment Needed: #2

Saddle, saddle pad, girth, bench or "wooden horse."
Drawing of horse.
Show and Tell the Following:
  I. Prepare the horse mentally and physically.
      Talk to horse.
      Rub under his mane.
      Stroke his neck.

Sample Outline

II. Stand left of horse.   #3
     Place the saddle pad below his withers.
     (Use diagram on the board to show where the withers are.)
III. Place saddle on top of pad.
     Watch toes!
IV. Fasten girth first on left, then right.
     Tighten from right.
     Tighten a second time.

                                                    #6
Conclusion:
Putting a saddle on a well-groomed, happy, and healthy horse is a cinch! I really could go on and talk about my horses all day. I could talk about bridles and bits. I could talk about breeds of horses, even how to braid a tail or mane, but then I wouldn't have time for a trail ride today, and that just won't do!

6 | **WRITE YOUR SPEECH.**

You may decide to give your speech using only your outline. However, if you decide to write out your speech, follow your outline and write it the same way you would any other piece of writing. Keep your purpose (to inform, demonstrate, or persuade) and your audience in mind. Also remember to use words and sentences that will sound good to your audience. (**SEE** "All About Writing" on pages 3–7 for additional help.

7 | **PRACTISE YOUR DELIVERY.**

You've heard that practise makes perfect, but how can you practise a speech? Simple. First look at the reminders in step 8 below; then do one or more of the following:

- **Practise in a quiet place where you can listen to yourself.**
- **Practise in front of friends or parents and ask for their suggestions.**
- **Practise with an audio or video tape recorder and pick out the spots you need to practise more.**

8 | **PRESENT YOUR SPEECH.**

When you are ready to give your speech, remember these points:

- **Look at the audience.**
- **Speak loudly and clearly.**
- **Speak in a slow, natural tone. Look at your notes only when you need a reminder.**
- **Use clear, correct language. Do *not* use slang, or such sounds as *ah, eh,* or *um.***
- **Stand up tall. Don't slump, sway, or lean.**

The Final Speech: A Student Model

If you follow all eight steps in the process, you should end up with a speech that is interesting to both you and your audience — Just like the model below.

Winnipeg's Royal Canadian Mint

Hello. My name is Jessica Friesen. I've lived in Winnipeg, Manitoba, all my life and I really enjoy this city. There are lots of places that are fun to visit in Winnipeg, but my personal favourite is The Royal Canadian Mint, the place where they make money.

Did you know people have used beads, cocoa beans, salt, seashells, stones, birds' scalps, and many other things for money? The world's first coins were probably made in Lydia, now Turkey, about 600 B.C. Since 1975, most Canadian coins have been made in Winnipeg, in one of the world's most modern mints.

Before a new coin is produced, an artist makes a large black-and-white drawing of it. Then the drawing is transferred to a set of steel tools, called dies, which are used to stamp out coins. During the first stage in making coins, called blanking, powerful punches pound out smooth disks, called blanks, from long metal strips. The three presses in Winnipeg are fast. They can stamp out up to 8800 blanks a minute.

Once the raised rim is put on the coin, they are heated up in gas-fired furnaces that operate at 760 to 980 degrees Celsius. These furnaces make the metal softer and easier to work. When they come out, they are washed, rinsed, and placed in hot-air dryers.

Finally, the coins go to the coining presses, where the designs are stamped on. The coins are held firmly in a collar and struck on the front and back sides at the same time. Each coining press produces 18 000 coins every hour. The Winnipeg Mint turns out almost three billion coins each year.

I hope you can come and visit the Mint some day. If you do, be sure to take the tour along the elevated walkways. Just remember not to help yourself to any samples along the way!

Performing Poems

Perform It!

You're Melinda Castillo and you've written this wonderful poem about spring. If you could just do something with this, you think, something more than putting it into your portfolio. You talk with your friends. You read them your poem. Several of them agree; your poem IS terrific! Now you need to figure out what to do!

Flamingo of Spring

the Flamingo of Spring
walks through winter.
the Flamingo of Spring
brightens everyone's daisies.
the Flamingo of Spring
welcomes the baby animals
to the world
the Flamingo of Spring
stands on one leg
in a shimmering lake.
the flowers open to
a beautiful song made
by the Flamingo of
Spring.

Moving Poetry from Page to

So what do you do if you have a wonderful
perform it! Perform it right there in your class
night, for a community group. You can form your
company and perform wherever you like. Here's what you
do: *form a team, find a poem, script the poem, score the poem,* and
perform the poem.

1 Form a Team. You can always perform alone, but it is
more fun performing as a team. Your team can be made up of
two, three, or four performers, but avoid teams of five members or
more. You may start out working with one partner. Later, you may
find that some poems really need one or two more partners.

2 Find a Poem to Perform. Look through your portfolio,
your classroom anthologies of student work, books of poems
you've published.

Collect Several Poems ● Read each poem carefully to your
self and then out loud to your partners. Collect a variety of poems,
maybe several that are funny, and one or two that are serious.
Don't worry too much about a poem's length. If you find a short
poem you really like, try to find another poem to go with it.

Choose the Right Poem ● Poems that contain a lot of
action are easiest to perform. Poems that tell about ideas and
feelings are sometimes harder to perform. However, such poems
can really get your imagination going. Here are some questions
you can ask about each poem to help you decide:

1. **Who is the main speaker in the poem?**
2. **What other characters (people, animals, things) appear?**
3. **Where and when does the poem take place?**
4. **What actions (physical or mental) are in your poem?**

TALK About It

If you have more characters in your poem than
you have team members, ask the players to
take two or more parts, using a different voice
for each character.

Script the Poem. After you have selected the poem you want to perform, make a copy for each person in your group. This will make it much easier to "script" the poem. (Scripting a poem means dividing it into speaking parts.) Let's imagine that your team has chosen to perform "I'm Glad," a short poem by an unknown author:

I'm Glad

I'm glad the sky is painted blue,
And the earth is painted green,
With such a lot of nice fresh air
All sandwiched in between.

You might think, "Four lines divided by four performers equals one line per performer. Simple!" But poetry is *not* simple mathematics!

A "Scripted" Poem ● Instead of dividing the lines by the number of actors, divide them according to the characters in the poem. Remember, characters can be people, places, things, or animals. In "I'm Glad," we find four *characters*: the sky, the air, the earth, and I (the narrator who tells the story).

Cast: 1 = Narrator
2 = The sky
3 = The earth
4 = The air

All:	"I'm Glad," author unknown
1:	I'm glad the sky is painted
2:	blue
1:	And the earth is painted
3:	green
1:	With such a lot of
4:	nice fresh air
2 & 3:	All sandwiched in between

Two Scripting Possibilities:

All:	"I'm Glad," author unknown
1:	I'm glad
2:	the sky is painted blue
1:	And
3:	the earth is painted green
1:	With such a lot of
4:	nice fresh air
2 & 3:	All sandwiched in between

4 **Score the Poem.** Next, your team must "score" its poem. (Scoring a poem simply means to name emotions [feelings] and motions [movements] for each line of poetry.) Scoring your poem will help you to understand and perform it better. Consider this familiar poem called "The 5:15" by an unknown author:

> The 5:15
> The peanut sat on the railroad track.
> Its heart was all aflutter.
> The 5:15 came rushing by —
> Toot! Toot!
> Peanut Butter!

A "Scored" Poem ● Here is one way to score this poem, which has been scripted for three characters:

> *Cast:* 1 = Peanut, 2 = Engineer, 3 = Bystander

	Line	Emotion	Motion
1:	The peanut sat on the railroad track	*(excited)*	sit on chair
1:	Its heart was all aflutter.	*(frightened)*	pat heart or bite nails
1:	The 5:15 came rushing by —	*(surprised)*	jump back as if to dodge passing train
2:	Toot! Toot!	*(threatening)*	raise and lower hand as if pulling chain of whistle
3:	Peanut Butter!	*(happy)*	pretend mouth is full of peanut butter

You don't need emotions and motions for every word or line. Sometimes you can simply tell the poem, letting the words stand on their own. Try to find a balance between telling and performing.

5 **Perform Your Poem.** After you have scripted and scored your poem, practise reading it out loud. You don't need a stage or special lights for your final performance. The front of the classroom will do just fine. (You can use simple costumes and props, if you want.)

Five Performance Tips

- **Stand and move with confidence.** Always stand up (or sit up) straight. Do not fidget. Standing (or sitting) tall will help you talk to your audience with confidence.

- **Face your audience.** As a rule, do not turn your back to the audience, even a little. It helps to think of your audience as one person (who happens to be very wide and hard of hearing).

- **Introduce the poem and the poet.** Before your performance, stand shoulder to shoulder facing the audience. As a team, using your clear, confident, outside voices, announce the title of the poem and then the poet's name. Then move quickly into your starting positions for the performance.

- **Use your "outside" voice.** Always speak clearly and loudly enough to be heard by *everyone*. Try to find a voice somewhere between soft-spoken and yelling. This clear, loud voice is your outside voice, the one you use while playing outside.

- **Exit quietly.** When your performance is over, pause for a moment, take a bow if you wish, then leave your performance space.

Now You Try It!

The following poem was written by a group of students. It is scripted for four people. Experiment with different ways of scripting and scoring this poem. (**SEE** pages 284–285).

The Salmon People

1 2 3 4:	I am salmon,
1:	I am fast;
2:	A fish that likes to swim in the past.
1 2 3 4:	I am going somewhere!
3:	To the place of my birth
4:	To the Adams River
1 2 3 4:	To the Salmon People who live in the ocean.
1:	I have magic wings that help me fly.
2:	I can swim through a river of stars.
3:	My skin is slippery like a wet bar of soap.
4:	My scales shine like fluorescent fingernails;
1 2 3 4:	Pink, orange, yellow, green, blue, and purple
1 2:	Salmon People have long gold and silver hair.
3 4:	Their skin is different colours;
1 2 3 4:	Mixed together like the rainbow.
1:	I need food.
2:	I'm going on a mission
2:	To survive.
3:	To talk to the people;
4:	Can the people help me?
1 2 3 4:	Be kind to the salmon.

Improving Viewing Skills

Becoming a Smart Viewer

According to a recent survey, Canadians watch an *average* of 22.8 hours of television a week. And that's the average. Some of watch as much as 40 hours of TV a week! Most of that time is spent watching entertainment (and commercials). The rest of it is spent getting information, either from the news or from educational specials.

Even if you spend very little time watching television, it's important for you to be a smart viewer. And that's just what this chapter can help you become!

As you watch television, it is shaping what you *know*, what you *believe*, and what you *buy*. You need to become an intelligent viewer — you need to know what to look for and what questions to ask.

Watching the News

Let's start with a sample news story. CGIP sends a camera person and a news reporter to Brown School to document your trip to a local pond. You've been studying pond life for weeks, and you can hardly wait to get out there to see and feel a *real* one. By 9:00 a.m. you're off. The day goes well, you *think*, and you're all excited because you know you'll see yourself on TV tonight.

Six o'clock comes, and you're sitting in front of the TV, hot dog and juice in hand — rah, rah — and before you know it…

THERE YOU ARE!

But guess what? The good TV folks didn't show you gently pulling your crayfish out of the pond and carefully drawing it; they showed you fooling around with Cary during one of those "off" moments. Instead, the news showed Devon doing what *he* was supposed to be doing! You're mad because you know very well they filmed *you* with the crayfish, too!

About It

The story you've just read teaches a simple lesson: All of us, from kids to camera people, report what *we* see and hear, and what *we* feel is most important. Sometimes we don't see the whole story. As long as we remember this, we can watch the news, or any TV program, intelligently.

Questioning the News

➤ *Is it complete?*

A news story must answer all the basic questions
(**5Ws and H**) about the event. It must tell...

Who was involved:	*Tom and Jerry, the class gerbils,*
What happened:	*escaped*
When it happened:	*last night.*
Where it happened:	*The cage is kept on the windowsill.*
Why it happened:	*When the janitor opened the window,*
How it Happened:	*the cage fell out the window, and its door came open. Tom and Jerry scrammed.*

➤ *Is it fair?*

It can be hard to decide when a news story is fair. The story
about the class studying pond life certainly didn't seem fair, at
least not to all the students. Here are some things to look for:

Sound Bites ● A sound bite is a short film clip of someone
speaking. Sometimes a sound bite is too short and doesn't tell the
whole story, or it makes the person look bad. Let's say you are
listening to a report on the two candidates for mayor of your town.
Are you seeing all of what each candidate said, or just a short part
of it? Do you think each candidate was treated fairly?

Equal Time ● Even though there is an *equal-time* law for
elections, this law doesn't have to be followed for news stories.
Let's say the story is about a tough new law against young
offenders. The story does not have to give equal time to people who
are for it *and* to people who are against it. But to be fair, it should.

Choice of Sources ● A fair story will include *reliable*
sources (people) who have different views on an issue. If a news
story uses the Minister of Justice as a source in favour of a tough
new youth crime law, and a convicted felon as a source against it,
is the story fair? Probably not.

What are a news reporter's responsibilities?
Is all the news you watch really news?
Which local TV station has the best newscast?

Watching Television Specials

Has your teacher ever asked you to watch a certain TV show? Maybe it was a special on the Canadian Space Program or the fall of the Berlin Wall. Television can "put you there" in ways that no other medium (books, magazines, etc.) can. However, even educational programs need to be viewed correctly.

Viewing Guidelines

✔ Before viewing, consider what you already know about the subject, and think of questions you would like answered.

✔ If your teacher gives you questions to answer during the show, make sure you understand them before you leave school.

✔ While watching the special, take a few notes — not only on the facts, but on how you feel about what you see.

✔ After the special, talk with somebody about it, or write about it in your journal.

Sample Journal Entry

Saturday, January 11, 1997
Lake Baykal The Deepest Lake in Russia

It's so deep and so cold, it's got life in it that's found nowhere else in the universe! That's because it was formed 25 million years ago. Here are some animals you can only find in Lake Baykal.
golomyanka and other kinds of fish
Baykal seal
It's beautiful and wild — 336 rivers flow into it, but only one flows out. It's frozen from January to May — that's a long time!

Improving Listening Skills

"Now Listen Carefully!"

Since this page and the next are about listening, maybe you could find a partner to read them out loud while you listen. But if that isn't possible, do the next best thing: continue reading.

Do you know that we spend more time listening than we do speaking, reading, and writing combined? Our ears make it possible for us to hear what is being said around us. But it is our minds that make it possible for us to *listen*. You see, listening is more than just hearing — it is thinking about what we hear. It is making sense of all the "noise" that comes at us 14 to 16 hours a day, seven days a week, week after week.

Good Listener Checklist

Because we are human, we don't always li[...]
listening?). We are easily distracted. We somet[...]
sometimes *hear* people when we should be *list*[...]
how can you become a better listener, both in [...]
Here's a whole page of suggestions. I hope they help!

✔ **Listen with a good attitude;** you'll learn more.

✔ **Listen with your ears *and* your eyes;** you'll hear more.

✔ **Listen for specific directions;** you'll know what you're supposed to do.

✔ **Listen for the main ideas;** you'll stay on track.

✔ **Listen for key words (like *first*, *second* or *before*, *after*);** you'll keep things in the right order.

✔ **Listen for the speaker's tone of voice;** you'll get the true meaning.

> A good listener is not only popular everywhere, but after a while he gets to know something.

✔ **Take notes or make drawings;** you'll remember things longer.

✔ **Think about what you hear;** you'll understand better if you relate ideas to different things you already know.

✔ **Picture what you hear;** you'll see things more clearly.

WRITE
About It

Write down questions about the things that aren't clear. Also, sum up everything in writing as a test of how well you listened.

Improving Your Thinking

Getting Organized

Thinking and Writing

Thinking Clearly

Getting Organized

Becoming a Better Thinker

All of us are thinkers. We think all the time (except maybe when we're sleeping). Because you are a student, you have to learn to think well. To think well, you have to be able to gather many different kinds of thoughts, or details, and organize them in the right way.

Then you have to use these organized thoughts to help you understand things better, solve problems, make decisions, and support your opinions.

That's what this section of your handbook is about: helping you become a better, more organized thinker.

Many of the ideas presented here will help you plan and organize your reports and other writing assignments.

Using Graphic Organizers

One very effective way to organize your thoughts is to use *graphic organizers*. (Graphic organizers are shapes created from lines, circles, and boxes.) When you are gathering ideas, you can use these shapes to help you collect and organize your details. Because you can *see* where each detail should go, it is much easier to keep your thoughts organized.

Collect Details ➤

If you are trying to collect details to describe something, you can draw a circle with lines or spokes around it. Write the name of the person or thing you want to describe in the circle (the key word). List the important details on the spokes around the circle.

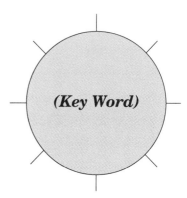

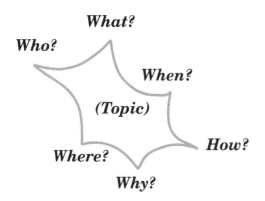

➤ Ask Questions

Another good way to organize your thoughts and details is to ask the 5Ws & H questions. You can use a web like the one shown here to help you see your answers.

Collect Information

When you need to collect and organize lots of information on a topic, you can use a "gathering grid." Simply draw a grid or chart with as many boxes as you need. Then label each box across the top and down the side to fit your topic. Fill in the grid as you collect your information. (**SEE** page 226 for a sample grid.)

Compare and Contrast ➤

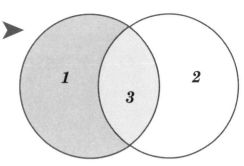

Venn Diagram

The design show here (called a Venn diagram) can be used to organize your thoughts when you need to compare or contrast two subjects.

Put the important details for one of these subjects in the area marked with a **1.** Put the details for the second subject in area **2.** In area **3,** list the details the two things have in common. Now you can clearly see the similarities and differences.

TAKE NOTE

When you want to compare, talk about the details in area **3.** When you want to contrast, talk about how the details in area **1** are different from the details in area **2.**

Outline ➤

Sometimes you will need to make an organized list of the details (facts, examples, reasons) you collect. One kind of list is the outline. Use it when you have lots of different ideas or topics that need organizing.

An outline also works well when you have a lot of notes or ideas that you need to organize for a report or speech. Simply put the topic at the top and organize your details underneath it.

(Topic)

I. _____
   A. _____
   B. _____
   C. _____

II. _____
   A. _____
   B. _____
   C. _____

Bright IDEA

Try to come up with graphic organizers of your own. Compare them with the ones your classmates have invented.

Becoming an Organized Thinker

Becoming a better, more organized thinker isn't easy — but it can be done. It simply takes time and a desire to improve. Here are some helpful guidelines to get you going.

1   **Be patient...** Don't expect quick, easy answers to every problem or challenge you face. Good thinking often takes time — time to plan, read, and listen.

2   **Set goals...** Think about what you can do now (*short-term goals*) and what you will have to do later (*long-term goals*). (*SEE* page 319.)

3   **Think logically...** Don't settle for the first answer that pops into your head. Look at all sides of a question; then support your thoughts with good reasons, examples, and facts. (*SEE* "Thinking Clearly" on pages 308-313.)

4   **Ask questions...** Ask questions about what you read, what you hear — even what you see! If you think you know what something is, then ask *why, who, when, where, how, how much, why not.*

5   **Think about your thinking...** Try to "watch" yourself as you think and work; then change the way you think if necessary (slow down, speed up, zoom in, back up).

6   **Write things down...** Writing can help you think more clearly. It can also help you discover things you didn't know you knew. It can even help you sort through your thoughts and do more with them than you ever imagined.

7   **Use graphic organizers...** Keep your thoughts organized using lists, outlines, or graphic organizer. (*SEE* pages 296-297.)

Your Basic Writing and Thinking Moves

The following chart shows you the kinds of "thinking moves" you can use to help you gather and organize your thoughts.

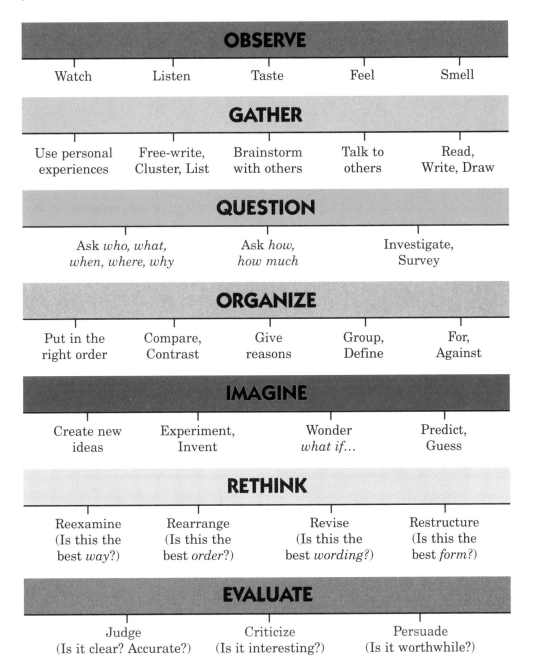

OBSERVE				
Watch	Listen	Taste	Feel	Smell

GATHER				
Use personal experiences	Free-write, Cluster, List	Brainstorm with others	Talk to others	Read, Write, Draw

QUESTION		
Ask *who, what, when, where, why*	Ask *how, how much*	Investigate, Survey

ORGANIZE				
Put in the right order	Compare, Contrast	Give reasons	Group, Define	For, Against

IMAGINE			
Create new ideas	Experiment, Invent	Wonder *what if...*	Predict, Guess

RETHINK			
Reexamine (Is this the best *way*?)	Rearrange (Is this the best *order*?)	Revise (Is this the best *wording*?)	Restructure (Is this the best *form*?)

EVALUATE		
Judge (Is it clear? Accurate?)	Criticize (Is it interesting?)	Persuade (Is it worthwhile?)

Thinking and Writing

Learning to Think

We go to school to learn how to read, how to write, how to speak. But before we can do any of these things — or at least do them well — we have to "learn" how to think. You will use many different kinds of thinking in school. Thinking is often divided into six general categories:

- ■ **Recalling**
- ■ **Understanding**
- ■ **Applying**
- ■ **Analyzing**
- ■ **Synthesizing**
- ■ **Evaluating**

An explanation of each of the six kinds of thinking follows. These explanations will help you understand the different kinds of thinking and how you can use them in your writing.

■ Recalling

The most basic type of thinking you do in school is **recalling** information. This is the type of thinking you do when you are asked to remember something you talked about in class or read about in a textbook. Because your teacher will expect you to recall the most important information, make sure that you listen and read carefully.

➤ Use Recall on Tests

When you answer test questions, you are *recalling* information. Let's say you are studying pollution in your science class. As one part of this unit, you read about acid rain, a serious pollution problem that is killing lakes around the world.

As a basic test question, your teacher might ask you to list five important facts that you have learned about this kind of pollution. The sample answer below shows the kind of information you might list (recall) to answer this test question.

Test Question: *List in complete sentences five important facts you have learned about acid rain.*

Answer

1. Acid rain is caused by pollution from cars and some electric-power plants.
2. When acid rain is still in clouds, it can blow far away from where the pollution started.
3. Acid rain kills plants and trees.
4. When acid rain falls on lakes and rivers, it kills fish.
5. The worst acid rain contains as much acid as lemon juice.

■ Understanding

Your teachers will often ask you to do more than just recall or make a list of what you remember about a topic. They will ask you to show that you **understand** the information well enough to talk or write about it.

➤ Read, Study, and Understand

To really *understand* information from a textbook, you must be a careful reader and take notes. Then, to test whether you understand the material you've read, do one of three things — summarize it in writing, review the main points out loud, or teach it to someone else. If you *can't* do at least one of these three, read it again.

➤ Write to Show Understanding

Understanding is also important when you work on paragraphs and essay test questions. Let's say your science teacher asks you to explain acid rain. Your teacher is really asking you to recall the important facts and details about this kind of pollution *and* show that you understand it by writing clearly about it. The paragraph below is a sample of what you might write. (Also **SEE** ages 330-331.)

Assignment: *In a paragraph, explain acid rain.*

Model Understanding Paragraph

Acid rain is a kind of pollution. It starts when chemicals from cars and power plants go into the air. In the atmosphere, the chemicals mix with the tiny drops of water that make up clouds. When rain falls from the clouds, the acid chemicals are in the rain. The acid kills plants, trees, and fish.

■ Applying

When you are asked to **apply** information, you are being asked to *use* what you've learned. If, for example, you have been learning to play an instrument, you may be asked to apply what you have learned by playing a scale or a short solo.

➤ Use What You've Learned

You will often be asked to *apply* what you have learned in school. Let's say that as part of a pollution unit, your science teacher hands you the following assignment:

Assignment: *Write a letter to a company in your area that might be causing pollution. Explain what you've learned about acid rain. Ask the company to explain to you what they are doing to prevent pollution at their plant.*

Model Letter

Dear Mr. Gray:

In school, I learned that power plants that make electric power by burning coal are a big cause of acid rain. Power plants release the chemicals that cause acid rain. The chemicals mix with clouds and can be blown far away, even to other countries, before the acid rain falls. When it falls, it can kill plants and animals.

I am worried that your power plant could be causing acid rain. Please write to me and tell me if your plant pollutes the air with the chemicals that cause acid rain. If so, please tell me what you are doing to stop polluting the air.

Sincerely,

■ Analyzing

As you get older, you will be asked to study information very carefully and in many different ways. This is called **analyzing**. When you analyze, ask yourself these three questions:

➤ Decide the Purpose

First: "What is the purpose of this assignment?" Is it to show how things are alike (comparing) or different (contrasting)? Is it to put similar ideas into groups (grouping)? Is it to give reasons (cause and effect)? Or is there another purpose?

➤ Select Facts and Details

Second: "Which facts and details are the right ones to use for this assignment?" Let's say the purpose of the assignment is to compare two planets you've been studying. You will want to select the *same kind* of information (facts and details) for both planets. Then you can make a comparison. (*SEE* page 297.)

➤ Organize the Facts and Details

Third: "How should the facts and details for this writing assignment be organized?" In order of importance? In time order (the order in which they happened)? In order of location (the order in which they are located)?

Assignment: *In a paragraph, discuss the causes of acid rain.*

Model Cause and Effect Paragraph

Acid rain is caused by air pollution. But not all air pollution causes acid rain. It is only caused by certain chemicals. When coal or gasoline is burned, chemicals called nitrogen oxides and sulphur dioxide are released into the air. They mix with the water droplets in clouds. When the water droplets fall as rain, the acid chemicals are still there. The acid in acid rain kills trees and fish.

■ Synthesizing

If your teacher were to stop in the middle of a story or an experiment and ask you what you think might happen next, you would be **synthesizing**. You would be using what you already know to create new information. You would be thinking like an artist, a songwriter, or an architect.

➤ Think About it

Suppose your teacher asks you to take the information you just learned in your pollution unit and do something unusual with it — something that will force people to think about it or look at it in a new way.

➤ Use a New Form

One thing you could do is use a different or creative kind of writing form. Instead of writing an ordinary paragraph, you could write a title-down paragraph (or a list poem). Or you could use one of the other forms of writing. (**SEE** pages 34-35.) By putting what you have learned into a new or an unusual form, you are forcing yourself (and your audience) to look at things differently. You are *synthesizing* information.

Title-Down Paragraph: **ACID RAIN**

Acid rain starts with air pollution.
Cards are one source of air pollution that causes acid rain.
Industry is another source of air pollution that causes acid rain.
Damage from acid rain lasts for years.

Rain that is polluted kills plants and animals.
Acid snow is just as harmful as acid rain.
In Canada, forests and lakes are dying from acid rain caused by
    industry.
Nitrogen oxides are one group of chemicals that cause acid rain.

■ Evaluating

Evaluating is one of the most advanced levels of thinking and writing you will be asked to use. When your teachers ask you to evaluate, they are asking you to judge or defend what you have learned. It's the kind of thinking a judge or lawyer has to do.

➤ Study the Subject

When you are asked to evaluate information, you are being asked to think like an expert. To become an expert, you must know all the important facts and details on the topic. You must know its good and bad points, its strengths and weaknesses.

➤ Write an Evaluation

To write an evaluation, start with a sentence that tells the reader how you feel about the subject. Then add facts and details that prove that your ideas are correct.

Let's say that as part of that unit on pollution, you are asked to *evaluate* the latest attempts to stop acid rain. After studying your notes and reading more on the subject, you feel you have enough information. The following paragraph is an example of what you might write for this assignment.

Assignment: *Evaluate the latest attempts to stop acid rain.*

Model Evaluating Paragraph

The latest attempts to stop acid rain are not strong enough. In most places, the main chemical in acid rain is sulphur, which forms a gas (sulphur dioxide) when it is burned at electric-power plants. Most new power plants must have "scrubbers" that keep sulphur from getting into the air, preventing acid rain. But studies show that unless more plants are required to use scrubbers, acid rain will keep getting worse.

Guidelines for Thinking and Writing

If you are asked to...	you should be ready to...
Recall *list* *label* *cluster* *name* *identify* *define* *memorize*	**Remember what you've learned** ■ by listing important details ■ by defining terms ■ by clustering information
Understand *review* *show* *summarize* *explain* *describe*	**Show that you understand what you've learned** ■ by giving examples ■ by explaining how something words
Apply *select* *choose* *organize* *illustrate* *demonstrate* *locate*	**Use what you've learned** ■ to select the most important details ■ to organize information ■ to make something work
Analyze *compare* *classify* *contrast* *divide* *tell why* *map* *break down* *examine*	**Examine material closely to understand it better** ■ by making connections between this and other things ■ by studying cause and effect
Synthesize *combine* *develop* *invent* *design* *compose* *create* *predict* *imagine*	**Reshape material into a new form** ■ by inventing a better way of doing something ■ by predicting what will happen next
Evaluate *judge* *rate* *recommend* *measure* *persuade* *argue* *convince*	**Judge the worth of the material** ■ by pointing out its strengths and weaknesses ■ by evaluating its clearness, accuracy, value, etc.

Thinking Clearly

Use Your Brain!

You don't have to *be* a brain to *use* your brain. In fact, as you read this page, you are already using your brain. You are observing, comparing, analyzing, evaluating, and solving problems. Plus, you've been using these skills sine you were very young, without even "thinking" about it.

So, even though you've been practising since you were very young, you will want to know how you can become an even better thinker — a clearer thinker. You can do it by...

- using facts and opinions correctly,
- avoiding fuzzy thinking,
- making good decisions,
- and solving problems.

This chapter will help you better understand and practise these four important thinking skills.

Why think? Thinking saves time, prevents accidents, leads to success, and helps you figure things out — that's why.

Using Facts and Opinions Correctly

An **opinion** is what someone *believes* is true. A **fact** is a statement that can be *proven* to be true. Look at the difference between the opinion and the facts below. The opinion states a personal belief about paper recycling. The facts are specific and can be proven. (Facts can be used to support an opinion.)

> *Opinion:* Recycling paper should be required by law.
>
> *Fact:* If paper is not recycled, trees must be cut down to make more paper.
>
> *Fact:* We are running out of places to dump our garbage, and much of our garbage is paper.

➤ Write an Opinion Statement

Once you've formed an opinion in your mind, you must word it well so that others will understand what you are saying. Follow the simple recipe below to help you write a good opinion statement.

> *Recipe:* A specific subject (*recycling paper*) + your specific opinion or feeling (*should be required by law*) = a good opinion statement.

Opinions that include strong words such as *all, best, every, never,* or *worst* are difficult to support. (Recycling *all* paper should be required by law.)

➤ Support Your Opinion

When you support or back up your opinion, make sure you use clear, provable facts. Otherwise, your reader probably won't believe you. Let's say you are supporting the opinion that paper recycling should be required by law. Look at the difference between the following ideas:

> *Provable Fact:* Recycling paper would save trees.
>
> *Not a Provable Fact:* Recycling paper would help everyone.

Avoiding Fuzzy Thinking

When you're trying to get others to agree with you, it's important to think clearly, and stick to the facts! There's really no room for fuzzy thinking. Here are some suggestions to help you keep your thinking clear.

Don't make statements that jump to conclusions.

"Because ozone is a gas found in smog, ozone is bad."

Discussion: This statement jumps to a conclusion. It says that ozone is bad because it is part of smog, which is bad. But ozone can be good. The natural ozone in the atmosphere protects the earth from the sun's rays.

Don't make statements that make things seem worse — or better — than they are.

"Scientists in Canada have discovered many ways to recycle millions of used automobile tires into things we can use."

Discussion: This statement makes things sound better than they really are. It might make you think that most tires are recycled into useful products. But Canadians throw away 26 million tires each year, and only about 3 million of them are actually recycled. Old tires can be used for things such as floor mats and soles for sandals, but recycling them is expensive and uses a lot of energy.

Don't make statements that are half-truths.

"Acid rain is 2000 times more acidic than unpolluted rain."

Discussion: This statement makes it sound like *all* acid rain is 2000 times more acidic than unpolluted rain. Some is, but some is only 10 times more acidic. The statement makes part of the truth sound like the whole truth.

Don't make statements just because most people agree with them.

"Acid rain is not a bad problem, because most people I talked to don't think it is."

Discussion: This statement is based on the idea that if most people believe something, it must be true. But "most people" can be wrong. They may not know how bad acid rain really is.

Don't make statements that compare things that aren't really like each other.

"When acid rain falls, it's like liquid fire falling on the earth."

Discussion: This statement compares acid rain to something that is really much worse. The worst acid rain is about as acidic as lemon juice. That's bad for the earth, but not as bad as liquid fire!

Don't make statements that are based on feelings, not on facts.

"All big factories should be shut down because they cause air pollution."

Discussion: This statement is based on feelings, and there are no facts to back it up. First, not all big factories cause air pollution. Second, there are other ways to stop air pollution besides shutting down factories.

MINI LESSON After you've read each of the six **don't** statements, go back and read them again. Then rewrite each of the six samples so that they are no longer fuzzy. Compare answers with your classmates.

Making Good Decisions

We make decisions every day. We decide what to wear to school, where to sit at lunch, what book to read for our next report. Many of these decisions can be made with very little planning.

Other decisions are much more difficult and take a good deal of time and thought. When you face a tough decision, here are some guidelines you can use:

1. Define your goals.
   ❏ What are you trying to figure out or accomplish?
   ❏ What decision do you have to make?

2. Make a list of your options or choices.
   ❏ What are some of the things you could do?

3. Study your options.
   ❏ Look carefully at each option.
   ❏ What are the pluses and minuses of each?

4. Rank the options.
   ❏ Put your options in order from best to worst, from easiest to most difficult, from quickest to longest, etc.

5. Choose the best option.
   ❏ Consider all your options; then choose the best one.

 The best option for you might not be the best option for someone else. Each person and each situation is different.

6. Review all the steps.
   ❏ Let some time pass. Then go through the process again to see if your thinking has changed.

Solving Problems

Just like doctors, lawyers, and auto mechanics, you have to solve problems every day. Some are big problems; some are small. And, like anyone else, you will need a plan for solving these problems. First, you will need to identify the problem. Next, you will need to collect information about the problem, think of possible solutions, and choose the best one.

Sometimes you do all of this in a split second; other times, it can take you days or even weeks to solve a problem. For these harder problems, here are some guidelines you can follow:

1. Identify or name the problem.

- ❏ What is the problem?

2. Collect information.

- ❏ What exactly is wrong or needs to be done?
- ❏ What caused the problem?

3. Think of possible solutions.

- ❏ What can be done right now?
- ❏ What can be done a little at a time?

4. Try out the solutions.

- ❏ Try to imagine each solution in action.
- ❏ Use trial and error to test your solutions if you can.

5. Choose the best solution.

- ❏ Think of what's best for others as well as for you.
- ❏ Put your plan into action.

6. Evaluate the result.

- ❏ If you had it to do over again, would you choose the same solution?

Improving Your Learning Skills

Writing as a Learning Tool

Completing Assignments

Working in Groups

Taking Tests

Keeping Good Notes

Writing as a Learning Tool

Dear Students,

Before you read the following pages, I would like to share a few thoughts with you about writing... and how you can use writing to learn.

When I first learned to write, I understood that it was important for communicating with others — friends, teachers, relatives. But now, after many years of writing and publishing books, I see that my writing helps me figure things out, find and organize my thoughts, and keep in touch with the outside world.

As a teacher and an author, I've learned this for myself, and as a father, I've enjoyed watching my daughters learn the same thing. The following stories may explain what I mean, and also help you use **writing as a learning tool**.

Sincerely

Toby Fulwiler

Megan's Story...

One day, when I was reading the newspaper, my eldest daughter, Megan, asked me, "Dad, how do you make a speech?" She was supposed to give a short speech to her class explaining how to do something, and she wanted to explain how to stencil. (She had been helping her mother stencil heart designs.)

Make a List

I suggested that she first make a list of all the things she wanted to tell about stencilling. "Just list what comes to mind," I said. Here's what she came up with:

> what stencilling is used for
> where you can buy supplies
> the origin of stencilling
> dictionary definition
> show sample
> make one

First Things First

A good list, I thought, and asked her another question. "In what order do you want to say these things?" Here is what she wrote:

> dictionary definition
> what stencilling is used for
> the origin of stencilling
> show sample
> make one
> where you can buy supplies

When Megan wrote her fist list, ideas spilled out of her head. As soon as she saw her ideas on paper, she saw how she could rearrange them. The first list made the second list possible!

Because writing, unlike speaking, stays put, it lets you see your thinking *outside* of your head. You can look at your ideas; you can do something with them.

Anna's Story...

Megan was the reader and writer in the family, but Anna, my second daughter, thought of herself as a nonwriter. As it turns out, Anna actually was a writer — an *undercover* writer.

One day Anna and I were watching a TV show, but she wasn't really paying attention. Instead, she was carefully unfolding small, crumpled sheets of paper and arranging them on her lap.

An "Undercover" Writer

I asked, *"What are you doing?"*

Without looking up, she replied, "Sorting my notes."

"What notes?"

"The ones from school."

"What do you mean?"

"The notes I get from my friends."

"How many do you have?"

She stopping unfolding and counted each sheet: "One hundred and twelve," she said.

"Wow! That's a lot, and you've only been in school a few weeks. What are they about?"

"Oh, you know, finding out what people are doing or who they're fighting with. I'm organizing them."

Writing for Real Reasons

Of course, Anna *wrote* notes, too, and these undercover notes taught her a lot. Without realizing it, she understood that writing means connecting with real people (her friends) for real reasons. The same was true for Megan. Once she listed ideas about her subject, her speech-making job became easier, and her stencil-making speech took shape.

WRITE
About It

Try some "real" writing yourself. Each day for a month, write out your ideas for doing tomorrow's school assignments. See if this doesn't help you do even better assignments the next day.

Completing Assignments

Learning Made Easier

How do you learn? Is learning easy for you? Do you sometimes wish it could be easier? Well, maybe we can help. Understanding *how* you learn can help you become a better learner.

When it comes to learning in school, there are three pieces to the puzzle: you, your teachers, and your texts.

Your teachers start the learning process by introducing a unit of study. Your texts (this includes books, CDs, videos, etc.) give you the information for the unit. Your job is to read and study this material until you become the best student you can be.

Let's Get Started!

We'll help you do your job by showing you how to set goals, manage your time, and complete your assignments. It's as easy as

1, 2, 3!

Setting Goals

Before you started school, you set goals for yourself all the time — like learning to ride a bike or dribble a basketball.

Now, years later, you're still setting goals — learning to play an instrument, earning money to buy something, turning your next assignment in on time. Setting goals for yourself and reaching them is what growing up is all about.

No one plans to fail; they just fail to plan.

Some Helpful Guidelines

1 Be realistic. Learn to set realistic goals for yourself. Becoming the editor of your school newspaper, although a big challenge, is a realistic aim. But can you learn to play the guitar in a day? Probably not. It's better to do some things step-by-step. For example, you might plan to do one part of a science project each day for a week. Or, each time you play in a sport, you might try to improve just one specific skill.

2 Work toward your goal. Continue working toward your goal — no matter what happens! If you choose to keep a journal, set aside a specific time each day to write in it. If you want to improve in a certain sport, set up a time to talk to your coach or an older friend about improving your skills.

TAKE NOTE Remember, there will be times when you won't be able to write or practise — when you are sick, for instance. Find another time to make it up.

3 Reward yourself. When you reach one of your goals, reward yourself in some small way. Let's say you've decided to keep a daily journal for the whole school year. When you have faithfully written in your journal every day for two weeks, do something special, or tell a parent or teacher. They'll be proud of you!

Managing Your Time

Are you a *procrastinator*? Do you sometimes put off doing things that you should do? Well, the truth is, we all procrastinate at times. But if you put things off all the time, then you need to learn about time management.

Steps in the Process

1 **Make a daily list.** Write down things you need to do today, perhaps in a small spiral notebook. Number your "To Do" list from the most important to the least important, and cross each one off as you complete it.

2 **Keep a weekly schedule.** A weekly planner shows you what you have to do during the week. It helps you plan your study time and your fun time. Use the following model or design your own.

WEEKLY PLANNER

Day	Assignment	Due Date	Activities	Study Time	Fun Time
Monday					
Tuesday					

Figure out what time of the day you think and work best. Use this time for your toughest assignments and most important work.

3 **Turn big jobs into little ones.** When you have a big assignment to do, it can seem really overwhelming. One way to make it seem easier is to turn it into smaller jobs. Figure out how many days you have to complete the assignment, and how much you need to do each day. Working 15 minutes a day for two weeks beats two or three hour of work the night before your project is due.

Doing the Assignments

1 Plan ahead.

- First of all, be sure you know exactly what your assignment is, and when you have to turn it in.
- Decide how much time you'll need to complete your assignment. Then, set aside study time in your daily schedule to get it done.
- Plan when and where you will do your assignment. This should be a quiet place where you can work without interruptions. (Ask your family to "hold your calls.")

2 Get off to a good start.

- Gather all the materials you will need to complete your assignment (paper, pens, folders, journal, notebook, handouts, dictionary, handbook).
- Read over all your teacher's directions so that you know exactly what you have to do for the assignment.
- Set a goal for yourself to get a certain amount of the assignment done before you take a break. Stick to that plan!

3 Get the job done.

- Use a study-reading strategy to help you complete your reading and studying. (**SEE** pages 238-242 in "Using Reading Strategies.")
- Keep an "Ask the Teacher" list for things you don't understand.
- Make sure your work is neat and doesn't contain any careless errors. Turn it in on time.

Working in Groups

Listening, cooperating, and clarifying are often called "people skills" because they help people work and learn better in groups.

Making Your Group Work

What was it like the last time you worked in a group? Did your teacher ask you to work with other students in the class? Did you work with a group of kids in the neighbourhood or at a club meeting? Did you have a good time? Did you accomplish something?

Getting Started

Working in a group can be fun if everyone gets along and gets the job done. In this chapter, we'll look at how you can use "people skills" to help make your next group a success. You can begin by *making a plan*.

Making a Plan

Every job you do should begin with a plan. Your group's task is no different. Members should ask themselves these questions:

- What is our task or assignment?
- What do we need to do in order to accomplish this task?
- What job or jobs will each group member do?
- What deadlines must we meet?

Try using an outline like the one below to help your group make its plan. Remember to share ideas and listen carefully to one another. Be sure everyone agrees with the plan and is willing to do the jobs assigned to them.

Group Plan

A. Our task is _____
(Is it to solve a problem, answer questions, research a topic?)

B. Things we need to do:

1. _____
2. _____
3. _____
(Add more lines if you need them.)

C. Jobs for each group member:

Name _____ Job _____
Name _____ Job _____
Name _____ Job _____
(Some sample jobs: writer or recorder, researcher, artist, coordinator)

D. This is our schedule:

By this date _____ , we will have this done:_____
By this date _____ , we will have this done:_____

Skills for Listening

Listening is important when you work in groups. People can only work together if they listen to one another. Imagine a group of fire fighters at a huge fire. If they didn't listen to one another, they could never cooperate well enough to put out the fire.

➤ **Just listen.** Remember, listening means *thinking about* what is being said. So, you can't truly listen and do something else at the same time. Don't draw pictures, write notes to your friends, or make animals out of paper clips while you're listening.

➤ **Listen actively.** You'll have to try hard to keep your mind on what's being said. It's natural for your mind to wander. Because you can think faster than people can talk, your mind races ahead and gets off the track. To stay on track, do the following:

■ **Look at the person who is speaking.**
This works because your mind thinks about what your eyes see.

■ **Listen for key words and phrases.**
For example: "The only solution is…"
or "Here's what I think we should do."

■ **Write down a few notes.**
It's not the same as writing notes to your friends, because you're writing about what's being said.

➤ **Ask questions.** If you don't understand something, ask about it. But don't interrupt the person who is speaking unless you're really lost. Wait until she or he is finished. Then ask a good, clear question such as, "Karen, you're saying we should do a report instead of making a model, because a report will be easier — right?"

THINK IT OVER

Listening is not as easy as it sounds!
To **hear**, you need only your ears.
To **listen**, you need your ears *and* your mind.

Skills for Cooperating

Cooperating means working with others to reach a shared goal.

➤ **Give your ideas and opinions.** It's important to let other group members know what you think. When you like someone's idea, say so! When you don't, it's okay to say so. But don't say, "That's a stupid idea!" Say, "I don't think that will work *because*..." (When you give your opinion, you should give your reasons, too.)

➤ **Be willing to change your opinions.** Listen to other opinions with an open mind. Remember, when you work with a group, you are trying to reach a decision everyone agrees with.

➤ **Don't get personal.** Try not to criticize or say something too personal. And if you hear a personal comment, remind the speaker that this is a group project and everyone needs to work together.

Skills for Clarifying

Clarifying means "clearing up." If someone in the group is confused, the group can't work together toward the goal. Here's how you can help clear up confusion:

➤ **Remember your goal.** Remind everybody what the group's goal is. Also, suggest steps that will help you reach the goal. For example: "First, let's decide whether to do a report or make a model. Then let's decide what each person's job will be."

➤ **Re-explain it.** If someone doesn't understand something, ask if anyone else in the group can think of a new way to explain it.

➤ **Stay on track.** Also, if someone gets off track, say something as simple as, "I think we should get back to the main point."

Making a Group Decision

Successful groups make decisions by *consensus*. *Reaching a consensus* means getting everyone in the group to agree with the decision. How do you get everyone to agree? Here are some tips:

Reaching a Consensus

- Ask everyone in the group for ideas about a certain problem, and listen while they explain them.
- Discuss each idea and how it will (or won't) help solve the problem.
- Select the idea everyone agrees will help the most.
- If more than one idea is selected, try to combine these ideas into one plan, a plan everyone can agree on.

THINK IT OVER

Remember, to reach a consensus, you must get everyone to agree with a group decision. That doesn't mean that everyone thinks it's the *best* idea; it means that it is the idea that everyone in the group agrees to accept.

Evaluating Your Work

Well, how did your group do? The proof that your group *succeeded* is a *successful* product. Before you hand in your assignment, judge the work your group accomplished. You can do this by having everyone answer and discuss these questions:

- Does our final product meet all the requirements of the assignment?
- Did group members do their jobs and contribute to the final product?
- Are we proud to say that this is our product?

If you have to answer "no" to any of these questions, you may want to go back and revise your work. Then answer the questions again.

Bright IDEA

Group Sharing

One kind of group work you'll do in school is "group sharing." One of the most common topics for group sharing is books you have read. Here are some guidelines to help you share with your group.

Before You Begin: Make a list of the things you plan to say about the book. Here are some ideas:

The Plot

What events stand out in your mind? Why?

What parts of the story remind you of your own life? In what way?

What other stories is this one like?

The Characters

Who are your favourite characters?

Do any of the characters remind you of people you know?

Overall Effect

Do you think the title fits the book?

What is the author trying to tell the reader about life?

Who else should read this book?

Helpful Hint After you have told a little about your book, you might actually read your favourite part to the group.

As You Share: Get into small groups (no more than six) and sit facing each other. Decide who's going to start.

- Listen carefully to one another and write down your reactions and questions.
- Add to what the others say about the book. Make sure you share your personal thoughts about the book as well.

Taking Tests

Getting Your Act Together

You're having a test? Well, it had to happen sooner or later! Taking a test is a good way for you — and your teacher — to find out what you have learned. (And what you haven't learned!) But tests don't have to be a big deal. If you follow these two simple rules, you'll do just fine: **be prepared** and **pay attention**.

Test-Taking Strategies

On the following pages, you'll find lots of good strategies and hints for helping you do your best on tests. There are hints for objective tests, hints for essay tests, and hints to help you remember things better. We hope they help!

> **To do well on tests, you must do well in class. You must organize yourself, your time, and your work — from the very first day.**

Preparing for the Test

Ask questions...

- What will be on the test? (Ask your teacher for examples.)
- What kind of test will it be? (Multiple choice? Essay?)

Organize your notes...

- Reread your class notes carefully. (Get any notes or materials you may have missed.)
- Rewrite your most important notes or put them on note cards.

Review for the test...

- Skim the lessons in your textbook. (Also look over old quizzes and worksheets.)
- Recite difficult material out loud as you review.

 Use lists, diagrams, rhymes, or any other special memory aids. (**SEE** pages 334-335.)

Taking the Test

Listen attentively...

- Listen carefully to your teacher. How much time will you have? Can you use your notes, a dictionary, or your handbook?

Read carefully...

- Skim the whole test quickly, so you know which questions will take the most time.
- Then go back and read the directions carefully. Be on the lookout for words like *always, only, all,* and *never.*
- Don't spend too much time on any one question.

Check closely...

- Double-check to be sure you have answered all the questions. (Check each answer if you have time.)
- Ask your teacher about any questions that still confuse you.

The Essay Test

When you answer an essay question, you are doing more than just writing. You are reading, thinking, organizing — *and* writing. Here are some suggestions to help you improve your essay answers.

Understanding the Essay Test Question

Your essay answer will be much better and clearer if you take the time to read before you write. The first step is to read the question carefully, at least twice, to be sure you understand what is being asked.

Pay special attention to the "key words" that are found in every essay question. These key words will tell you what kind of thinking and writing you'll need to do to answer the question correctly.

Key Words

Compare/contrast ● (*Compare and contrast* the water quality before and after the chemical plant moved to our town.) To *compare*, you should use examples to show how two things are alike in several ways. To *contrast*, you show how they are different.

Define ● (*Define* ultraviolet light.) To *define*, you must tell what the word or subject in the question means. You do this by showing just what this thing is, and what it does.

Describe ● (*Describe* the sun's spectrum.) To *describe*, you must tell how something or someone looks, feels, sounds, etc.

Explain ● (*Explain* how photosynthesis works.) To *explain*, you must tell how something happens or show how something works (step-by-step).

List ● (*List* why you think Canada is the best place in the world to live.) To *list*, you must include a number of examples, reasons, or other details, in list form.

Prove ● (*Prove* that Canada produces the best hockey players in the world.) To *prove*, you must present facts and details (proof) showing clearly that something is true.

Planning and Writing the Essay Answer

1 Reword the question. After you've read the question carefully, you can change it into the first sentence of your answer. This is easy... all you need to do is drop the key word and rearrange the remaining words into a topic sentence. (Sometimes you may need to add words, too.)

Question: *List* three reasons why the Stanley Steamer was so popular in Canada in the early 1900s.

Topic Sentence: *The Stanley Steamer was one of the most popular cars in Canada during the 1900s for three reasons.*

TAKE NOTE The question was changed into a topic sentence by dropping the key word (*list*) and arranging the rest of the words into a sentence.

2 Organize the main points. Put all the details in the best order before you start writing your answer.

> 1. *Stanley Steamers were popular cars.*
>   A. *Inexpensive to operate.*
>   B. *Quiet and smooth-running.*
>   C. *Easy to drive.*

3 Write your essay answer. Your first sentence will be your topic sentence. The other sentences will add the information you need to make your answer clear and complete. Use connecting words to make sure your answer reads smoothly. Double-check your answer, by rereading the question and your notes or outlines, to be sure you included everything you needed to.

> *The Stanley Steamer was one of the most popular cars in Canada during the early 1900s for three reasons. Because they used inexpensive kerosene to heat water and produce steam, these cars were very cheap to run. They were quiet, smooth-running machines that produced no smells or vibrations. Since they had no gears to shift, they were easy to operate. All the driver had to do was release the handbrake and push the throttle lever.*

The Objective Test

To really shine on an objective test, keep the following hints in mind as you take the test.

TRUE/FALSE TEST

➤ Read the entire question before answering. For an answer to be true, the *entire answer* must be true. If only part of it is true, you must choose false.

➤ Watch for words like *all, every, always, never.* Statements with these words in them are often false.

Questions: Read carefully each sample true/false question below. Then decide how you would answer each.

_____ 1. Plastic can never be recycled.

_____ 2. All plastic can be recycled.

_____ 3. Vinyl is a kind of plastic used to make tires.

Answers: All are false. Some plastic — but not *all* — can be recycled. In number 3, the first half is true (vinyl is a kind of plastic), but vinyl is *not* used to make tires.

MATCHING TEST

➤ Before you make any matches, read both lists quickly.

➤ Check off each answer as you make your match, unless you are told that you might need to use an answer more than once.

Questions: Match the product (on the left) to the recycled material that it is made from (on the right).

_____ Asphalt   a. Motor oil

_____ Mulch for plants   b. Christmas trees

_____ Motor oil   c. Tires

Answers: (c) Asphalt, (b) Mulch, (a) Motor oil

MULTIPLE CHOICE TEST

➤ Read the directions carefully to see if you are looking for the *correct* answer or the *best* answer.

➤ Answer each question in your mind *before* looking at the choices. Then read *all* the choices before answering.

TAKE NOTE Look for negative words like *not, never, except, unless.* They can change the entire meaning of the question.

Questions: Read the following questions carefully. How would you answer each?

1. Plastic can never be recycled to make
   (a) packaging (b) park benches (c) tires

2. Motor oil can't be recycled except to make
   (a) tires (b) plastic jars (c) motor oil

Answers: 1. (c) Plastic is *never* recycled to make tires. 2. (c) Motor oil *can't* be recycled except to make motor oil.

FILL IN THE BLANKS

➤ Count the number of blanks in each question. It could tell you the number of words that are needed in your answer.

Questions: Read the statements below. Can you predict the kinds of words that would probably fit in each blank?

1. Paper makes up about _____ of our garbage.

2. _____ makes up about 1/3 of our garbage.

3. _____ and _____ cannot be recycled, even though they are made from paper.

Answers: 1. 41% *(a percentage or fraction)* 2. packaging *(a general noun)* 3. juice cartons, pet-food bags *(specific nouns)*

REMEMBERING for Tests

Knowing how to take a test is important — remembering all the material you covered on the test is even more important. Luckily, there are some tricks you can use that will help you improve your memory. Here are a few you can begin using immediately!

Use Maps or Organizers ● A map is a drawing made up of circles, lines, and other shapes to help you organize your thoughts. (**SEE** pages 296-297.)

Use Acronyms ● Acronyms are words made up of the first letters of a title or a group of words. NATO, for example, is an acronym for North Atlantic Treaty Organization. To help you remember things better, you can create your own acronyms.

> *HOMES... Huron, Ontario, Michigan, Erie, Superior*
> (the Great Lakes)

> *ROY G. BIV... Red, Orange, Yellow, Green, Blue, Indigo, Violet*
> (the colours of the rainbow)

Use Poems or Songs ● Sometimes a simple (even silly) song or poem can help you remember things. Using a familiar tune or poem, substitute information to be learned. Do you remember any of these?

A B C D E F G H I

i before e, except after c...
In 1492, Columbus sailed the ocean blue.

Talk to Others ● It may seem too simple to help much, but talking to others about things you need to remember can be very helpful. Here are some of the ways you can talk and learn.

- *Form a study group.*
- *Teach what you need to learn to someone else.*
- *Recite what you need to remember out loud.*
- *Ask questions.*

Draw or Visualize ● Use drawings or pictures in your mind to help you remember. Here's an example of a drawing used to help remember prepositions. (No matter where you put a balloon, you should be able to think of a preposition to tell you where it's located.)

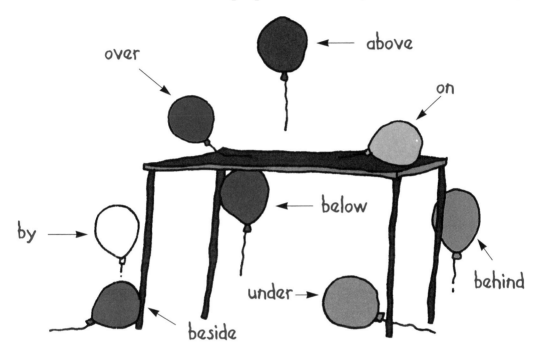

Rewrite It ● There are many different ways you can use writing to help you learn and remember. Here are just a few:

Write about it in a journal or learning log. (*SEE* pages 338-339 for more suggestions.)

Write down what you need to remember and hang it in front of you like a poster on the wall.

Note cards can be carried around and used like flash cards to drill yourself throughout the day.

Keeping Good Notes

A Plan of Action!

If you were told to get bagels, orange juice, a dozen eggs, a litre of milk, and a bag of popcorn at the store, you *might* remember everything. If you had a list handed to you, remembering would be a lot easier. And, if *you* wrote the list, you might not even need to look at it once you got to the store. That's how powerful writing is as a learning tool.

Don't *Just* Write

Note taking is a very important writing and learning tool. But it's not just writing down everything you hear — it's listening carefully and writing down *just* the important ideas. That's what being a good note taker is all about.

To get started, all you need is a notebook and some helpful hints.

If you get the notebook, we'll provide the hints!

> *Being able to take good notes is a wonderful skill, one you'll use more and more throughout your school years.*

Guidelines for Improving Note-taking Skills

The guidelines that follow will help you improve your note-taking skills. Read and follow each hint carefully. (**SEE** "Improving Listening Skills" on pages 292-293 for more suggestions.)

Pay attention!

1. Listen carefully.
2. Put the date and subject at the top of each page.
3. Write neatly and quickly!

Be brief!

1. Write down just the important ideas — **not** every single word.
2. Use abbreviations and symbols (#, $, &, =).
3. Summarize what is put on the board or overhead projector.
4. Draw pictures if they make the ideas clearer.

Be organized!

1. Use numbers or words to help organize your notes (1st, 2nd, before, after).
2. Circle words you have questions about.
3. Read over your notes; recopy those that are hard to read.
4. Use a **pen** or **marker** to highlight the main points.

Keeping a Learning Log

One kind of notebook is called a **learning log**. A learning log is a place for you to write down your thoughts and feelings about a subject. It is also a place to write questions you may have about a subject, to write reactions to reading assignments, to keep track of new vocabulary words, or to write whatever else you want.

The following guidelines will help you begin your own learning lot. It will work best if you write freely and use your own words.

1 **Divide Your Notebook:** Divide your notebook into sections for each subject you would like to write about. Write the date each time you make an entry.

2 **Plan to Write:** Set aside a time for your writing. Plan to spend more time writing about a subject that is especially tough for you.

3 **Write Nonstop:** Write in short, nonstop bursts. See if you can "get it all down" without stopping. Some writings will take only 3–5 minutes to finish, but others will take longer. Don't stop until you've written down all your thoughts.

Sample Response to a Class Discussion

Jan. 6, 1997

What a crazy world! We want big factories to provide good jobs. We want lots of heat and light in our homes, and we love to ride around in our cars. But scientists say that the acid rain produced by factories, power plants, and cars may be wrecking our buildings and highways. And what's really bad is that this acid rain is also hurting our lakes, streams, and rivers. Many are just dead bodies of water. So should people give up jobs and cars? Should we ... ?

More Learning Log Activities

Here are some other ideas for keeping a learning log. Try them all! Then decide which ones work best for you.

First Thoughts ● Make a list of key words that come to mind after a lesson. These key words will help you focus on the most important ideas.

Nutshelling ● Have you ever heard the phrase "in a nutshell"? It means you say a lot in a few words. Try *nutshelling*: In one sentence, write the meaning of an important class discussion or a chapter you have read.

Stop 'n' Write ● Stop whatever you are studying and write about it. This is a quick way to be sure your mind is on your work.

Notes to the Teacher ● Jot down any questions you may have about the subject and give them to your teacher before or after class. Ask your teacher to react to your questions.

Clustering ● If you already use clustering, you know how valuable it can be to help you explore your thoughts about a subject. It is also a good activity to use in a learning log. (***SEE*** page 26.)

Unsent Letters ● Write a letter to any person on a topic related to the subject. Writing a letter will help you think about the topic in a very personal way.

Draw ● You can even use your learning log to draw or illustrate something you learned or thought about in class.

Bright IDEA

You can also use your learning log to check your progress in your subjects. Are you doing well in all areas (reading and understanding, daily assignments, quizzes)? What needs improving? What can you do to improve?

Proofreader's Guide: Check It Out!

Writers Express

THESAURUS

Check It Out!

MARKING PUNCTUATION

Period

01 ▶ A **period** is used to end a sentence. It is also used after initials, after abbreviations, and as a decimal point.

02 ▶ **At the End of a Sentence**

A period is used at the end of sentences making statements or requests.

My mother has a secret recipe for chocolate chip cookies. (statement)

Please pass the cookies. (request)

03 After an Initial

Place a period after an initial in a person's name.

K.C. Irving

Michael J. Fox

04 As a Decimal

Use a period as a decimal point and to separate dollars and cents.

Robert is 99.9 percent sure that it costs $2.50 to get into the movies today.

05 After Abbreviations

A period is placed after each part of an abbreviation.

Mr. Mrs. Ms. Dr. Ph.D.

06 After Final Abbreviations

Only one period should be used at the end of the sentence when an abbreviation is the last word.

When Pina is nervous, she bites her nails, wiggles her thumbs, taps her toes, etc.

Ellipsis

07

An **ellipsis** (three periods) may be used to show omitted words or sentences or to indicate a pause in dialogue.

Tip: When typing an ellipsis, leave one space before, after, and between each period.

08 To Show Omitted Words

An ellipsis is used to show that one or more words have been left out of a quotation.

Complete Quote: **"All I know is that I saw something that hummed and glowed and looked like a giant sugar bowl with no handles, hovering above the water tower."**

Shortened Quote: **"All I know is that I saw something that hummed and glowed ... hovering above the water tower."**

09 At the End of a Sentence

If the words left out are at the end of a sentence, use a period followed by three dots.

Complete Quote: **"That is the last thing I remember about my walk last night. Then I woke up here."**

Shortened Quote: **"That is the last thing I remember .... Then I woke up here."**

10 Pause in Dialogue

An ellipsis is used to indicate a pause in dialogue.

"That's ... incredible!" I cried.

11 ▶ **Commas** are used to keep words and ideas from running together, making your writing easier to read. Commas tell the reader where to pause.

12 ▶ **Items in a Series**

Commas are used between words, phrases, or clauses in a series.

| I know someone who likes pepperoni, pineapple, and olives on her pizza. (words)

| In summer I like to go skateboarding, ride my bike, and play basketball. (phrases)

13 ▶ **In Dates**

Commas are used to separate the day from the year in dates.

| We are having our next reunion on July 1, 1999 at Wells Park.

Tip: Do not use a comma if you write the date with the day first, followed by the month and the year: 1 July 1999.

14 ▶ **In Addresses**

Commas are used to separate items in addresses.

| Raffi's new address is 188 Salisbury Drive, Saskatoon, SK S7H 3J8.

Tip: Do not use a comma at the end of a line or to separate the province from the postal code:

188 Salisbury Drive
Saskatoon, SK S7H 3J8

15 ▶ **To Set Off Interruptions**

Commas are used to set off a word, phrase, or clause that interrupts the main thought of a sentence.

| As it turned out, however, Mrs. Cheung sold the car for $250.

16 ▶ **Between Two Independent Clauses**

A comma may be used between two independent clauses which are joined by coordinating conjunctions such as the following: *and, but, or, nor, for, so,* and *yet.*

| My friend never does any homework, yet he hopes to get good grades.

| I always bring a lot of work home, and I expect to get good grades.

Tip: Do not connect two independent clauses with a comma unless you also use a conjunction. (See page 372 for more information about independent clauses.)

17 ▶ To Set Off Dialogue

Commas are used to set off the exact words of the speaker from the rest of the sentence.

> **As Oscar the Grouch says,**
> **"One man's trash is another**
> **man's treasure."**

No comma is needed when *reporting* rather than *repeating* what a speaker said.

> **Carla said that the Frisbee**
> **just missed her nose.**

18 ▶ In Direct Address

Commas are used to separate a noun of direct address (the person being spoken to) from the rest of the sentence.

> **Carla, watch out!**

19 ▶ In Letter Writing

Commas are used after the salutation, or greeting, in a friendly letter and after the closing in all letters.

> **Dear Uncle Roberto,** (greeting)
>
> **Your niece,** (closing)

20 ▶ To Separate Adjectives

Commas are used to separate two or more adjectives that equally modify the same noun.

> **I like to wear old, mouldy**
> **socks when I play basketball.**

Tip: Use these tests to discover if adjectives modify equally:

➤ Switch the order of the adjectives; if the sentence is still clear, the adjectives modify equally.

➤ Insert *and* between the adjectives; if the sentence reads well, use a comma when *and* is omitted.

21 ▶ To Set Off Interjections

A comma is used to separate an interjection or weak exclamation from the rest of the sentence.

> **Wow, you really did it this time!**
>
> **Hey, will you do me a favour?**

22 ▶ To Set Off Appositives

An appositive is a word or phrase that renames the noun or pronoun before it.

> **My father, a great cook, makes**
> **the best pizza in town.** ("a great
> cook" is an appositive phrase)

23 ▶ To Set Off Long Phrases and Clauses

Use a comma to separate a long modifying phrase or clause from the independent clause following it.

> **After five long days in school,**
> **I am tired of sitting at a desk.**
> (phrase)
>
> **When you practise as much as**
> **I do, in-line skating is easy.**
> (clause)

Semicolon

24 The **semicolon** is a cross between a period and a comma. It is sometimes used in place of a period; other times, it serves the same function as a comma.

25 Between Independent Clauses

A semicolon is used to join two or more independent clauses that are not connected with a coordinating conjunction. (This mean that each clause could stand alone as a separate sentence.)

> My aunt has a new motorcycle; I wish I were old enough to drive it.

> She takes me for rides on it; however, I would still rather be driving it.

Tip: See page 372 for more information about independent clauses; see page 387 for an explanation of coordinating conjunctions.

26 To Separate Phrases

A semicolon is used to separate a series of phrases that already contain commas.

> We should buy less processed food; grow some of our own fruits, vegetables, and grains; and drink more clean water, fresh juices, and low-fat milk.

Note: The second and third phrases above already contain commas.

Colon

27 A **colon** is used in a sentence to introduce a list or draw attention to information that follows. Colons are also used between the numbers in time.

28 To introduce a List

A colon is used to introduce a list.

> Motorcycles are used for the following reasons: transportation, recreation, and racing events.

29 After a Salutation

A colon may be used after the salutation of a business letter.

> Dear Ms. Davidson:

30 Between Numbers in Time

A colon is used between the parts of a number that indicate time.

> The race begins at 1:30 p.m.

> I'll meet you at 12:00 noon.

31 As a Formal Introduction

A colon may be used to introduce an important quotation in a serious report, essay, or news story.

> In his final letter, Norman Bethune, a physician who worked in China, wrote: "My only regret is that I shall now be unable to do more."

Hyphen

32 A **hyphen** is used to divide or join words. Hyphens are also used to create new words.

33 To Divide a Word

A hyphen is used to divide a word when you run out of room at the end of a line. A word may be divided only between syllables. (The word *con-tri-bu-tion* can be divided in three places.)

> In 1883, Jan Matzeliger helped to make an important contri- bution to civilization.

Tip: Here are some other guidelines for hyphenating words:

➤ *Never* divide a one-syllable word: **helped, great.**

➤ *Never* divide a one-letter syllable from the rest of the word: **i-dentity**.

➤ *Never* divide contractions: **haven't, shouldn't**

34 In Compound Words

A hyphen is used to make some compound words.

> **Matzeliger was not well-known, even though he invented a machine used to make shoes.**

35 In Fractions

A hyphen is used between the numbers in a fraction.

> **Matzeliger's machine shaped the upper one-half of the shoe and then attached it to the sole.**

36 To Form an Adjective

The hyphen is used to join two or more words that work together to form a single adjective *before* a noun.

> **Matzeliger's shoe-stitching machine revolutionized the process of making shoes.**

37 To Create New Words

A hyphen is used to form new words beginning with the prefixes *self, ex, great, all,* and *half.* A hyphen is also used with suffixes such as *free* and *elect.*

> **great-aunt, half-baked, all-purpose, self-esteem, sugar-free, president-elect.**

Dash

38 A **dash** may be used to show a change in thought or direction in a sentence, or to show that a speaker has been interrupted.

39 In a Sentence Break

A dash may be used to show a sud- den break in a sentence.

> **The skateboard — if you didn't notice — has a wheel missing.**

40 In Interrupted Speech

A dash is used to show that some- one's speech is being interrupted by another person.

> **Well, hello — yes, I — that's right — yes, I — sure, I'd love to — eight o'clock is perfect!**

Apostrophe

41 An **apostrophe** is used to form plurals, to show that a letter or letters have been left out of a word, or to show possession.

42 To Form Plurals

An apostrophe and *s* are used to form the plural of a letter, a number, or a sign.

A's (letter)

8's (number)

+'s (sign)

43 In Contractions

An apostrophe is used to show that one or more letters have been left out to form a contraction.

Contraction	*Short For*
don't	**do not**
it's	**it is; it has**
they'll	**they will**
he'd	**he had**
they're	**they are**
o'clock	**of the clock**

44 In Place of Numbers or Letters

An apostrophe is also used to show that one or more letters or numbers have been left out of numerals or words.

class of '99 (*19* is left out)

rarin' to go (*g* is left out)

45 In Singular Possessives

The possessive form of singular nouns is usually made by adding an apostrophe and *s*.

My sister's hobby is jazz dancing.

When a singular noun ends with an *s* or *z* sound, the possessive may be formed by adding just an apostrophe.

Lucas' hobby is collecting pencil stubs.

EXCEPT When a singular noun is a one-syllable word, add both an apostrophe and an *s*.

Gus's mother took him fishing.

46 In Plural Possessives

The possessive form of plural nouns ending in *s* is usually made by adding just an apostrophe.

the girls' log-rolling team

For plural nouns not ending in *s*, an apostrophe and *s* must be added.

children's book

47 In Shared Possessives

When possession is shared by more than one noun, add an apostrophe and *s* to the last noun.

Jim, Joe, and Jerry's fish.

Quotation Marks

48 ▶ **Quotation marks** are used to enclose the exact words of the speaker, to show that words are used in a special way, and to punctuate titles.

49 ▶ Direct Quotations

Quotation marks are placed before and after the spoken words.

"Terry Fox is a true Canadian hero," the teacher reminded her students.

50 ▶ Placement of Punctuation

Periods and commas are always placed *inside* quotation marks.

The child said, "Tell me a story."

"I'm so tired," said the mom.

A question mark or an exclamation point is placed *inside* the quotation marks when it punctuates the quotation; it is placed *outside* when it punctuates the main sentence.

"Should I tell you a story?" asked the child.

"Please do!" answered the mom.

Did the dad say, "I want to listen, too"?

51 ▶ Special Words

Quotation marks may be used to set apart a word that is being discussed.

The word "got" is often used incorrectly.

52 ▶ To Punctuate Titles

Quotation marks are used to punctuate titles of songs, poems, short stories, essays, chapters of books, and articles found in magazines, newspaper, or encyclopedias. (See page 351 for other information about titles.)

"O Canada" (song)

"When I Went Up to Ottawa" (poem)

"Roses and Onions" (chapter)

Tip: When you write a title, capitalize the first word, last word, and every word in between except for articles (a, an, the), short prepositions (by, for, to), and short conjunctions (and, or).

Question Mark

53 ▶ A **question mark** is used after a direct question (an interrogative sentence) and to show doubt about the correctness of something.

54 ▶ Direct Question

A question mark is used at the end of a direct question.

Have you ever flown in an airplane?

55 ▶ Correctness

A question mark is placed in parentheses to show that the writer isn't sure a fact is correct.

You'll see virtual reality TV shows by the year 2000 (?).

Exclamation Point

56 An **exclamation point** is used to express strong feeling. It may be placed after a word, a phrase, or a sentence.

Not! (word)

Happy birthday! (phrase)

I can't wait for Friday! (sentence)

Italics

57 **Italic** is a printer's term for a slightly slanted style of type. (The word *friend* is typed in italics.) **Italics** are used to indicate titles and special words.

Tip: In handwritten material each word or letter that should be in italics is *underlined*. If you use a computer, you may be able to print italics.

58 For Titles

Italics (or underlining) are used for titles of plays, books, newspapers, magazines, television programs, movies (videos), record albums (cassettes and CDs), and other complete works.

The Wiz OR <u>The Wiz</u> (play)

Keeper of the Isis Light (book)

Ghostwriter (television program)

Home Alone (movie)

59 For Specific Words

Use italics (or underlining) to indicate names of aircraft and ships.

Columbia OR <u>Columbia</u> (spacecraft)

Bluenose (Nova Scotian schooner)

Use italics (or underlining) to indicate foreign words.

Canada's motto is *a mari usque ad mare*, meaning "from sea to sea."

Use italics (or underlining) to indicate words discussed as words, rather than for their meaning.

The word *freedom* means different things to different people.

Parentheses

60 Parentheses are used around words included in a sentence to add information or to help make an idea clearer.

61 To Add Information

Parentheses are used to add information.

The map (figure 2) will help you understand the explorer's route.

62 To Make an Idea Clearer

Parentheses are used to make an idea clearer.

Five of the students provided background music (humming very quietly) for the singer.

Unsolved Mysteries

Do you know the difference between an *acronym* and an *aardvark*? No? Do you know when to capitalize *mother, father, aunt,* or *uncle?* Not sure? Do you know when to add *s* to a word and when to add *es?* Another unsolved mystery?

Well, this is your lucky day. We're about to take some of the mystery out of these and other questions about the mechanics of writing:

EDITING FOR MECHANICS

Capitalization

63 ▶ Proper Nouns and Proper Adjectives

Capitalize all proper nouns and proper adjectives. A proper noun names a specific person, place, thing, or idea. A proper adjective is formed from a proper noun.

Proper Nouns:
Edmonton Eskimos
Céline Dion

Proper Adjectives:
Saskatchewan wheat
Manitoba blizzard

64 ▶ Names of People

Capitalize the names of people and also the initials or abbreviations that stand for those names.

Marnie McBean, Lui Passaglia, Monica Hughes, Lester B. Pearson

65 ▶ Words Used as Names

Capitalize words such as *mother, father, aunt,* and *uncle* when these words are used as names.

Will you ask Mother what we're having for lunch? (*Mother* is used as a name; you could use her first name in its place.)

Will you ask my mother what we're having for lunch? (In this sentence, *mother* describes someone but is not used as a name.)

66 ▶ Titles Used with Names

Capitalize titles used with names of persons.

Prime Minister Chrétien
Dr. Frederick Banting
Mayor Jean Drapeau
(Do not capitalize titles when they are used alone: the prime minister, the doctor, the mayor.)

68 ▶ Historical Events

Capitalize the names of historical events, documents, and periods of time.

Treaty of Versailles, British North America Act, Stone Age

69 ▶ Abbreviations

Capitalize abbreviations of titles and organizations.

M.D. (Doctor of Medicine)

RCMP (Royal Canadian Mounted Police)

70 ▶ Organizations

Capitalize the name of an organization, association, or team and its members.

Girl Guides of Canada, the New Democratic Party, Vancouver Canucks, Montreal Expos

67 ▶ Capitalizing Geographic Names

Planets and heavenly bodies	**Earth, Jupiter, Milky Way**
Continents	**Europe, Asia, South America, Australia, Africa**
Countries	**Morocco, Haiti, Greece, Chile, United Arab Emirates**
Provinces	**Alberta, British Columbia, Quebec, Ontario**
States	**New Mexico, Alabama, West Virginia, Delaware, Iowa**
Cities and towns	**Montreal, Prince George, Pincher Creek, Charlottetown**
Bodies of water	**Georgian Bay, Great Slave Lake, Saskatchewan River, Indian Ocean, Gulf of St. Lawrence, Black Creek**
Landforms	**Rocky Mountains, Cypress Hills, Canadian Shield**
Public areas	**Stanley Park, Upper Canada Village**
Roads and highways	**Trans Canada Highway, Dundas Street, Trinity Lane**
Buildings	**CN Tower, McMahon Stadium, the Taj Mahal**

CHECK IT OUT

71

Capitalize	Do Not Capitalize
January, March . . . . winter, spring
Mother (as a name). . . . . **my mother** (describing her)
Prime Minister Chrétien . . . . Jean Chrétien, our **prime minister**.
Mayor Heble . . . . Mrs. Heble, the **mayor**
Lake Ontario. . . . . the **lake** area
Saskatchewan **River** . . . . the North and South Saskatchewan **rivers**
the North (section of the country). . . . . **north** (a direction)
planet Earth . . . . the **earth** we live on

72 ▶ Titles

Capitalize the first word of a title, the last word, and every word in between except articles (a, an, the), short prepositions, and short conjunctions.

▌ *National Geographic World* (magazine)

▌ *Suzanne* (song)

▌ *Bob's Birthday* (movie)

▌ *This Can't Be Happening at Macdonald Hall!* (book)

Tip: Don't lowercase every short word in a title. Even though *Can't* and *Be* are short, they are not articles, prepositions, or conjunctions.

73 ▶ First Words

Capitalize the first word of every sentence.

▌ **The first basketball game is on Monday after school.**

Capitalize the first word of a direct quotation.

▌ **Jamir shouted, "Keep that ball moving."**

74 ▶ Days and Months

Capitalize the names of days of the week, months of the year, and special holidays.

▌ **Wednesday, March, Remembrance Day, Easter, Passover, Kwanzaa**

Tip: Do not capitalize the seasons.

▌ **winter, spring, summer, fall**

75 ▶ Names of Religions, Nationalities, Languages

Capitalize the names of religions, nationalities, and languages.

▌ **Buddhist, Hindu** (religion)
▌ **Australian, Somali** (nationality)
▌ **English, Spanish** (language)

76 ▶ Official Names

Capitalize the names of businesses and the official names of their products.

▌ **Burger King, Post Sugar Crisps, Popsicle, Crest toothpaste**

Tip: Do not capitalize a general descriptive word like *toothpaste* when it follows the product name.

Plurals

77 The **plurals** of most nouns are formed by adding *s*.

| balloon → balloons
| shoe → shoes

78 Nouns Ending in *sh, ch, x, s,* and *z*

The plurals of nouns ending in *sh, ch, x, s,* and *z* are made by adding *es* to the singular.

| brush → brushes
| bunch → bunches, box → boxes,
| dress → dresses, buzz → buzzes

79 Nouns Ending in *o*

The plurals of most words ending in *o* are formed by adding *s.*

| patio → patios, rodeo → rodeos

The plurals of most nouns ending in *o* (with a consonant letter just before the *o*) are formed by adding *es.*

| echo → echoes, hero → heroes

EXCEPT Musical terms and words of Spanish origin always form plurals by adding *s*; consult a dictionary for other words of this type.

| piano → pianos, solo → solos,
| taco → tacos, burrito → burritos

80 Nouns Ending in *ful*

The plurals of nouns that end with *ful* are formed by adding an *s* at the end of the word.

| two cupfuls, five platefuls

81 Nouns Ending in *f* or *fe*

The plurals of nouns that end in *f* or *fe* are formed in one of two ways.

1. If the final *f* is still heard in the plural form of the word, simply add *s*.

| goof → goofs, chief → chiefs
| safe → safes, fife → fifes

2. If the final *f* has the sound of *v* in the plural form, change the *f* to *v* and add *es*.

| calf → calves, loaf → loaves
| wife → wives, knife → knives

82 Nouns Ending in *y*

The plurals of common nouns that end in *y* (with a consonant letter just before the *y*) are formed by changing the *y* to *i* and adding *es*.

| sky → skies, bunny → bunnies

The plurals of nouns that end in *y* (with a vowel before the *y*) are formed by adding only *s*.

| money → monkeys
| donkey → donkeys

83 Compound Nouns

The plurals of compound nouns are usually formed by adding *s* or *es* to the important word in the compound.

| sisters-in-law
| maids of honour

84 Irregular Nouns

Some nouns form a plural by taking on an irregular spelling.

| child → children, goose → geese
| mouse → mice

Numbers

85 **Numbers** from one to nine are usually written as words; all numbers 10 and over are usually written as numerals.

one   three   10   115   2000

EXCEPT Numbers being compared should be kept in the same style.

| Students from 8 to 11 years old are invited.

86 **Very Large Numbers**
You may use a combination of numbers and words for very large numbers.

| 15 million, 1.2 million

87 **Sentence Beginnings**
Use words, not numerals, to begin a sentence.

| Fourteen new students joined the jazz band.

88 **Numerals Only**
Use numerals for any numbers in the following forms:

money...**$3.00**
decimal.......................................**25.5**
percentage........................**6 percent**
chapter............................**chapter 8**
page ....**pages 17–20**
address......................**445 Acorn Dr.**
date..**July 1**
time ....**1:30 p.m.**
statistic ....**a vote of 5 to 2**

Abbreviations

89 An **abbreviation** is the shortened form of a word or phrase. Most abbreviations begin with a capital letter and end with a period.

Tip: The following abbreviations are always acceptable in both formal and informal writing:

| Mr.   Mrs.   Ms.   Dr.
| a.m.   p.m.   B.C.   A.D.   M.D.

In formal writing, do not abbreviate the names of provinces, countries, months, days, or units of measure.

90 **Acronyms**
An acronym is a word formed from the first letter or letters of words in a phrase. Acronyms do not end with a period.

| **MADD** (**M**others **A**gainst **D**runk **D**riving)
| **NATO** (**N**orth **A**tlantic **T**reaty **O**rganization)
| **radar** (**ra**dio **d**etecting **a**nd **r**anging)

91 **Initialism**
An initialism is like an acronym except the initials that form this abbreviation are not pronounced as a word.

| **TV** (**t**ele**v**ision)
| **CD** (**C**ompact **D**isc)
| **MIA** (**M**issing **I**n **A**ction)
| **UN** (**U**nited **N**ations)

POSTAL ABBREVIATIONS FOR NORTH AMERICA

Alberta	AB	Newfoundland	NF	Prince Edward Island	PE
British Columbia	BC	Northwest Territories	NT	Quebec	PQ
Manitoba	MB	Nova Scotia	NS	Saskatchewan	SK
New Brunswick	NB	Ontario	ON	Yukon	YT

Alabama	AL	Kentucky	KY	North Dakota	ND
Alaska	AK	Louisiana	LA	Ohio	OH
Arizona	AZ	Maine	ME	Oklahoma	OK
Arkansas	AR	Maryland	MD	Oregon	OR
California	CA	Massachusetts	MA	Pennsylvania	PA
Colorado	CO	Michigan	MI	Rhode Island	RI
Connecticut	CT	Minnesota	MN	South Carolina	SC
Delaware	DE	Mississippi	MS	South Dakota	SD
District of Columbia	DC	Missouri	MO	Tennessee	TN
Florida	FL	Montana	MT	Texas	TX
Georgia	GA	Nebraska	NE	Utah	UT
Hawaii	HI	Nevada	NV	Vermont	VT
Idaho	ID	New Hampshire	NH	Virginia	VA
Illinois	IL	New Jersey	NJ	Washington	WA
Indiana	IN	New Mexico	NM	West Virginia	WV
Iowa	IA	New York	NY	Wisconsin	WI
Kansas	KS	North Caroline	NC	Wyoming	WY

OTHER COMMON ABBREVIATIONS

a.m. ante meridiem

ASAP as soon as possible

B.A. Bachelor of Arts

cm centimetre

COD cash on delivery

e.g. for example

etc. and so forth

FM frequency modulation

FYI for your information

i.e. that is

kg kilogram

km kilometre

km/h kilometres per hour

kw kilowatt

L litre

m metre

M.A. Master of Arts

M.D. Doctor of Medicine

Ph.D. Doctor of Philosophy

pd. paid

pg. page (or **p.**)

p.m. post meridiem

R.S.V.P please reply

vs. versus

WYSIWYG what you see is what you get

CHECKING YOUR SPELLING

1 You'll need to be patient. **Learning to become a good speller takes time.**

2 **Check your spelling** by using a dictionary or list of commonly misspelled words (like the list that follows).

3 **Check a dictionary for the correct pronunciation** of each word you are trying to spell. Knowing how to pronounce a word will help you remember how to spell it.

4 Also **look up the meaning** of each word. (Knowing how to spell a word is of little use if you don't know what it means.)

5 **Practise seeing the word in your mind's eye**. Look away from the dictionary page and write the word on a piece of paper. Check the spelling in the dictionary. Repeat this process until you can spell the word correctly.

6 **Make a spelling dictionary**. Include any words you misspell in a special notebook. (**SEE** page 271.)

 **YOU DON'T SSSSSAY**

Just as you must watch and practise to become a better basketball player, you must read and write to become a better speller.

A

	afraid	angel	arrival
	after	angle	article
about	against	animal	artificial
above	agreement	anniversary	athlete
absent	allowance	anonymous	athletic
accept	all right	another	attention
accident	almost	answer	attitude
accompany	alone	anybody	attractive
accurate	along	apartment	audience
ache	a lot	apologize	August
achieve	already	application	aunt
across	although	appreciate	author
actual	always	April	automobile
address	American	aren't	autumn
adventure	among	argument	avenue
advertisement	amount	arithmetic	awful
advise	ancient	around	awhile

B

baggage
balloon
banana
bargain
basement
beautiful
because
become
been
before
beginning
behind
believe
belong
between
bicycle
birthday
biscuit
blanket
blizzard
bought
breakfast
brilliant
brother
brought
bruise
buckle
building
built
burglar
business
busy
button
buy

C

cafeteria
calendar
called
campaign
candidate
canoe
canyon
captain
careful
careless
casserole
caterpillar
caught
celebration
cemetery
century
certain
certificate
change
character
chief
children
chimney
chocolate
choir
choose
church
city
civilization
classmates
classroom
climate
closet
cocoa
cocoon
colour
come
coming
committee
community
company
complete
concert
congratulate
cooperate
cough
could
couldn't
country
courage
courteous
courtesy
cousin
criticize
cupboard
curious
customer

D

dairy
dangerous
daughter
day
dear
December
decorate
definition
delicious
describe
desert
dessert
developed
didn't
different
difficulty
disappear
disastrous
discover
discussion
distance
divide
division
doctor
does
done
doubt

E

early
earth
easy
edge
either
electricity
elephant
emergency
encourage
enormous
enough
entertain
environment
every
everybody
exactly
excellent
exercise
exhausted
expensive
experience
explain
expression
eyes

F

face
familiar
family
famous
fashion
faucet
favourite
February
fierce
fifty
finally
first
football
foreign
forty
forward
found
fountain
fourth
fragile
Friday
friend
from
front
fuel
full

G

gadget
generally
generous
genius
gentle
geography
getting
goes
gone
government
grade
graduation
grammar
grateful
great
grocery
group
guarantee
guard
guardian
guess
gymnasium

H

half
handkerchief
handsome
happened
happiness
haven't
having
hazardous
heard
heavy
height
history
holiday
honour
horrible
hospital
hour
humorous
hundreds

I

icicle
immediately
immigrant
impatient
important
impossible
individual
innocent
instead
intelligent
interested
island

J

January
jewellery
journal
journey
judgment
juicy
July
June

K

kitchen
knew
knife
knives
know
knowledge

L

language
laughed
league
leave
length
lesson
letter
light
lightning
likely
listen
literature
little
loose
lovable

M

magazine
making
manufacture
many
March
marriage
material
mathematics
May
maybe
mayor
might
millions
minute
mirror
Monday
money
morning

N

natural
necessary
neighbourhood
neither
never
nice
noisy
none
no one
nothing
November
nuclear
number

mountain
music
musician
mysterious

O

obey
occasion
o'clock
October

office
often
once
operate
opposite
other
outside

P

package
paragraph
parallel
party
pasture
patience
peace
people
picture
piece
place
played
pleasant
please
pleasure
point
poison
practise/practice
prejudice
preparation
present
president
pretty
principal
privilege
problem
products
psychology
pumpkin

Q

quarter
quickly
quiet

R

quit
quite
quotient

raise
ready
really
reason
receive
recognize
remember
responsibilities
restaurant
right
rough
route

S

safety
said
salad
salary
sandwich
Saturday
says
scared
scene
school
sentence
September
several
shoes
should
since
skiing
something
sometimes
soon
special
started
store
straight
studying

suddenly
sugar
summer
Sunday
suppose
sure
surprise
surround
swimming
system

T

table
teacher
tear
temperature
terrible
Thanksgiving
their
there
they're
though
thought
thousands
through
Thursday
tired
together
tomorrow
tonight
toys
travelling
trouble
truly
Tuesday
turn

U

unconscious
unfortunately
until
unusual
upon

use
usually

V

vacation
vacuum
vegetable
vehicle
very
violence
visitor
voice
volume

W

wasn't
weather
Wednesday
weight
weird
welcome
welfare
were
we're
what
when
where
which
while
whole
whose
women
world
wouldn't
write
writing
wrote

Y

yellow
young
your
you're

USING THE RIGHT WORD

You will want to use "the right words" whenever you write. This section will help you do just that. Begin by looking over the commonly misused words on the next eight pages. Then, whenever you have a question about which word is the *right* word, come back to this section for help. P.S. Remember to look for your word in a dictionary if you don't find it here.

a, an	I played **a** joke on my dad. 　　(**A** *is used before words beginning with a consonant sound.*) I placed **an** ugly rubber fish under his pillow. 　　(**An** *is used before words beginning with a vowel sound.*)
accept, except	Please **accept** (receive) my apology. Everyone has **except** (other than) you.
affect, effect	Jorge's funny face **affected** the whole class. 　　(**Affect** *is always a verb meaning "to influence."*) The **effect** (result) was a class full of giggling students.
allowed, aloud	We are **allowed** (permitted) to read to partners in class. But we may not read **aloud** in the library. 　　(**Aloud** *is an adverb meaning "clearly heard."*)
a lot	**A lot** of my friends like jeans with holes in them. 　　(**A lot** *is always two words.*)

I have **already** finished all of my homework.
    (**Already** is an adverb telling when.)
Now I'm **all ready** to shoot some baskets.
    (**All ready** is a phrase meaning "completely ready.")
	already, all ready

Since the road was blocked, we took an **alternate** route.
    (**Alternate** is an adjective meaning "other.")
We had no alternative but to turn back.
    (**Alternative** is a noun meaning "choice.")
	**alternate,
	alternative**

An **ant** is an insect. An **aunt** is a close relative.	**ant, aunt**
I **ate** a bowl of popcorn He had **eight** pieces of licorice.	**ate, eight**
She put her **bare** feet into the cool stream. She didn't see the **bear** fishing on the other side	**bare, bear**
I **blew** on my frozen fingers. The tip of my index finger looked almost **blue**.	**blew, blue**
A **board** is a piece of wood. When Tom is **bored**, he pounds nails into boards.	**board, bored**
Pump the **brake** to slow down. Otherwise, you or your bike may **break**.	**brake, break**

Please **bring** me my glasses.
    (**Bring** means "moving toward the speaker.")
Take your dishes to the kitchen.
    (**Take** means "to carry off.")
	bring, take

Did a Frisbee just fly **by** my window? I had better **buy** some new glasses.	**by, buy**

Can I go off the high diving board?
    (I am asking if I have the "ability" to do it.)
May I go off the high diving board?
    (I am asking for "permission" to do something.)
	can, may

Each flower costs 25 **cents**. The **scent** (smell) of the flowers was sweet. He **sent** her 75 **cents** worth of scented flowers.	**cent, scent, sent**

Koji **chose** to take drum lessons last year.
He will **choose** a different instrument this year.
    (**Chose** [choz] is the past tense of the verb
      choose [chooz].)
	chose, choose

close, clothes	***Close*** the window. Then put the ***clothes*** in the dryer.
coarse, course	A cat's tongue feels ***coarse*** to the touch. I took a ***course*** called "Caring for Cats."
creak, creek	Old houses ***creak*** when the wind blows through them. The water in the nearby ***creek*** is clear and cold.
dear, deer	Bambi is my ***dear*** friend. The ***deer*** enjoyed the corn in our garden.
desert, dessert	A cactus grows in the ***desert*** near our house. My favourite ***dessert*** is cactus pie.
dew, do, due	The ***dew*** on the grass was cool on my feet. I ***do*** my homework right after school. The report is ***due*** on Wednesday.
die, dye	The plant will ***die*** if it isn't watered. The red ***dye*** in the sweatshirt turned everything in the wash pink.
doesn't, don't	Mom ***doesn't*** dance. (***doesn't*** = *does not*) I ***don't*** either. (***don't*** = *do not*)
eye, I	For the play, Massoud wore a patch over his left ***eye***. ***I*** have a patch on my jeans.
fewer, less	There are ***fewer*** drums than drummers in the school band. 　　(***Fewer*** *refers to something you can count.*) So I get ***less*** and ***less*** time to practise. 　　(***Less*** *refers to something you cannot count.*)
find, fined	Did you ***find*** your book? Yes, but the librarian ***fined*** my because it was overdue.
fir, fur	***Fir*** trees are evergreen trees. Would you ever wear a ***fur*** coat?
for, four	You can eat the caramel corn ***for*** a snack. The ***four*** of you can also share the chips.
good, well	Rosie looks ***good*** in that outfit. 　　(**Good** *is an adjective describing Rosie.*) It fits her ***well***. 　　(**Well** *is an adverb modifying "fits."*)

A *hare* looks like a large rabbit My *hair* looks like a wet rabbit.	**hare, hair**
It takes a long time for a blister to *heal*. José has a blister on his *heel*.	**heal, heel**
How could I *hear* you? I was over *here*, and you were over there.	**hear, here**
We *heard* the noise, all right! It sounded like a *herd* of charging elephants.	**heard, herd**
An *heir* is a person who inherits something. *Air* is what we breathe.	**heir, air**
Say *hi* to the pilot for me. How *high* is this plane flying?	**hi, high**
A bagel has a *hole* in the middle of it. Michael ate a *whole* bagel.	**hole, whole**
It takes one *hour* to get to school by bus. *Our* school has very slow buses.	**hour, our**
Our bus needs *its* heater repaired. *It's* not only cold but noisy. (*It's* is the contraction of "it is.")	**its, it's**
I finally *knew* everyone's name. Then two *new* kids were added to our class.	**knew, new**
The *knight* guarded the tower gates. Thursday is the knight's *night* off.	**knight, night**
I have a *knot* in my shoelaces I am *not* able to get it untied.	**knot, not**
Do you *know* how to turn on the computer? *No*, we'll have to ask Pierre.	**know, no**
Alina *knows* all about computers. Her *nose* is always in a computer manual.	**knows, nose**

Please *lay* the sleeping bag on the floor.
    (*Lay* means "to place.")
I must *lie* down for a while.
    (*Lie* means "to recline.")
	lay, lie

Paints used to contain *lead*. I have to *lead* my dog around the show ring. The drill team *led* the parade.	**lead, led**

learn, teach	I don't want to **learn** another fact about the moon.
	     (**Learn** means "to get information.")
	 I know so much I could **teach** the class myself.
	     (**Teach** means "to give information.")

loose, lose	Joe's pet tarantula is **loose**!
	     (**Loose** [loos] means "free or untied.")
	 No one but Joe could **lose** a big, fat spider.
	     (**Lose** [looz] means to "misplace or fail to win.")

made, maid	Yes, I have **made** a big mess. I need a **maid** to help me clean it up.
mail, male	Some people receive **mail** on their computers. Men are **male**; women are female.
main, Maine, mane	She does many things, but her **main** job is writing. The state of **Maine** has a rugged coastline. The hair on a horse's neck is called a **mane**.
meat, meet	I like **meat** and potatoes for breakfast. I'll **meet** you at the table.
metal, medal	Gold is a precious **metal**. So is the **medal** I won for finishing first.
miner, minor	Some coal **miners** suffer from black lung disease. **Minors** are individuals who are not legally adults.
oar, or, ore	You use an **oar** to row a boat. Kim **or** Rosa will do the rowing. Iron **ore** is a mineral containing metal.
one, won	He has **one** hot bike! He **won** it by guessing the number of beans in a jar.
pain, pane	A bee sting usually causes **pain**. A broken window **pane** can, too.

A **pair** (two) of pigeons roosted on our windowsill. To **pare** an apple means to peel it. A **pear** is a sweet, juicy fruit.	**pair, pare, pear**
The school bus **passed** a stalled truck. In the **past**, most children walked to school.	**passed, past**
Ms. Nguyen likes **peace** and quiet in her room. I like a **piece** of cake in my lunch.	**peace, piece**
Toni wanted a **plain** (basic) white dress. The coyote ran across the flat **plain**. A stunt **plane** can fly upside down.	**plain, plane**
A **pore** is an opening in the skin. Please **pour** me another glass of Gatorade. That store has a **poor** choice of books.	**pore, pour, poor**
Practice makes perfect. I want to **practise** my trumpet. 　　(**Practice** is a noun, **practise** is a verb.)	**practice, practise**
My **principal** is a strong leader. 　　(**Principal** as a noun is a school administrator; 　　as an adjective, it means "most important.") She asks students to follow this **principle**: Respect each other, and I'll respect you. 　　(**Principle** means "idea" or "belief.")	**principal, principle**
Libraries are supposed to be **quiet** places. **Quit** talking, or we will get in trouble. There is **quite** a bit of whispering going on.	**quiet, quit, quite**
The **rain** made the field very muddy. Queen Victoria's **reign** was long. Pull the **reins** to stop the horse.	**rain, reign, rein**
Please don't **raise** (lift) the shades. The sun's **rays** are very bright this afternoon. To **raze** means "to tear something down."	**raise, rays, raze**
Have you **read** any books by Martha Brooks? Why do we always have **red** Jell–O?	**read, red**
Is this the **right** place to turn right? I'll **write** you a letter and let you know.	**right, write**
My house is one block from the main **road**. I **rode** my bike to the pond. Then I **rowed** the boat to my favourite fishing spot 　　and threw in a line.	**road, rode, rowed**

scene, seen	The movie has a great chase **scene**. Have you **seen** it yet?
sea, see	A **sea** is a body of salty water. It's difficult to **see** any salt, though.
seam, seem	The **seam** in my jacket is ripped. I **seem** to remember catching it on the door handle.
sew, so, sow	Will you please **sew** my ripped jacket? I have time, **so** I will do it for you now. Good. Then I can go **sow** seeds in the garden.
sit, set	Can I **sit** in one of those folding chairs? Yes, if you help me **set** them up first.
some, sum	I have **some** math problems to do. What is the **sum** of 58 + 17?
son, sun	Jacques Villeneuve is the **son** of Gilles Villeneuve. The **sun** is the source of the earth's energy.
sore, soar	His feet were so **sore** he could hardly walk. His hopes **soared** when he heard a car coming.
stationery stationary	I use my best **stationery** (paper) when I write to my pen pal. A **stationary** bike stays in place while you pedal it.
steal, steel	You can **steal** third base, but don't take it home! Many knives are made of **steel**.
tail, tale	A snake uses its **tail** to move its body. "Sammy the Spotted Snake" is my favourite tall **tale**.
than, then	Your dog is bigger **than** my dog. (**Than** is used in a comparison.) **Then** my dog immediately ran the other way. (**Then** tells when.)
their, there, they're	What should we do with **their** tickets? (**Their** shows ownership.) Put them over **there** for now. **They're** going to the game later. (**they're** = they are)

He **threw** the ball at the basket. It swished **through** the net.	**threw, through**
Eva threw the ball **to** Maria Lea is **too** tired to guard her. (**Too** means "also" or "very.") Maria easily scored **two** points.	**to, too, two**

My little sister's **waist** is as small as one of my legs.
You look like you are going to **waste** away.
    (The verb *waste* means "to shrink"; the noun
    waste refers to useless material.)
	waist, waste

I can't **wait** for the field trip. My brother lifts **weights** to get strong.	**wait, weight**
There are many different **ways** to lose weight. I **weigh** more than he does.	**way, weigh**
How long have you had a **weak** back? I've had a weak back for about a **week**.	**weak, week**
The crossing guards **wear** yellow ponchos. **Where** do you think they got them?	**wear, where**
I like rainy **weather**. My dad goes golfing **whether** it's nice out or not.	**weather, whether**
Which book should I read? You'll like *The Lion, the* **Witch***, and the Wardrobe*.	**which, witch**
The man **who** answered the door was my dad. The movie, **which** was very funny, ended too soon. The puppy **that** I really wanted was sold already.	**who, which, that**
Who ordered this pizza? The pizza was ordered by **whom**?	**who, whom**

Who's that knocking at the door?
    (**Who's** is the contraction for "who is.")
Whose door are you talking about?
    (**Whose** shows ownership.)
	who's, whose

Baseball bats are made of **wood**. **Would** you like to play baseball after school?	**wood, would**

You're talking to the right person!
    (**You're** is the contraction for "you are.")
You can pick up **your** pizzas after school.
    (**Your** shows ownership.)
	you're, your

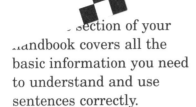
UNDERSTANDING SENTENCES

*section of your
handbook covers all the
basic information you need
to understand and use
sentences correctly.

Here's what you'll
find inside:

5 Things You Should Know!

1. A sentence is made up of one or more words that express a complete thought.
2. A sentence has two basic parts — a subject and a predicate (verb).
3. A sentence makes a statement, asks a question, gives a command, or shows strong emotion.
4. A sentence begins with a capital letter and ends with a period, a question mark, or an exclamation point.
5. More information on sentences is included on pages 42–45 and 85–89.

Parts of a Sentence

SUBJECT

Simple Subject	A **subject** is the part of a sentence that is doing something.
	    *Maria **baked a chocolate cake.***
	A subject can also be the word that is talked about.
	    My** friend **is a marvelous cook.

Complete Subject	The **complete subject** is the simple subject and all the words that describe it.
	    *My best friend **baked a chocolate cake.***
	    (*My best friend* is the complete subject.)

Compound Subject	A **compound subject** is made up of two or more simple subjects. *Maria **and her** sister **also baked some blueberry muffins.***

PREDICATE

Simple Predicate	A **predicate** (verb) is the part of the sentence that says something about the subject.
	    Maria** baked **the cake for my birthday.
	    (*Baked* tells what the subject did.)

Complete Predicate	The **complete predicate** is the simple predicate with all the words that describe it.
	    ***Maria** baked the cake yesterday.*
	    (The complete predicate is *baked the cake yesterday.)*
	    ***My friend Maria** is a marvelous cook.*
	    (The complete predicate is *is a marvelous cook.)*

Compound Predicate	A **compound predicate** is made up of two or more simple predicates. ***Maria** frosted **and** decorated **the cake.***

MODIFIER

A Modifier	A **modifier** is a word or group of words that add details to the sentence. Modifiers are either adjectives or adverbs.

CLAUSES

A Clause	A **clause** is a group of related words that has both a subject and a predicate. *We ride **our bikes to school.*** (*We* is the subject and *ride* is the predicate in this clause.) ***when the** weather is **nice*** (*Weather* is the subject and *is* is the predicate in this clause.)
Independent	An **independent clause** expresses a complete thought and can stand alone as a sentence. ***We ride our bikes to school.***
Dependent	A **dependent clause** does not express a complete thought and cannot stand alone as a sentence. ***when the weather is nice*** **NOTE:** A *dependent clause* can be combined with an **independent clause** to form a complex sentence. (See page 373 for more information.) ***We ride our bikes to school** when the weather is nice*

PHRASES

A Phrase	A **phrase** is a group of related words that does not have a subject, or a predicate, or both. Phrases do not make a complete thought, so they are not sentences. ***the junior high school students*** (This is a noun phrase.) ***wrote their reports*** (This is a verb phrase.) ***about Louis Riel*** (This is a prepositional phrase. See page 386.) **NOTE:** If you put these three phrases together, they would form a complete sentence. ***The junior high school students wrote their reports about Louis Riel.***
Kinds of Phrases	Phrases are named by how they are used in a sentence. Noun: ***The junior high school students*** Verb: ***wrote their reports*** Prepositional: ***about Louis Riel***

TYPES OF SENTENCES

Simple	A **simple sentence** has just one independent clause (one complete thought). It may, however, have a compound subject or compound predicate, and even a phrase or two.
	My knees ache. (A basic simple sentence)
	My face and neck look red and feel hot. (This simple sentence has a *compound subject* and a *compound predicate*.)
	I just skated for two hours. (This simple sentence includes *a prepositional phrase*.)
Compound	A **compound sentence** is made up of two or more simple sentences joined together by a comma and a connecting word, or by a semicolon.
	I've skied in the Laurentians, but I have only seen a picture of the Rockies.
	St. Sauveur is 30 kilometres from my home; Banff is 3000 kilometres away.
Complex	A **complex sentence** contains one *independent* clause and one or more *dependent* clauses.
	Because it was raining, the race was called off.

KINDS OF SENTENCES

Declarative	**Declarative sentences** make statements.
	The capital of New Brunswick is Fredericton.
Interrogative	**Interrogative sentences** ask questions.
	Did you know that forestry and tourism are British Columbia's major industries?
Imperative	**Imperative sentences** give commands.
	You must never swim alone.
	NOTE: Imperative sentences sometimes use an understood subject [*you*].
	Never swim alone. Stay here.
Exclamatory	**Exclamatory sentences** show emotion or surprise.
	I just saw a killer whale!

The Parts of Speech

All the words in our language have been divided into eight groups. These word groups are called the *parts of speech*.

Each part of speech includes words that are used in the same way in a sentence. With this information in hand (**or in eight hands**), you should be ready to learn more about the words in our language.

UNDERSTANDING OUR LANGUAGE

8 *Things You Should Know!*

1. **Nouns** name a person, place, thing, or idea. (*Bill, billboard*)
2. **Pronouns** are used in place of nouns. (*I, me, you*)
3. **Verbs** express action or state of being. (*is, are, run, jump*)
4. **Adjectives** describe a noun or pronoun. (*tall, quiet, neat*)
5. **Adverbs** tell something about a verb, an adjective, or another adverb. (*gently, easily, fast*)
6. **Prepositions** show how a noun is related to some other word in the sentence. (*on, near, over*)
7. **Interjections** show emotion or surprise. (*Wow, Oh, Yikes!*)
8. **Conjunctions** connect words or groups of words. (*and, or, because*)

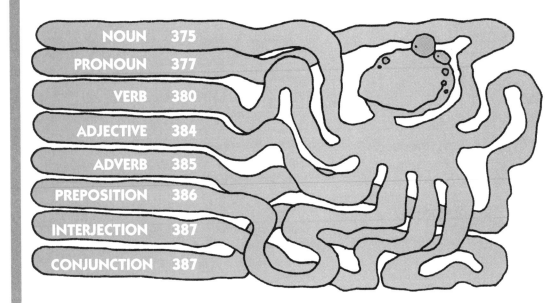

Noun

A **noun** is a word that names a person, place, thing, or idea.

Person	Maria, friend, Josh, parent
Place	home, Kelowna, city, backyard
Thing	baseball, homework, secret
Idea	happiness, trouble, friendship

KINDS OF NOUNS

Common and Proper Nouns

A **common noun** is the *general* name of a person, place, thing, or idea. (Common nouns are not capitalized.)

A **proper noun** is the *specific* name of a person, place, thing, or idea. (Proper nouns are always capitalized.)

Common Nouns	Proper Nouns
woman	Sylvie Frechette
fort	Fort Garry
mountains	the Rocky Mountains
team	Edmonton Oilers
park	Point Pelée National Park

Concrete and Abstract Nouns

Concrete nouns name things that can be touched or seen. **Abstract nouns** name things that *cannot* be touched or seen.

Concrete	magazine, cactus, Toyota
Abstract	love, happiness, democracy

Singular and Plural Nouns

A **singular noun** names one person, place, thing, or idea. A **plural noun** names more than one person, place, thing, or idea.

Singular	note, paper, pen pal, hope
Plural	notes, papers, pen pals, hopes

USES OF NOUNS

Subject Nouns	A **subject noun** is a noun that does something or is being talked about. *Josh **told Maria the secret.*** (The noun *Josh* did something: *told the secret.*)
Predicate Nouns	A **predicate noun** is a noun that renames the subject. It is linked to the subject by a linking verb. ***The note is a** secret.* (The noun *secret* renames the subject *note*; it is another name for the subject. *Secret* is linked to *note* by the verb *is.*)
Possessive Nouns	A **possessive noun** is a noun used to show possession or ownership. ***Josh told Maria the secret in** Gloria's **note.*** (The *'s* added to *Gloria* shows that the note belongs to her.)

NOUNS AS OBJECTS

Direct Objects	A noun is a **direct object** when it receives the action of the verb. ***Josh told the** secret.* (*Secret* is a direct object because it receives the action of the verb.)
Indirect Objects	A noun is an **indirect object** when it names the person to or for whom something is done. ***Josh told** Maria **the secret***. (*Maria* is an indirect object because something has been done to her.)
Objects of a Preposition	A noun is an **object of a preposition** when it is part of a prepositional phrase. (See page 386.) ***Josh told Maria the secret in Gloria's** note.* (The noun *note* is the object of the preposition *in.*)

Pronoun

A **pronoun** is a word used in place of a noun.

Carlotta dropped her lunch tray.

She dropped her lunch tray. (*She* is a pronoun that replaces the noun *Carlotta.*)

NOTE: The most common pronouns are called personal pronouns. All of the personal pronouns are discussed and listed on this page.

USES OF PERSONAL PRONOUNS

Subject Pronouns

A **subject pronoun** is used as the subject of a sentence.

I can never remember jokes. (Singular)

They really make people laugh. (plural)

Singular	I, you, he, she, it
Plural	we, you, they

Object Pronouns

An **object pronoun** is used after an action verb or in a prepositional phrase.

Mr. Otto teases me. (*Me* comes after the action verb *teases.*)

My friends made a funny card for him. (*Him* is the object in the prepositional phrase *for him.*)

Singular	me, you, him, her, it
Plural	us, you, them

Possessive Pronouns

A **possessive pronoun** shows ownership.

Jackie finished writing her story. (*Her* comes before the noun *story.*)

The idea for it was mine. (*Mine* can stand alone.)

Before a noun
my, your, his, her, its, our, their

Stand alone
mine, yours, his, hers, its, ours, theirs

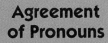

Agreement of Pronouns	The pronouns in your sentences must *agree* with the words they replace.
	Shi Ting's skateboard ***works great now that*** it ***is oiled.*** (The pronoun *it* and the word it replaces, *skateboard*, are both singular, so they agree.)
	The other kids' boards ***look like*** they ***could use some oil, too.*** (The pronoun *they* and the word it replaces, *boards*, are both plural, so they agree.)
	An **antecedent** is the name for the noun that a pronoun replaces.
	Shi Ting ***practises whenever he can.*** (*Shi Ting* is the antecedent of the pronoun *he*.)

PERSON OF A PRONOUN

First-Person Pronoun	The *person* of a pronoun tells us whether the pronoun is speaking, listening, or being spoken about.
	A **first-person pronoun** is used in place of a speaker.
	I ***like blue-moon ice cream.*** (*I* replaces the speaker's name.)
	We ***like ice cream in waffle cones.*** (*We* replaces the names of two or more speakers.)
Second-Person Pronoun	A **second-person pronoun** is used in place of a person (or thing) spoken to.
	Todd, have you ***decided on a flavour?*** (*You* replaces the name *Todd*, the person being spoken to.)
	You ***guys do not need triple-dip cones.*** (*You* replaces *guys*, the people being spoken to.)
Third-Person Pronoun	A **third-person pronoun** is used in place of the person (or thing) being spoken about.
	Jonathan said that he ***was ordering pumpkin ice cream.*** (*He* replaces *Jonathan*, the person being spoken about.)
	The four guys said they ***needed some water.*** (*They* replaces *guys*, the people being spoken about.)

TYPES OF PRONOUNS

Personal	A **personal pronoun** is the most common type of pronoun. (See a complete list on page 377.)
Relative	A **relative pronoun** connects one part of a sentence with a word in another part of the sentence. *Any student who wants to join our music group should see Carlos.*
	who, whose, which, what, that, whoever, whatever, whichever
Demonstrative	A **demonstrative pronoun** points out or identifies a noun without naming it. *That sounds like a great idea!*
	this, that, these, those
Interrogative	An **interrogative pronoun** asks a question. *Who is going to play the keyboard?*
	who, whose, whom, which, what
Intensive and Reflexive	An **intensive pronoun** stresses the word it refers to. A **reflexive pronoun** refers back to the subject. *Carlos himself taught the group a new song.* (intensive) *The performers admired themselves in the mirror.* (reflexive)
	myself, himself, herself, yourself, itself, themselves, ourselves
Indefinite	An **indefinite pronoun** does not name the word it replaces. *Somebody needs to videotape the practice.*
	all, another, any, anybody, anyone, anything, both, each, either, everybody, everyone, everything, few, many, most, much, neither, nobody, none, no one, nothing, one, other, several, some, somebody, someone, something

Verb

A **verb** shows action or links the subject to another word in the sentence. The verb is the main word in the predicate part of the sentence. (See page 371 for more about the predicate.)

> *The boys fight often.* (The verb shows action.)
> *I am sad about that.* (The verb links two words.)

TYPES OF VERBS

Action Verbs

An **action verb** tells what the subject is doing. Action verbs make writing clear and specific.

> *I watched the entire game.*
> *Janet left after the third quarter.*

Linking Verbs

A **linking verb** links a subject to a noun or an adjective in the predicate part of the sentence.

> *That car is a Dodge Neon.* (The verb *is* links the noun *Dodge Neon* to the subject *car*.)
> *A Dodge Neon looks funny.* (The verb *looks* links the adjective *funny* to the subject *Dodge Neon*.)

> **"Be" Verbs**
> is, are, was, were, am, been

> **Other Linking Verbs**
> smell, look, taste, remain, feel, appear, sound, seem, become, grow, stand, turn

Helping Verbs

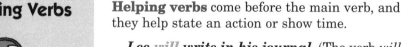

Helping verbs come before the main verb, and they help state an action or show time.

> *Lee will write in his journal.* (The verb *will* helps state a future action, *will write*.)
> *Lee has been writing in his journal.* (The verbs *has been* help state a continuing action, *has been writing*.)

> **Helping Verbs**
> is, are, was, were, am, been, shall, will, could, would, should, must, can, may, might, have, had, has, do, did

FORMS OF VERBS

Singular and Plural Verbs

A **singular verb** must be used when the subject in a sentence is singular.

> ***Ben** likes **peanut butter and olive sandwiches.*** (The subject *Ben* and the verb *likes* are both singular.)

A **plural verb** must be used when the subject is plural.

> ***Black olives** taste **like wax.*** (The subject olives and the verb taste are both plural.)

NOTE: When a subject and verb are both singular or plural, they agree in number. (See page 88.)

Active and Passive Voice

A verb is **active** if the subject is doing the action in the sentence.

> ***Gus** threw **a rotten tomato.*** (*Threw* is active because the subject *Gus* is doing the action.)

A verb is **passive** if the subject does not do the action.

> ***A rotten tomato** was thrown **by Gus.*** (*Was thrown* is passive because the subject *tomato* is not doing the action.)

Regular Verbs

Most verbs in our language are **regular**. You add *ed* to regular verbs to state a past action or when you use a helping verb *(has, have, had)*.

> **Regular Verbs**
> I play.   Earlier I played.   I have played.
> He walks. Earlier he walked. He has walked.

Irregular Verbs

Some verbs in our language are **irregular**. An irregular verb does not end in *ed* when you state a past action or when you use a helping verb. For most irregular verbs, the word changes.

> **Irregular Verbs**
> I ride.   Earlier I rode.   I have ridden.
> She eats. Earlier she ate. She has eaten.

NOTE: The chart on the next page lists the common irregular verbs in our language.

Common Irregular Verbs

The **principal parts** of the common irregular verbs are listed below. The part used with the helping verbs *has, have,* or *had* is called the **past participle**.

REMEMBER: With most irregular verbs, the word changes when you state an action in the past or when you use a helping verb.

Present Tense	Past Tense	Past Participle
I hide.	Earlier I hid.	I have hidden.

Principal Parts of Irregular Verbs

Present Tense	Past Tense	Past Participle	Present Tense	Past Tense	Past Participle
am, be	was, were	been	lie (recline)	lay	lain
begin	began	begun	ride	rode	ridden
bit	bit	bitten	ring	rang	rung
blow	blew	blown	rise	rose	risen
break	broke	broken	run	ran	run
bring	brought	brought	see	saw	seen
burst	burst	burst	set	set	set
catch	caught	caught	shake	shook	shaken
come	came	come	shine (light)	shone	shone
dive	dived, dove	dived	shrink	shrank	shrunk
do	did	done	sing	sang, sung	sung
draw	drew	drawn	sink	sank, sunk	sunk
drink	drank	drunk	sit	sat	sat
drive	drove	driven	speak	spoke	spoken
eat	ate	eaten	spring	sprang, sprung	sprung
fall	fell	fallen	steal	stole	stolen
fight	fought	fought	swear	swore	sworn
fly	flew	flown	swim	swam	swum
freeze	froze	frozen	swing	swung	swung
give	gave	given	take	took	taken
go	went	gone	tear	tore	torn
grow	grew	grown	throw	threw	thrown
hang	hung	hung	wake	woke, waked	waked
hide	hid	hidden, hid	wear	wore	worn
know	knew	known	weave	wove	woven
lay (place)	laid	laid	write	wrote	written
lead	led	led			

THE TENSE OF A VERB

Tense	We call the time of a verb its **tense**. Tense is shown by endings (*talked*), by helping verbs (*will talk*), or by both (*have talked*). There are three common tenses: **present, past**, and **future**. There are also three special tenses: **present perfect, past perfect**, and **future perfect**.
Present Tense	The **present tense** of a verb states an action that is happening now, or that happens regularly. *I like **soccer.*** *We practise **every day.***
Past Tense	The **past tense** of a verb states an action that happened at a specific time in the past. *She liked **soccer.*** *Beth was **the goalie.***
Future Tense	The **future tense** of a verb states an action that will take place. The future tense is made by using the helping verbs *will* or *shall* before the main verb. *I will like **soccer even better next year.*** *We shall practise **every day.***

SPECIAL TENSES

Present Perfect Tense	The **present perfect tense** of a verb states an action that is still going on. It is formed by using *has* or *have* before the main verb. *Raji has slept **for two hours.***
Past Perfect Tense	The **past perfect tense** of a verb states an action that began and was completed in the past. It is formed by using *had* before the main verb. *Roxanne had slept **for eight hours.***
Future Perfect Tense	The **future perfect tense** of a verb states an action that will begin in the future and end at a specific time in the future. It is formed by adding *will have* or *shall have* before the main verb. *Riley will have slept **for 12 hours.***

Adjective

An **adjective** is a word that describes a noun or pronoun.

> *Male peacocks have beautiful feathers.*
>
> *The feathers are colourful.* (An adjective after a linking verb is called a *predicate adjective.*)

Articles

The **articles a, an,** and **the** are adjectives.

> *Owlet is the name for a baby owl.*

FORMS OF ADJECTIVES

Positive

The **positive** form of an adjective describes a noun without comparing it to anyone or anything else.

> *A hummingbird is small.*

Comparative

The **comparative** form of an adjective compares two people, places, things, or ideas.

> *A hummingbird is smaller than a sparrow.* (The ending *er* is added to one-syllable adjectives.)
>
> *A hummingbird is more graceful than a pelican.* (*More* is added before most adjectives with two or more syllables.)

Superlative

The **superlative** form of an adjective compares three or more people, places, things, or ideas.

> *A hummingbird is the smallest bird I've seen.* (The ending *est* is added to one-syllable adjectives.)
>
> *A swan is the most graceful bird in the zoo.* (*Most* is added before most adjectives with two or more syllables.)

Special Forms

The adjectives listed in this chart use different words to make comparison:

Positive	Comparative	Superlative
good	better	best
bad	worse	worst
many	more	most

Adverb

An **adverb** is a word that describes a verb, an adjective, or another adverb. Most adverbs tell **where, how,** or **when.**

> **The first pitch curved** *inside*. (tells *where*)
>
> **Roberto hit the next pitch** *hard*. (tell *how*)
>
> **Robert ran** *immediately*. (tells *when*)

NOTE: Adverbs often end in *-ly*, but not always. Words like *not, never, very,* and *always* are common adverbs.

FORMS OF ADVERBS

Positive

In the **positive** form, an adverb does not make a comparison

> **Roberto plays** *hard* **from the first pitch to the last out.**

Comparative

The **comparative** is formed by adding *er* to one-syllable adverbs or the word *more* or *less* before longer adverbs.

> **He plays** *harder* **than his cousin.**
>
> **He plays** *more often* **than his cousin.**

Superlative

The **superlative** is formed by adding *est* to one-syllable adverbs or the word *most* or *least* before longer adverbs.

> **Roberto plays** *hardest* **in close games.**
>
> **Roberto plays** *most often* **in centre field.**

Special Forms

The adverbs below use different words to make comparisons:

Positive	Comparative	Superlative
well	better	best
badly	worse	worst

NOTE: Do not confuse *good* and *well*. *Good* is an adjective and *well* is usually an adverb.

> **She has a** *good* **swing.**
>
> **She runs bases** *well*, **too.**

Preposition

A **preposition** is a word that relates a noun or pronoun to another word in the sentence.

One cat rested on the desk top.

Another cat watched from a desk drawer.

Object of the Preposition

The **object of the preposition** is the noun or pronoun that comes after the preposition.

One other cat lay under the desk. (*Desk* is the object of the preposition *under*.)

Prepositional Phrase

A **prepositional phrase** includes a preposition, the object of the preposition, and any describing words that come in between.

A fourth cat sat beside the old oak desk.

COMMON PREPOSITIONS

about	for	on	past	under
above	from	on top of	since	underneath
across	in	onto	through	until
after	in front of	out of	to	up
against	inside	outside	toward	upon
along	instead of	over		with
among	into			within
around	like			without
at	near			
before	of			
behind	off			
below				
beneath				
beside				
between				
by				
down				
during				
except				

Interjection

An **interjection** is a word or phrase used to express strong emotion or surprise. A comma or an exclamation point is used to separate an interjection from the rest of the sentence.

Wow, **look at those mountains!**

Hey! **Keep your eyes on the road!**

Conjunction

A **conjunction** connects individual words or groups of words.

The river is wide *and* **deep**

We can fish in the morning *or* **in the evening.**

KINDS OF CONJUNCTIONS

Coordinate

A **coordinate conjunction** connects equal parts: two or more words, two or more phrases, and so on.

The river winds down the valley *and* **through the prairies.** (The conjunction *and* connects two prepositional phrases.)

> and, but, or, nor, for, so, yet

Correlative

A **correlative conjunction** is used in pairs.

Either **snow** *or* **wind may delay the trip.** (*Either* and *or* work as a pair in this sentence.)

> either, or; neither, nor; both, and; just, as

Subordinate

A **subordinate conjunction** connects two clauses to make a complex sentence.

Our trip was delayed *when* **the snowstorm hit.**

We stayed in town *until* **the snow stopped.**

> after, although, as if, because, before, if, in order that, since, so, that, though, unless, until, when, where, while

Your Handbook Index

The **index** is your personal guide to using the *Writers Express* handbook. It will help you find specific information. For example, if you want to find a list of state abbreviations so you can address a letter, you can look under *abbreviations* or under *state*. Both entries will tell you where to turn in your handbook to find the information. (See if you can find the correct page for state abbreviations using the index.)

A

B

C

Symbols of Correction

agr.	agreement	p.	punctuation
awk.	ackward expression	?	unclear
cap. (≡)	capitalization	R	repetitious (redundant)
CS	comma splice	RO	run-on sentence
d.m.	dangling modifier	sp.	spelling
d. neg.	double negative	t.	verb tense
frag.	sentence fragment	◯	check this out
gram.	grammar	trans.	transition
l.c. (/)	make lower case letter	⁊	take something out
mis. mod.	misplaced modifier	TS	topic sentence
n.c.	not clear	u.	usage
∧	omission (add something)	w.c.	word choice
¶	paragraph	wordy	more words than needed
pro. ref.	pronoun reference	X	find and correct error